Recent Advances in Image Restoration with Applications to Real World Problems

Edited by Chiman Kwan

Published in London, United Kingdom

IntechOpen

Supporting open minds since 2005

Recent Advances in Image Restoration with Applications to Real World Problems
http://dx.doi.org/10.5772/intechopen.90607
Edited by Chiman Kwan

Contributors
Chiman Kwan, Bulent Ayhan, David Gribben, Jude Larkin, Ying Qu, Hairong Qi, Gemine Vivone, Rocco Restaino, Paolo Addesso, Jocelyn Chanussot, Daniele Picone, Xin Li, Ahmed Sidiya, Rongjun Qin, Shuang Song, Xiao Ling, Mostafa Elhashash, Hessah Albanwan, Jiang Li, Mohammad Shahab Uddin

First published in London, United Kingdom, 2020 by IntechOpen
IntechOpen is the global imprint of INTECHOPEN LIMITED, registered in England and Wales, registration number: 11086078, 5 Princes Gate Court, London, SW7 2QJ, United Kingdom
Printed in Croatia

British Library Cataloguing-in-Publication Data
A catalogue record for this book is available from the British Library

Additional hard and PDF copies can be obtained from orders@intechopen.com

Recent Advances in Image Restoration with Applications to Real World Problems
Edited by Chiman Kwan
p. cm.
Print ISBN 978-1-83968-355-8
Online ISBN 978-1-83968-356-5
eBook (PDF) ISBN 978-1-83968-357-2

An electronic version of this book is freely available, thanks to the support of libraries working with Knowledge Unlatched. KU is a collaborative initiative designed to make high quality books Open Access for the public good. More information about the initiative and links to the Open Access version can be found at www.knowledgeunlatched.org

For EU product safety concerns:
IN TECH d.o.o., Prolaz Marije Krucifikse Kozulić 3, 51000 Rijeka, Croatia, info@intechopen.com or visit our website at intechopen.com.

Meet the editor

Chiman Kwan received his BSc in electronics from the Chinese University of Hong Kong in 1988, and his MS and Ph.D. degrees in electrical engineering from the University of Texas at Arlington in 1989 and 1993, respectively. Currently, he is the Chief Technology Officer of Signal Processing, Inc. and Applied Research LLC, working on projects related to control, signal processing, image processing, fault diagnostics and prognostics, and remote sensing. The past 30 years of research results with numerous collaborators have been published in the form of 1 book, 4 book chapters, 15 patents, 70+ invention disclosures, 360+ journal and conference papers, over 500+ technical reports, and 120 competitively selected projects from government and private companies totaling more than 36 million dollars.

Contents

Preface

In 2012, my colleagues and I worked on a project from NASA on change detection using hyperspectral images. Since then, we have worked on a few other projects funded by DOE on land cover classification, NASA on Mars rover image processing, and DARPA on border monitoring. There are some common technical challenges in the above applications. For example, the images have either low spatial resolution or low spectral resolution. Through those projects, we have started to realize the power of some new technology breakthroughs in image restoration techniques and their impact on some real applications such as change detection, land cover classification, etc. For example, the demosaicing of NASA's Mastcam images is still being done using a technology developed in 2004. After we applied the latest deep learning based demosaicing, we were able to dramatically improve the quality of demosaiced images. Similar breakthroughs in image processing have been ongoing in the past 10 years. It is the above remarkable progress in image processing that motivated me to conceive the idea of editing this book.

I would like to thank all the contributors for spending their precious time to prepare these book chapters, which are by no means a thorough overview of the recent advances in image restoration, but rather a glimpse of this important research area. There are eight chapters divided into five sections in this book.

Section 1 contains Chapter 1, which provides a short overview of image restoration applications in recent years. Some interesting applications in Mars rover Curiosity are mentioned.

Section 2 contains Chapters 2 and 3 on image enhancement of multispectral and hyperspectral images. Chapter 2 presents some new results on the pansharpening of hyperspectral images using multi-platform data. This is a challenging problem because the high resolution images and the low resolution hyperspectral images come from different imagers that have different spectral characteristics such as viewing angles, collection times, bandwidths, etc. More research is needed in this area. Chapter 3 summarizes the application of some recently developed deep neural network models to enhance the left Mastcam images with help from the right Mastcam images. Actual Mastcam images were used to demonstrate the performance of the proposed algorithms.

Section 3 contains Chapters 4 and 5 on the application of generative adversarial network (GAN) in image enhancement. Chapter 4 addresses an important practical problem in machine learning/deep learning. The problem is about the lack of training data in target detection and recognition using infrared videos. Three performance metrics were used to compare the two conversion algorithms. It was concluded that CycleGAN consistently performed better than pix2pixGAN in all three metrics. Chapter 5 presents a novel unsupervised learning approach combining a style-based generator with relativistic discriminator. The unsupervised approach is capable of improving the matching performance of widely used face recognition systems.

Section 4 contains Chapters 6 and 7 on multiview imaging and 3D reconstruction. Chapter 6 discusses various spatio-temporal fusion methods for remote sensing images. Pixel, feature, and decision level fusion approaches were summarized. A few results from the authors' past papers were also included. Chapter 7 presents a new framework for fusing results from cross-view images for 3D mesh reconstruction. Real satellite and ground-view images were used to demonstrate the proposed framework. It was found that the reconstruction accuracy has been improved by close to 1 meter in one of the areas.

Section 5 contains Chapter 8 on digital terrain and digital surface model generation. Chapter 8 summarizes the investigation of various inpainting algorithms for accurate digital terrain model generation. This is necessary because, in urban and sub-urban areas, the terrain may be covered by trees and manmade structures. A benchmark dataset was used in the investigation.

Chiman Kwan
Signal Processing, Inc.,
Rockville, Maryland, USA

Section 1

Introduction

Chapter 1

Introductory Chapter: Recent Advances in Image Restoration

Chiman Kwan

1. Recent advances

In this chapter, we do not intend to provide a comprehensive survey of existing recent image restoration papers in the literature. Instead, we attempt to provide a glimpse of recent advances from our own perspectives and applications. In particular, we will focus on the following areas. Moreover, we will connect those research areas to some real-world applications.

1.1 Image enhancement

Images can be enhanced from several perspectives: spatial, spatial-spectral, spectral, and spatio-temporal.

1.1.1 Spatial domain

Here, we focus on methods that use only a single image to improve the spatial resolution. The simplest method is the bicubic interpolation, which does not utilize any external information such as point spread function (PSF) [1]. A total of 16 neighbors are used to generate a prediction, and the performance is better than bilinear interpolation, which uses only four neighbors. Recently, there are some new developments. A notable one is the algorithm described in [2], which utilizes the PSF to improve the resolution of a single image. The super-resolution algorithm in [3] is based on edge interpolation. There is also a group of methods based on deep learning [4–6]. Vast amounts of training images are needed to train the algorithm. Another group is using dictionary-based approach [7, 8]. Both the deep learning and dictionary approaches require many training images, which may be difficult to obtain.

In Sidiya and Li's chapter [9] in this book, a generative adversarial network (GAN)-based approach was introduced to face image enhancement. The key distinction from conventional GAN is that it is an unsupervised approach, meaning that no ground truth images are required for training. Experimental results showed that the proposed unsupervised approach is only 1–2 dBs inferior to state-of-the-art supervised algorithms. The chapter also pointed out some failure cases, which the authors knew the reasons and will further improve the results in the future.

In Qin et al.'s chapter [10], the authors present a new framework for fusing results from cross view images for 3D mesh reconstruction. Real satellite and ground-view images were used to demonstrate the proposed framework. It was found that the reconstruction accuracy has been improved by close to 1 meter in one of the areas.

IntechOpen

1.1.2 Spatial-spectral resolution enhancement: Pansharpening

In many applications, we may have a high-resolution (HR) image with only a few bands and another image having low resolution but many bands. Pansharpening is an image fusion approach that fuses one high spatial resolution image with another low-resolution (LR) multispectral (MS) image. Earlier pansharpening algorithms are limited to images where the panchromatic band overlaps with the MS bands. However, recent advancements have extended the approach to non-overlapping bands [11–13].

There are two recent survey papers in pansharpening [13–16]. In recent studies, pansharpened images were observed to improve the performance of some applications [17].

Another chapter in this book by Qu et al. [18] summarizes a Dirichlet-Net for pansharpening. The algorithm was applied to Mastcam image enhancement.

In Restaino et al.'s chapter [19], the authors report an interesting study of using multi-platform data for pansharpening. That is, the low-resolution hyperspectral data and the high-resolution pan or multispectral data come from different satellites.

1.1.3 Spectral enhancement using synthetic bands

In some applications, only MS images are available. It may be useful to synthesize some hyperspectral images using those images so that the performance of some applications can be improved. Recently, there have been some new algorithms such as the Extended Morphological Attribute Profiles (EMAP) algorithm [20] for synthesizing spectral bands.

Here, rather than explaining the details of EMAP, we would like to mention a few recent applications of EMAP. The first one is to use EMAP for soil detection. The original MS images have eight bands. After applying EMAP, 80 synthetic bands were generated. The soil detection performance was improved quite significantly. More details can be found in [21–23]. Another application is on change detection using heterogeneous images. That is, the images at two different times may not come from the same imager. In [24], we have demonstrated that EMAP has improved the change detection performance in 36 out of 50 cases. In a third application on land cover classification [25], we have observed that, with the help of EMAP, using only 4 bands (RGB and NIR) can achieve reasonably accurate land cover classification performance that is only a few percentage points lower than that of using 144 bands of data.

1.1.4 Spatio-temporal fusion

Here, we consider an interesting application scenario. At time t_1, we have one high-resolution (HR) MS image and a LR MS image. However, at time t_2, we only have a LR MS image. It will be important to use the aforementioned images and synthesize a HR MS image at t_2.

Such scenarios do exist. As shown in **Figure 1**, one example is the fusion of Landsat (30 m spatial resolution with 16-day revisit period) and MODIS (500 m spatial resolution with almost daily revisit). More details can be found in [26, 27]. Another application scenario is the fusion of Worldview with Planet images [28]. A third temporal fusion study is for Landsat and Worldview images [29]. Once the fused images are available, more frequent change detection can then be performed for a given area.

Albanwan and Qin's chapter on spatio-temporal [30] discusses various spatio-temporal fusion methods for remote sensing images. Pixel, feature, and decision level fusion approaches were summarized. A few past results from the authors' past papers were also included.

1.2 Image denoising

Image noise can be introduced during the image acquisition process. For example, in low lighting conditions, pixel amplitude-dependent noise (Poisson noise) are introduced. In the past, people have investigated sparsity-based methods [31, 32] and deep learning methods [33, 34]. There are also joint denoising and demosaicing algorithms [35].

1.3 Image demosaicing

Many commercial cameras have incorporated the Bayer pattern [36], which is also known as color filter array (CFA) 1.0. An example of CFA 1.0 is shown in **Figure 2a**. There are many repetitive 2x2 blocks and, in each block, two green, one red, and one blue pixels are present. To save cost, the Mastcam onboard the Mars rover Curiosity [37–40] also adopted the Bayer pattern. Due to the popularity of CFA 1.0, Kodak researchers invented a red-green-blue-white (RGBW) pattern or CFA 2.0 [41, 42]. An example of the RGBW pattern is shown in **Figure 2b**. In each 4 × 4 block, eight white pixels, four green pixels, and two red and blue pixels are present. Having more white pixels is believed to help improve the sensitivity of the camera, which is important in low lighting conditions. Numerous other CFA patterns have been invented in the past few decades [43–45].

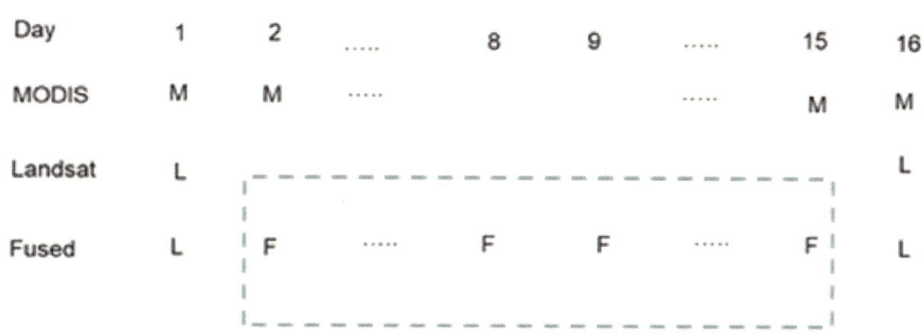

Figure 1.
Fusion of Landsat and MODIS images to create a high spatial and high temporal resolution image sequence.

Figure 2.
Three CFA patterns. (a) CFA 1.0; (b) CFA 2.0.

It will be good to illustrate the differences between a state-of-the-art method (Demonet [35]) and the NASA's current demosaicing algorithm known as Malvar-He-Cutler (MHC) [46]. From **Figure 3**, it can be seen that the demosaiced images by MHC contain some color distortion artifacts whereas the Demonet images do not have noticeable color distortions.

There are some new developments in demosaicing CFA 2.0 or RGBW. In [47], a new pansharpening approach was proposed to demosaic RGBW patterns. In [48], a further improved version by combining deep learning and pansharpening was proposed. In [49], a comparative study of the performance of CFA 1.0 and CFA 2.0 for low lighting images was carried out. It was found that CFA 2.0 has advantages over CFA 1.0 in low lighting conditions. It was also observed that denoising can further enhance the demosaicing performance. Finally, a new CFA 3.0 was proposed in [50] in which a comparative study among CFAs 1.0, 2.0, and 3.0 was conducted. It was observed that CFA 2.0 has better performance in terms of peak signal-to-noise ratio (PSNR) in low lighting conditions than CFAs 1.0 and 3.0. CFA 3.0 has better performance than CFA 1.0.

Figure 3.
Comparative of demosaicing images. Left column: NASA's existing software; right column: State-of-the-art deep learning approach.

1.4 Image deblurring

Image blurring can be caused by camera motion and built-in factors such as point spread functions in various stages of image formation. In the book [51], a few PSFs are mentioned, including optical, motion, detector, and electronics. For motion-induced blurring, researchers have developed estimation methods [52] to restore the original images.

For NASA's Mastcam application, an interesting approach was proposed in [53] to improve the left Mastcam images. The idea was to use the left and right Mastcam images to estimate the deblurring kernel, and then a deconvolution is applied to deblur the left images.

1.5 Image inpainting

Image inpainting is a well-known technique for image restoration. One can remove some image contents and then replace those missing contents with fictitious information. Some conventional techniques include Field of Experts (FOE) [54], Laplacian method [55], *Local Matrix Completion Sparse* (LMCS) [56], and Transformic [57]. More recent methods used GAN for inpainting [58]. We briefly describe these methods below.

FOE: The Field of Experts method (FOE) was developed by Roth et al. [54]. This method uses pre-trained models that are used to filter out noise and obstructions in images.

Laplacian: This method [55] fills in each missing pixel using the Laplacian interpolation formula by finding the mean of the surrounding known values.

Local Matrix Completion Sparse (LMCS) [56]: In LMCS, which was developed by us, a search is performed for each missing pixel to find a pixel with the most similar neighbors. After the search, the missing pixel is replaced with the found pixel. This method performs very well with images containing repeating patterns.

Transformic [57]: The Transformic method was developed by Mansfield et al. [57]. It is similar to the LMCS in that it searches the whole image for a patch that is similar to the neighbors of the missing pixel. However, this method transforms and rotates the searched area to find a better match.

Generative Inpainting (GenIn) [58]: A new inpainting method, Generative Inpainting (GenIn), which is a deep learning-based method [58], was considered in our research. It was developed at the University of Illinois that aims to outperform typical deep learning methods that use convolutional neural network (CNN) models. GenIn builds on CNN and generative adversarial networks in an effort to encourage cohesion between created and existing pixels.

We briefly mention a few recent applications. In [59], the LMCS technique was applied to automatic target recognition. A recent application of LMCS, Transformic, and deep learning can be found in [60] for error concealment in infrared images.

In the chapter by Kwan et al. [61], a number of conventional and deep learning methods were applied to digital terrain model (DTM) extraction.

1.6 Compression artifact reduction

It is surprising that JPEG image compression codec is still being used in some applications nowadays. For instance, the Mars rover Curiosity has a number of imagers, which are all using JPEG for image compression. The current practice at NASA is to use low compression ratios, which can only achieve around three times of compression efficiency. Since the invention of JPEG in early 1990s, there have been quite a few newer and more powerful compression standards in the literature. In the past few years, there are studies on evaluating a number of compression codecs that can achieve perceptually lossless compression [62–64]. The findings showed that it is feasible to attain 10 to 1 compression with almost no loss of image quality.

2. Future directions

Although there are some encouraging progress in image restoration in recent years, there are still some tough problems ahead. We list a few directions below.

2.1 Image enhancement

Earlier, we have seen that temporal resolution can be enhanced by fusing two sequences of images: one with high revisit times but low resolution and another just the opposite. After fusion, a sequence of high spatial resolution and high temporal resolution images emerges. The new sequence of images can be used for more frequent change detection, land cover classification, etc. However, based on our investigations, the change detection performance is still limited [65]. The reason is that the enhanced images fail to capture the changes sometimes. More research is needed.

Moreover, spectral enhancement sometimes have mixed results. In some applications, we do not see improvement for some reasons [66]. This implies that more research is needed to determine that under what conditions the EMAP-based methods can provide improvement and under what conditions not.

2.2 Image deblurring

For real blurred images collected from cameras, we noticed that some of the open-source codes still could not get good deblurring results. This is perhaps due to the fact that the camera motion may be nonlinear (jerky motion) and existing kernel estimation methods cannot handle such nonlinear motions. Again, more research is needed in this area.

2.3 Image demosaicing

As mentioned earlier, color images using color filter arrays collected in low lighting environments contain Poisson noise that seriously affect the image quality. Image denoising needs to combine with demosaicing in order to yield high-quality images. We believe there is still room for improvement in this area. One possible direction is to investigate deep learning approaches.

2.4 Change detection using heterogeneous images

In many remote sensing applications, we may have high-resolution images at one time but may only have low-resolution images at another time. It will be good to perform change detection across multiple platforms. There are some recent advances [24, 67–72] in change detection using multimodal or heterogeneous images. For example, Ziemann et al. [68] studied change detection using a mixture of multi-spectral and synthetic aperture radar (SAR) images. However, more research is still needed to yield consistent results.

Acknowledgements

This work was supported in part by DOE grant DE-SC0019936 and NASA contract number 80NSSC17C0035.

Author details

Chiman Kwan
Signal Processing, Inc., Rockville, Maryland, USA

*Address all correspondence to: chiman.kwan@signalpro.net

References

[1] Kwan C, Dao M, Chou B, Kwan LM, Ayhan B. Mastcam image enhancement using estimated point spread functions. In: Proceedings of the IEEE Ubiquitous Computing, Electronics & Mobile Communication Conference; New York, NY, USA; 19-21 October 2017

[2] Chan SH, Wang X, Elgendy OA. Plug-and-play ADMM for image restoration: Fixed point convergence and applications. IEEE Transactions on Computational Imaging. 2017;**3**:84-98

[3] Yan Q, Xu Y, Yang X, Truong TQ. Single image superresolution based on gradient profile sharpness. IEEE Transactions on Image Processing. 2015;**24**:3187-3202

[4] Dong C, Loy CC, He K, Tang X. Learning a deep convolutional network for image super-resolution. In: Proceedings of the European Conference on Computer Vision; Zurich, Switzerland; 6-12 September 2014. pp. 184-199

[5] Dong C, Loy CC, Tang X. Accelerating the super-resolution convolutional neural network. In: Proceedings of the European Conference on Computer Vision; Amsterdam, the Netherlands; 8-16 October, 2016. pp. 391-407

[6] Hoque MRU, Burks R, Kwan C, Li J. Deep learning for remote sensing image super-resolution. In: IEEE Ubiquitous Computing, Electronics & Mobile Communication Conference; New York City; 10-12 October 2019. pp. 286-292

[7] Timofte R, de Smet V, Van Gool L. A^{+}: Adjusted anchored neighborhood regression for fast super-resolution. In: Proceedings of the Asian Conference on Computer Vision; Singapore; 1-5 November, 2014. pp. 111-126

[8] Chang H, Yeung D, Xiong Y. Super-resolution through neighbor embedding. In: Proceedings of the 2004 IEEE Computer Society Conference on Computer Vision and Pattern Recognition; Washington, DC, USA; 27 June–2 July 2004

[9] Sidiya AC, Li X. Style-based unsupervised learning for real-world face image super-resolution. In: Kwan C, editor. Recent Advances in Recent Advances in Image Restoration with Applications to Real World Problems. Rijeka, Croatia: InTech; 2020

[10] Qin R, Song S, Ling X, Elhashash M. 3D reconstruction through fusion of cross-view images. In: Kwan C, editor. Recent Advances in Recent Advances in Image Restoration with Applications to Real World Problems. Rijeka, Croatia: InTech; 2020

[11] Loncan L, de Almeida LB, Bioucas-Dias JM, Briottet X, Chanussot J, Dobigeon N, et al. Hyperspectral pansharpening: A review. IEEE Geoscience and Remote Sensing Magazine. 2015;**3**:27-46

[12] Meng X, Xiong Y, Shao F, Shen H, Sun W, Yang G, et al. A large-scale benchmark data set for performance evaluation of pansharpening. IEEE Geoscience and Remote Sensing Magazine. 2020. DOI: 10.1109/MGRS.2020.2976696

[13] Vivone G, Alparone L, Chanussot J, Dalla Mura M, Garzelli A, Licciardi GA, et al. A critical comparison among pansharpening algorithms. IEEE Transactions on Geoscience and Remote Sensing. 2015;**53**(5):2565-2586

[14] Dao M, Kwan C, Ayhan B, Bell JF. Enhancing Mastcam images for Mars rover mission. In: Proceedings of the 14th International Symposium on Neural Networks; Hokkaido, Japan; 21-26 June 2017. pp. 197-206

[15] Kwan C, Budavari B, Dao M, Ayhan B, Bell JF. Pansharpening of Mastcam images. In: Proceedings of the IEEE International Geoscience and Remote Sensing Symposium (IGARSS); Fort Worth, TX, USA; 23-28 July 2017. pp. 5117-5120

[16] Kwan C, Choi JH, Chan S, Zhou J, Budavari B. Resolution enhancement for hyperspectral images: A super-resolution and fusion approach. In: Proceedings of IEEE International Conference on Acoustics, Speech, and Signal Processing; New Orleans; 2017. pp. 6180-6184

[17] Dao M, Kwan C, Koperski K, Marchisio G. A joint sparsity approach to tunnel activity monitoring using high resolution satellite images. In: Proceedings of IEEE Ubiquitous Computing, Electronics & Mobile Communication Conference; 2017. pp. 322-328

[18] Qu Y, Qi H, Kwan C. Application of deep learning approaches to enhancing Mastcam images. In: Kwan C, editor. Recent Advances in Recent Advances in Image Restoration with Applications to Real World Problems. Rijeka, Croatia: InTech; 2020

[19] Restaino R, Vivone G, Addesso P, Picone D, Chanussot J. Resolution enhancement of hyperspectral data exploiting real multi-platform data. In: Kwan C, editor. Recent Advances in Recent Advances in Image Restoration with Applications to Real World Problems. Rijeka, Croatia: InTech; 2020

[20] Bernabé S, Marpu PR, Plaza A, Mura MD, Benediktsson JA. Spectral–spatial classification of multispectral images using kernel feature space representation. IEEE Geoscience and Remote Sensing Letters. 2014;**11**:288-292

[21] Dao M, Kwan C, Bernabé S, Plaza AJ, Koperski K. A joint sparsity approach to soil detection using expanded bands of WV-2 images. IEEE Geoscience and Remote Sensing Letters. December 2019;**16**(12):1869-1873. DOI: 10.1109/LGRS.2019.2911923

[22] Kwan C. Remote sensing performance enhancement in hyperspectral images. Sensors. 2018;**18**:3598

[23] Lu Y, Perez D, Dao M, Kwan C, Li J. Deep learning with synthetic hyperspectral images for improved soil detection in multispectral imagery. In: Proceedings of IEEE Ubiquitous Computing, Electronics & Mobile Communication Conference; New York City; 2018

[24] Kwan C, Ayhan B, Larkin J, Kwan LM, Bernabé S, Plaza A. Performance of change detection using heterogeneous images and Extended Multi-Attribute Profiles (EMAPs). Remote Sensing. 2019;**11**(20):2377

[25] Kwan C, Gribben D, Ayhan B, Bernabe S, Plaza A, Selva M. Improving land cover classification using extended multi-attribute profiles (EMAP) enhanced color, near infrared, and LiDAR data. Remote Sensing. 2020;**12**(9):1392

[26] Gao F, Masek J, Schwaller M, Hall F. On the blending of the Landsat and MODIS surface reflectance: Predicting daily Landsat surface reflectance. IEEE Transactions on Geoscience and Remote Sensing. 2006;**44**:2207-2218

[27] Kwan C, Budavari B, Gao F, Zhu X. A hybrid color mapping approach to fusing MODIS and Landsat images for forward prediction. Remote Sensing. 2018;**10**. DOI: 10.3390/rs10040520

[28] Kwan C, Zhu X, Gao F, Chou B, Perez D, Li J, et al. Assessment of spatiotemporal fusion algorithms for Worldview and planet images. Sensors. 2018;**18**:1051

[29] Kwan C, Chou B, Yang J, Perez D, Shen Y, Li J, et al. Landsat and Worldview image fusion. In: Proceedings of the Signal Processing, Sensor/Information Fusion, and Target Recognition XXVIII; Baltimore, MD, USA; 15-17 April, 2019

[30] Albanwan H, Qin R. Spatiotemporal fusion of remote sensing. In: Kwan C, editor. Recent Advances in Recent Advances in Image Restoration with Applications to Real World Problems. Rijeka, Croatia: InTech; 2020

[31] Kwan C, Zhou J. Method for image denoising. Patent #9,159,121; 13 October 2015

[32] BM3D Denoising. Available from: http://www.cs.tut.fi/~foi/invansc/ [Accessed: 22 October 2019]

[33] Zhang K, Zuo W, Zhang L. FFDNet: Toward a fast and flexible solution for CNN based image denoising. 2018. arXiv:1710.04026 [cs.CV]

[34] Dong W, Wang H, Wu F, Shi G, Li X. Deep spatial–spectral representation learning for hyperspectral image denoising. IEEE Transactions on Computational Imaging. 2019;**5**(4):635-648

[35] Gharbi M, Chaurasia G, Paris S, Durand F. Deep joint demosaicking and denoising. ACM Transactions on Graphics. 2016;**35**

[36] Bayer BE. Color imaging array. US Patent 3,971,065; July 20, 1976

[37] Bell JF III et al. The Mars science laboratory curiosity rover mast camera (Mastcam) instruments: Pre-flight and in-flight calibration, validation, and data archiving. Earth and Space Science. July 2017;**4**(7):396-452

[38] Dao M, Kwan C, Ayhan B, Bell JF. Enhancing Mastcam images for Mars rover mission. In: 14th International Symposium on Neural Networks; 2017. pp. 197-206

[39] Kwan C, Budavari B, Dao M, Ayhan B, Bell JF. Pansharpening of Mastcam images. In: Proceedings of IEEE International Geoscience and Remote Sensing Symposium; 2017. pp. 5117-5120

[40] Ayhan B, Dao M, Kwan C, Chen H, Bell JF, Kidd R. A novel utilization of image registration techniques to process Mastcam images in Mars rover with applications to image fusion, pixel clustering, and anomaly detection. IEEE Journal of Selected Topics in Applied Earth Observations and Remote Sensing. 2017;**10**(10):4553-4564

[41] Hamilton J, Compton J. Processing color and panchromatic pixels. U.S. Patent 20070024879A1; 2007

[42] Kijima T, Nakamura H, Compton JT, Hamilton JF, DeWeese TE. Image sensor with improved light sensitivity. U.S. Patent 0 268 533; 2007

[43] Zhang C, Li Y, Wang J, Hao P. Universal demosaicking of color filter arrays. IEEE Transactions on Image Processing. 2016;**25**:5173-5186

[44] Condat L. A generic variational approach for demosaicking from an arbitrary color filter array. In: Proceedings of the IEEE International Conference on Image Processing (ICIP); Cairo, Egypt; 2009. pp. 1625-1628

[45] Menon D, Calvagno G. Regularization approaches to demosaicking. IEEE Transactions on Image Processing. 2009;**18**:2209-2220

[46] Malvar HS, He L-W, Cutler R. High-quality linear interpolation for demosaciking of color images. In: Processing of the IEEE International Conference on Acoustics, Speech, and Signal Processing; Montreal, Québec, Canada; 17-21 May 2004. pp. 485-488

[47] Kwan C, Chou B, Kwan LM, Budavari B. Debayering RGBW color filter arrays: A pansharpening approach. In: Proceedings of IEEE Ubiquitous Computing, Electronics & Mobile Communication Conference; New York City; 2017. pp. 94-100

[48] Kwan C, Chou B. Further improvement of debayering performance of RGBW color filter arrays using deep learning and pansharpening techniques. Journal of Imaging. 2019;**5**(8):68

[49] Kwan C, Larkin J. Demosaicing of Bayer and CFA2.0 patterns for low lighting images. Electronics. 2019;**8**(12):1444

[50] Kwan C, Larkin J, Ayhan B. Demosaicing of CFA 3.0 with applications to low lighting images. Sensors. 2020;**20**:3423

[51] Schowengerdt RA. Remote Sensing: Models and Methods for Image Processing. New York: Academic Press; 1997

[52] Xu L, Zheng S, Jia J. Unnatural L0 sparse representation for natural image deblurring. In: Proceedings of 2013 IEEE Conference on Computer Vision and Pattern Recognition; Portland, OR; 2013. pp. 1107-1114

[53] Kwan C, Dao M, Chou B, Kwan LM, Ayhan B. Mastcam image enhancement using estimated point spread functions. In: Proceedings of IEEE Ubiquitous Computing, Electronics & Mobile Communication Conference; New York City; 2017. pp. 186-191

[54] Roth S, Black MJ. Fields of experts. International Journal of Computer Vision. 2009;**82**:205

[55] Doshkov D, Ndjiki-Nya P, Lakshman H, Köppel M, Wiegand T. Towards efficient intra prediction based on image inpainting methods. In: 28th Picture Coding Symposium; Nagoya; 2010. pp. 470-473. DOI: 10.1109/PCS.2010.5702539

[56] Zhou J, Kwan C. High Performance Image Completion using Sparsity based Algorithms. Orlando, FL: SPIE Commercial + Scientific Sensing and Imaging Conference; 2018

[57] Mansfield A, Prasad M, Rother C, Sharp T, Pushmeet K, Van Gool L. Transforming Image Completion. British Machine Vision Conference. University of Dundee; 29 August - 2 September 2011

[58] Yu J, Lin Z, Yang J, Shen X, Lu X, Huang T. Generative image inpainting with contextual attention. 2018. arXiv:1801.07892 [cs.CV]

[59] Zhou J, Ayhan B, Kwan C, Tran T. ATR performance improvement using images with corrupted or missing pixels. In: Proceedings of SPIE 10649, Pattern Recognition and Tracking XXIX; 30 April, 2018. p. 106490E

[60] Chen Y, Kang JU, Zhang G, Xie Q, Cao J, Kwan C. High-performance concealment of defective pixels in infrared imagers. Applied Optics. 2020;**59**(13):4081-4090

[61] Kwan C, Gribben D, Ayhan B, Larkin J. Practical digital terrain model extraction using image inpainting techniques. In: Kwan C, editor. Recent Advances in Recent Advances in Image Restoration with Applications to Real World Problems. Rijeka, Croatia: InTech; 2020

[62] Kwan C, Larkin J. Perceptually lossless compression for Mastcam images. In: Proceedings of IEEE Ubiquitous Computing, Electronics & Mobile Communication Conference; New York City; 2018. DOI: 10.1109/UEMCON.2018.8796824

[63] Kwan C, Larkin J, Chou B. Perceptually lossless compression of

Mastcam images with error recovery. In: Proceedings of SPIE 11018, Signal Processing, Sensor/Information Fusion, and Target Recognition XXVIII; 2019. DOI: 10.1117/12.2518482

[64] Kwan C, Larkin J, Budavari B, Chou B. Compression algorithm selection for multispectral Mastcam images. Signal & Image Processing. 2019;**10**(1). DOI: 10.5121/sipij.2019.10101

[65] Kwan C, Chou B, Yang J, Perez D, Shen Y, Li J, et al. Fusion of Landsat and worldview images. In: Proceedings of SPIE 11018, Signal Processing, Sensor/Information Fusion, and Target Recognition XXVIII; 2019. DOI: 10.1117/12.2518949

[66] Kwan C, Chou B, Gribben D, Hagen L, Yang J, Ayhan B, et al. Ground object detection in Worldview images. In: Proceedings of SPIE 11018, Signal Processing, Sensor/Information Fusion, and Target Recognition XXVIII; 2019. DOI: 10.1117/12.2518489

[67] Gong M, Zhang P, Su L, Liu J. Coupled dictionary learning for change detection from multisource data. IEEE Transactions on Geoscience and Remote Sensing. 2016;**54**:7077-7091

[68] Ziemann A, Theiler J. Multi-sensor anomalous change detection at scale. In: Proceedings of the SPIE Conference Algorithms, Technologies, and Applications for Multispectral and Hyperspectral Imagery XXV; Baltimore, MD, USA; 26-30 April 2019

[69] Liu Z, Li G, Mercier G, He Y, Pan Q. Change detection in heterogeneous remote sensing images via homogeneous pixel transformation. IEEE Transactions on Image Processing. 2018;**27**:1822-1834

[70] Zhan T, Gong M, Jiang X, Li S. Log-based transformation feature learning for change detection in heterogeneous images. IEEE Geoscience and Remote Sensing Letters. 2018;**15**:1352-1356

[71] Tan K, Jin X, Plaza A, Wang X, Xiao L, Du P. Automatic change detection in high-resolution remote sensing images by using a multiple classifier system and spectral–spatial features. IEEE Journal of Selected Topics in Applied Earth Observations and Remote Sensing. 2016;**9**:3439-3451

[72] Ayhan, B, Kwan, C. A New Approach to Change Detection Using Heterogeneous Images. In: Proceedings of the IEEE 10th Annual Ubiquitous Computing, Electronics & Mobile Communication Conference, New York, NY, USA, 10-12 October 2019.

Section 2

Enhancement of Multispectral and Hyperspectral Images

Chapter 2

Resolution Enhancement of Hyperspectral Data Exploiting Real Multi-Platform Data

Rocco Restaino, Gemine Vivone, Paolo Addesso, Daniele Picone and Jocelyn Chanussot

Abstract

Multi-platform data introduce new possibilities in the context of data fusion, as they allow to exploit several remotely sensed images acquired by different combinations of sensors. This scenario is particularly interesting for the sharpening of hyperspectral (HS) images, due to the limited availability of high-resolution (HR) sensors mounted onboard of the same platform as that of the HS device. However, the differences in the acquisition geometry and the nonsimultaneity of this kind of observations introduce further difficulties whose effects have to be taken into account in the design of data fusion algorithms. In this study, we present the most widespread HS image sharpening techniques and assess their performances by testing them over real acquisitions taken by the Earth Observing-1 (EO-1) and the WorldView-3 (WV3) satellites. We also highlight the difficulties arising from the use of multi-platform data and, at the same time, the benefits achievable through this approach.

Keywords: hyperspectral image sharpening, Hyperion data, WorldView-3 images, data fusion, remote sensing

1. Introduction

Hyperspectral (HS) data often provide great insights in the field of Earth Observing (EO) for the analysis and monitoring of the planet surface [1, 2]. As they embed a very detailed spectral information of the observed scene, their employment has become necessary in many applications, including natural vegetation classification and monitoring, geological map construction, chemical properties detection, land cover observation, and water resources management [1, 2]. The widespread use of hyperspectral data pushed toward the development of acquisition devices with increasing capabilities, the most recent of which are characterized by a ground spatial interval (GSI) even below 10 m [2].

However, this spatial resolution is still insufficient in many fields, as, for instance, geology [3], agriculture [4], and land cover classification [5]. Data fusion techniques provide a possible solution to this issue that has been validated in several studies performed on both on real and simulated datasets [6–8]. In principle, high spatial resolution improvement factors can be attained for hyperspectral data, but the scarcity of exploitable companion high-resolution (HR) data represents a major issue. In fact, it is just possible to find very few examples of hyperspectral sensors co-located onboard of the same platform with high spatial resolution devices, such as panchromatic (PAN) and/or multispectral (MS) sensors. Since the Earth Observing-1, which mounted both a panchromatic and a multispectral camera onboard, is currently dismissed, the only remaining satellites to assure the availability of companion panchromatic sensors are the new Prisma and HypXIM, which are characterized by a six and four times higher spatial resolution with respect to the HS instrument, respectively.

The presence of a high-resolution sensor mounted on the same platform represents the ideal setting for the data fusion problem since the two images to combine are almost simultaneously acquired from the same point of view. However, in addition to the cited difficulty in finding platforms with this feature, the resolution ratio between the HS images and the companion high-resolution image is constrained to be very small, ranging from a value of 3 (EO-1 case) to 6 (Prisma case). Further resolution enhancement would require an additional upsampling procedure at one point in the algorithmic stack, thus strongly compromising the quality of the final fused product.

An alternative is constituted by the fusion of data acquired by multiple platforms, which, on the other hand, implies further difficulties related to the different observation geometry and the unavoidable lack of simultaneity between the acquisitions. Although this approach has been deeply investigated in the literature, the studies have almost always utilized simulated data [9, 10], thus ignoring the two cited issues that affect real data. A previous study based on real acquisitions was performed in [11] with temporally aligned images acquired by drones and aircrafts.

The current study focuses on multi-platform real data and aims at illustrating the state of the art of the, both classical and recent, low-level data fusion algorithms applicable to these data. Classical algorithms were adapted from the pansharpening literature, namely, from studies concerning the fusion of a panchromatic and a multispectral image [12]. They can be straightforwardly applied to the HS/PAN fusion problem [9, 12, 13], but they require a preliminary assignation phase when the high-resolution image is constituted by a multispectral image [14]. Indeed, a specific channel of the MS image has to be assigned to each hyperspectral band to complete the fusion process by means of classical techniques. The assignation algorithm (AA) significantly impacts the final results, and, for this reason, several algorithms have been proposed for completing this task [14, 15]. The latter fusion algorithms have been properly developed for the fusion of the HS and MS data and thus can be straightforwardly applied to the problem at hand. They include proper modifications of classical algorithms (hypersharpening) [16, 17] and applications of more general statistical approaches, as, for instance, the Bayesian framework [18], which is employed with naive [18, 19] and sparse Gaussian priors [20] and with alternative regularization terms [21, 22].

Three different datasets collected form the Earth Observing-1 and the World-View-3 (WV3) satellites were employed in this study to evaluate the performance of the fusion algorithms. The tests were conducted according to the reduced resolution (RR) assessment procedure, based on Wald's protocol [23]. Specifically, the available HS image is employed as reference (or ground truth (GT)), and the images to fuse are constituted by properly degraded versions of the available data. This facilitates the use of accurate indexes for evaluating the quality of the final products thanks to the presence of a reference image. The availability of real data allowed to draw conclusions about the behavior of the different types of fusion algorithms and, in the case of classical pansharpening, about the assignation approaches.

The work is organized as follows. Section 2 describes the problem under consideration, including some details on the main fusion techniques employed in hyperspectral image sharpening. The conducted experimental analysis is detailed in Section 3, whereas the outcomes are reported in Section 4. Finally, conclusions are drawn in Section 5.

2. The hyperspectral sharpening framework

The data fusion procedure to sharp hyperspectral images consists in augmenting the spatial information contained in a low-resolution (LR) hyperspectral image, by injecting information from high-resolution data.

In the following, we will denote a generic acquisition composed by N_A channels as a set of bidimensional matrices, as follows: $\mathbf{A} = \{\mathbf{A}_k\}_{k=1,\dots,N_A}$. More in detail, the HS datacube will be denoted by $\mathbf{H} = \{\mathbf{H}_k\}_{k=1,\dots,N_H}$, an MS acquisition by $\mathbf{M} = \{\mathbf{M}_k\}_{k=1,\dots,N_M}$, and a PAN image by $\mathbf{P} = \{\mathbf{P}_k\}_{k=1}$. The enhancement ratio, namely, the ratio between the spatial resolution of the original HS image and the desired spatial resolution, is indicated by R. We restrict the analysis of the fusion problem to the combination of two images, i.e., the details to be injected are extracted by a single image.

2.1 Classical pansharpening approaches

Classical pansharpening algorithms are designed to operate with a monochromatic image, which acts as source to extract details to be injected into the LR image. Consequently, as long as the HR image is still monochromatic, the framework of classical pansharpening can be directly applied to this scenario, with the straightforward adjustment of using the HS image as the LR source image to fuse. Conversely, when the details are extracted from a multichannel image, the application of pansharpening approaches requires an assignment procedure between each HS band and a specific channel of the high-resolution MS image.

Data fusion through classical pansharpening approaches can be formalized by the following equation [24]:

$$\widehat{\mathbf{H}}_k = \widetilde{\mathbf{H}}_k + \mathbf{G}_k \circ \left(\mathbf{Y}_k - \mathbf{Y}_k^{LP}\right), \tag{1}$$

which represents the sharpening procedure of a generic k-th channel of the HS image. In Eq. 1, the estimated HR hyperspectral image is indicated by $\widehat{\mathbf{H}}$, while $\widetilde{\mathbf{H}}$ denotes an upsampled (interpolated) version of the original image $\mathbf{H}$ to match the scale of $\widehat{\mathbf{H}}$. The details, represented by the difference between the HR image $\mathbf{Y}$ and its low pass version $\mathbf{Y}^{LP}$, are additively injected in the latter image by properly weighting them through an element-by-element matrix product (indicated by the $\circ$ operator) by the injection coefficient matrix $\mathbf{G}$. It is worth to remind that both the details and the matrix $\mathbf{G}$ in (1) are band-dependent, since some methods require a preliminary equalization of the HR image and $\mathbf{G}$ is often optimized for each channel.

2.1.1 Component substitution and multi-resolution analysis algorithms

It is possible to specify different techniques of classical pansharpening methods according to the particular definition of the *injection gain matrix* $\mathbf{G}$ and the method used for calculating the low-resolution image $\mathbf{Y}^{LP}$. In the literature, the key taxonomy for the macro-categorization is related to the techniques to $\mathbf{Y}^{LP}$, as two separate classes of methods arise with very distinguished properties. In particular, $\mathbf{Y}^{LP}$ can be obtained either by properly combining the channels of $\tilde{\mathbf{H}}$ or by spatially degrading the HR image $\mathbf{Y}$. The first approach defines the so-called component substitution (CS), or spectral, methods, whose name is to underline that the fusion is obtained by substituting the HS intensity component with the HR image [25]. This class includes both archetypical methods, such as the Brovey transform (BT) [26], the intensity-hue-saturation [27, 28], the principal component decomposition [29–31], or the Gram-Schmidt (GS) expansion [32], and more recent approaches, such as the Gram-Schmidt adaptive (GSA) method [33], which is able to achieve state-of-the-art performance [24].

The second class of approaches is known in the literature as multi-resolution analysis (MRA), or spatial, methods, since they operate directly in the spatial domain to obtain $\mathbf{Y}^{LP}$ through a multi-scale decomposition. The MRA class includes a wide plethora of methods, which exploit a variety linear filters (box filters [34, 35], Gaussian filters [36], and à trous wavelet filters [37]) or nonlinear decompositions (morphological filters) [38].

The two classes have different characteristics, both in terms of visual aspect of sharpened images and in terms of robustness against nonideal working conditions. Specifically, methods belonging to the CS class usually yield final products featuring an accurate reproduction of the spatial details with an intrinsic robustness to limited spatial misalignments between the two images to fuse [39]. Images produced by MRA approaches are instead characterized by a higher spectral coherence with the original LR image, possibly even reducing temporal misalignments among data to be combined [40].

2.1.2 Assignation algorithms

As seen in the previous section, in the case of HS/PAN fusion, the only possible choice for HR data $\mathbf{Y}$ in (1) is represented by the PAN image. Conversely, for the HS/MS fusion, any of the MS channels can act as HR data, demanding an assignation algorithm to couple a specific MS band with a given HS channel. This problem was addressed in previous papers by defining a series of criteria for selecting the most suitable MS channel [15, 41]. The possible approaches can be either data-independent, exclusively utilizing the characteristics of the sensors, or data-dependent, for which the assignment depends on the particular datasets. The analysis reported in [14] highlights the superior performances of the second approach but at the cost of requiring an additional computational effort to evaluate the new assignation for each new dataset.

Among the data-independent approaches, acceptable performance can be obtained by minimizing the distance between the centroid of the relative spectral response (RSR) of the sensor acquiring the $\mathbf{H}_k$ channel and the centroids of the RSRs of the HR sensor. This method, nicknamed CEN-AA, assigns to $\mathbf{H}_k$ the channel $\mathbf{M}_n$ that verifies the condition:

$$n = \arg\min_j |\mu_{\mathbf{H}_k} - \mu_{\mathbf{M}_j}|, \tag{2}$$

wherein

$$\mu_{\mathbf{A}_i} = \int f \frac{R_{\mathbf{A}_i}(f)}{\int R_{\mathbf{A}_i}(f)df} df \tag{3}$$

defines the centroid of the generic relative spectral response (RSR) $R_{\mathbf{A}_i}(f)$ of a given channel $\mathbf{A}_i$.

For the AA step, the overall best results in terms of data fidelity of the reconstructed fused image are obtained by employing the algorithms proposed in [15, 41]. The first consists in maximizing the cross correlation (CC) between $\mathbf{H}_k$ and the MS channels and is thus denoted in the following as CC-AA. Formally, it consists in coupling $\mathbf{H}_k$ with the HR image $\mathbf{Y} = \mathbf{M}_n$ such that:

$$n = \arg\max_j CC\left(\mathbf{H}_k, \mathbf{M}_j^{\downarrow R}\right) = \arg\max_j \frac{\left\langle \mathbf{H}_k, \mathbf{M}_j^{\downarrow R} \right\rangle}{\sqrt{\langle \mathbf{H}_k, \mathbf{H}_k \rangle \left\langle \mathbf{M}_j^{\downarrow R}, \mathbf{M}_j^{\downarrow R} \right\rangle}} \tag{4}$$

where $\mathbf{M}_j^{\downarrow R}$ indicates the image obtained by degrading the resolution of $\mathbf{M}_j$ by means of a filter matched to the modulation transfer function (MTF) of the j-th MS channel and a downsampling by a factor R; $\langle \mathbf{A}_j, \mathbf{A}_k \rangle$ represents the scalar product among the vectorized version of two generic channels $\mathbf{A}_j$ and $\mathbf{A}_k$.

The alternative approach, defined in [41] and assessed in [14], aims at evaluating the spectral coherence of each available HR channel if it acts as a substitute of $\mathbf{H}_k$. In order to quantify this criterion, let us build the supporting images $\mathbf{R}^{j,k}$ by substituting the $\mathbf{M}_j$ bands at the place of $\mathbf{H}_k$, which are compared to the original image $\mathbf{H}$. Formally, $\mathbf{R}^{j,k}$ is defined as:

$$\mathbf{R}_i^{j,k} = \begin{cases} \mathbf{M}_j^{(k)}, & i = k, \\ \mathbf{H}_i, & i \neq k, \end{cases} \tag{5}$$

where $\mathbf{M}_j^{(k)}$ is obtained by equalizing the first two statistical moments of $\mathbf{M}_j^{\downarrow r}$ w.r.t. $\mathbf{H}_k$. The AA rule is defined by setting $\mathbf{Y}$ equal to the channel $\mathbf{M}_n$ that satisfies the equation:

$$n = \arg\min_j SAM\left[\mathbf{H}, \mathbf{R}^{j,k}\right], \tag{6}$$

in which $SAM[\mathbf{A}, \mathbf{B}]$ denotes the *spectral angle mapper* (SAM) between $\mathbf{A}$ and $\mathbf{B}$ [42]. Accordingly, this approach is named *SAM-AA* by the authors.

2.2 Methods designed for hyperspectral image sharpening

Several different option have been recently developed ad hoc for the sharpening of HS data by using complementary images of different nature. A first option is to modify the existing pansharpening algorithms to account for the specific characteristics of the HS data. A different approach consists in developing a completely novel method by resorting to a suitable mathematical framework, as the widely exploited statistical Bayesian formalization.

2.2.1 Hypersharpening

A very effective method for sharpening HS images relies upon the construction of a simulated HR image assigned for each channel and obtained as a certain combination the available HR channels.

This approach proposed in [16] under the name of hypersharpening consists in defining the synthetic HR image $\mathbf{Y}_k$ to use in (1) for a given $\mathbf{H}_k$ through the expression:

$$\mathbf{Y}_k = \sum_{m=1}^{N_M} w_{k,m}\mathbf{M}_m, \tag{7}$$

in which the weights $w_{k,m}$ are optimized through linear regression as described in [16]. Equalizing the mean and variance of $\mathbf{Y}_k$ with respect to $\mathbf{H}_k$ yields an improved version of hypersharpening, as proposed in [17].

The term $\mathbf{Y}_k^{LP}$ in (1) is suggested to be obtained with the same strategies proposed by MRA methods, by degrading $\mathbf{Y}_k$ via an appropriate filter such as the MTF-matched generalized Laplacian pyramid. The fusion formula (1) is completed by defining the injection gain matrix that is derived through the regression-based model. Namely, $\mathbf{G}_k$ is a constant matrix with entries:

$$g_k = \frac{\text{cov}\left(\tilde{\mathbf{H}}_k, \mathbf{Y}_k^{LP}\right)}{\text{cov}\left(\mathbf{Y}_k^{LP}, \mathbf{Y}_k^{LP}\right)}, \tag{8}$$

where $cov(\cdot,\cdot)$ denotes the covariance operator.

2.2.2 Bayesian approaches

Most novel methods for sharpening HS images exploit the Bayesian statistical formalization of the fusion problem. In this approach, both the LR and HR available data are modeled as transformations, operating, respectively, in the spatial and in the spectral domains of an unknown ideal HR hyperspectral image denoted as $\mathbf{Z}$ [9].

Accordingly, the equation relating the target HR and the available LR image is written as:

$$\mathbf{h} = \mathbf{zBS} + \mathbf{n}_H, \tag{9}$$

where the lowercase letters denote the version of the matrices in lexicographic order (obtained by concatenating the columns of each channel), $\mathbf{B}$ is the blurring matrix, $\mathbf{S}$ is the downsampling matrix, and $\mathbf{n}_H$ is the noise accounting for the unmodeled effects corrupting the relationship. (9) is coupled either to:

$$\mathbf{p} = \mathbf{R}_P\mathbf{z} + \mathbf{n}_P, \tag{10}$$

or to

$$\mathbf{m} = \mathbf{R}_M\mathbf{z} + \mathbf{n}_M, \tag{11}$$

in the HS/PAN and HS/MS cases, respectively. They express the functional models relating $\mathbf{z}$ to $\mathbf{p}$ or $\mathbf{m}$ and include the factors $\mathbf{R}_P$ and $\mathbf{R}_M$ that model the RSRs of the HR sensors and the noise addends $\mathbf{n}_P$ and $\mathbf{n}_M$, accounting for the inaccuracy of the first terms.

The Bayesian approach based on the maximum a posteriori probability (MAP) consists in estimating the target vector $\mathbf{z}$ through the formula:

$$\hat{\mathbf{z}} = \text{argmax}_{z}p(\mathbf{z}|\mathbf{h}, \mathbf{v}). \tag{12}$$

in which we denote by $\mathbf{v}$ the available HR image ($\mathbf{m}$ or $\mathbf{p}$). A reliable solution of (12) can be found by regularizing the problem by adding a penalization term to the quantity $p(\mathbf{z}|\mathbf{h}, \mathbf{v})$. Examples of widely employed regularization terms include Gaussian priors [43, 44] or vector total variation (VTV) [22].

3. Quality assessment of fusion products

In this section, we present the performance assessment setup procedure for sharpening the HS data. The objective is to test the viability of fusion algorithms to reach a resolution enhancement factor R that goes beyond the limitations of single-platform setups. In the specific testbed, the HS data are constituted by acquisitions taken by the Hyperion sensor, which is characterized by a GSI of 30 m. The satellite platform also features the a PAN sensor, called ALI, whose GSI is 10 m, which corresponds to a nominal enhancement factor $R = 3$. For more ambitious factors, two extra scenarios are considered; in particular a very interesting comparison can be taken at $R = 6$ and $R = 12$ by analyzing different behaviors for single- and multi-platform with a selection of 12 state-of-the-art fusion algorithms. Specifically the single-platform case requires a preliminary interpolation of the ALI images, here performed via a convolution with a 45-tap interpolation kernel. The multi-platform case will employ, as companion source image, the MS imagery acquired by the WorldView-3, which instead have to be downsized to the target resolution, as it is characterized by a smaller GSI than the target one reached by all the considered R. The decimation procedure is performed by employing a filter, mimicking the modulation transfer function of the MS sensor and a downsampling.

We want to remark here that this study will ignore the contribution of the ALI MS and WV3 PAN sensors. The former has the same GSI of the Hyperion sensor, making its information mostly redundant. Regarding the latter, we want to remark that the native GSI of the MS WV3 sensors already exceeds that of the target resolution characterized, for all R under examination. Consequently, it is preferable to employ the MS sensor, as it is already characterized by a better spectral resolution, as shown in previous studies [14, 41].

3.1 Assessment procedure

The assessment procedure has been carried out at *reduced resolution*, namely, the original HS image is used as reference, and the images to fuse are obtained by degrading the available images by a factor equal to the resolution enhancement factor R. The adopted Wald's protocol [23] requires the reproduction of the characteristics of the fusion problem at a lower resolution. Accordingly, all the available images are degraded by using an MTF-shaped filter matched to the specific sensor and a downsampling system with factor R.

The reduced resolution assessment protocol allows the use of many accurate quality indexes, since the ground truth image is available. In this work we consider the *spectral angle mapper* [42] for evaluating the spectral distortion and the *erreur relative globale adimensionnelle de synthèse* (*ERGAS*) [45] for assessing the radiometric distortion. The vectorial $Q2^n$-index [46] index is used for obtaining a comprehensive measure of the overall image quality. Finally, we employed the *universal image quality index* (*UIQI*) or *Q-index*, proposed by Wang and Bovik [47], for performing a band-by-band comparison of the final product with the reference image.

3.2 Datasets

Three datasets are used for illustrating the capabilities of data fusion algorithms in producing very high-resolution hyperspectral images. The images have been acquired by the *Earth Observing-1* and *WorldView-3* sensors. The different settings allow to examine the features of the sharpening algorithms in the presence of the most common issues implied by multi-platform data fusion, namely, the different points of view and the temporal changes in the illuminated scenes between the two acquisitions. In this study we employ the visible near-infrared (VNIR) bands B09-B57, acquired by the sensor Hyperion, as HS data. The single-platform companion data are constituted by the PAN images collected by the ALI sensor, having a 10 m spatial resolution. All EO-1 data share a radiometric resolution of 15 bits. The multi-platform data have been acquired by the WV3 satellite. They are represented by an MS image composed of eight channels (coastal, blue, green, yellow, red, red edge, NIR1, and NIR2) with a radiometric resolution of 11 bits and an original spatial resolution of 1.2 m.

The employed datasets are briefly described below:

- *Harlem dataset*: the images have been collected in New York, USA, in the neighborhoods of the Harlem River. The size of the Hyperion and PAN ALI data, acquired on July 21, 2016, is 144 × 144 pixels and 432 × 432 pixels, respectively, while the native dimension of the WV3 MS image, acquired on June 9, 2016, is 4320 × 4320 pixels.

- *Agnano dataset*: the images refer to the area of the Agnano Racecourse, next to the city of Naples, Italy. The size of the Hyperion data is 144 × 72 pixels, and thus the corresponding ALI and WV3 images are composed by 432 × 216 pixels and 4320 × 1660 pixels, respectively. The acquisition dates of the EO-1 and WV3 sensors are May 20, 2015, and June 8, 2015, respectively.

- *Capodichino dataset*: the images refer to the east surrounding Naples, Italy, around Capodichino Airport. The images are composed of the same number of pixels of the *Agnano dataset* and were acquired on May 20, 2015, and on February 4, 2002, by the EO-1 and WV3 satellites, respectively.

3.3 Fusion algorithms

We compare several fusion algorithms to fully assess the quality of HS products achievable through data acquired by a single or multiple platforms. We firstly focus on the use of classical pansharpening approaches, which constitute an almost ready-to-use solution and then present the purposely designed methods. Among the wide plethora of available pansharpening methods [24], we employed the following CS and MRA methods: *Brovey transform* [26], *Gram-Schmidt* spectral sharpening [32], and the *Gram-Schmidt adaptive* [33] belonging to the CS class, the *additive wavelet luminance proportional* (AWLP) [37], the *generalized Laplacian pyramid* [48] with MTF-matched filter [49] using both the *high-pass modulation* scheme [50] (GLP-HPM), and the *regression-based* injection model (GLP-CBD) [51] belonging to the MRA class.

Among the second group of approaches, we consider the *hypersharpening* (Hyper) method, developed in [16, 17], and four Bayesian techniques, namely, the *coupled nonnegative matrix factorization* (CNMF) [21], the *naive Gaussian prior* (Bay-N) [43], the *sparsity promoted Gaussian prior* (Bay-S) [44], and the *hyperspectral superresolution* (HySure) [22].

Finally, we report the results related to a method for upscaling the original image at the target scale by a simple interpolation of the original HS image. We denote as EXP this method that is carried out through a 45-tap interpolation filter and that constitutes also the baseline for more complex sharpening methods presented here.

4. Experimental results

The performance of the fusion algorithms are evaluated both by calculating the numerical values of the chosen quality indexes and by assessing the final products by visual inspection.

The first proposed dataset is about *Harlem* that has the purpose of illustrating the capabilities of producing a significant improvement of the spatial quality of the original HS images through the compared algorithms. To this aim, we report in **Figure 1** the results related to all the tested enhancement factors (R = 3,6,12), using one exemplary algorithm of each class. The RGB images are built by averaging a group of channels in the red, green, and blue frequency ranges (B29–B33, B17–B22, and B11–B15, respectively) to construct the required channels. Naturally, all the reference images (or *ground truth*) coincide, since they are represented by the original HS image; see **Figure 1(a)**, **(m)**, and **(y)**. On the contrary, the simulated LR HS images, whose upsampled versions (EXP) are reported in **Figure 1(g)**, **(s)**, and **(ae)**, get more and more degraded as the enhancement factor increases.

Some introductory considerations can be drawn from the images in **Figure 1** obtained by using the SAM-AA for coupling the MS bands to the HS channels. In fact, the first remarkable result is the high quality of the final products achievable also at very high enhancement factors. More in detail, the images obtained by using classical GLP-CBD and the Hyper approach (which constitutes a generalization of the former approach, since both employ a regression-based injection scheme) produce the most appealing sharpened image. They are able to greatly enhance the spatial content of the original HS image, preserving an appreciable coherence of the colors.

On the other hand, the images achievable by using the ALI PAN have a satisfactory aspect only for R=3, as it was arguable by the 10 m resolution of the employed HR sensor. The effect of the interpolation is clearly visible in **Figure 1(n)** and **(z)**, and, thus, this approach could be preferable only when spatial or temporal misalignments among the multi-platform data cannot be avoided.

Those results are perfectly matched to the index values contained in **Table 1**. Actually, the numerical values point out that in most cases, the use of perfectly aligned images coming from a different satellite can produce images with superior quality also in the case of R=3. In this case, the closer correspondence between the details extracted in the MS channel and the missing spatial information of the HS image can justify the outcome.

Finally, we note that the comparison among the assignation algorithms mainly underlines that the two methods optimizing the assignation according to the specific dataset get almost the same results.

The other two scenes allow to gain more insight about the comparison of the sharpening algorithms and of the assignation algorithms. The EO-1 data have been extracted by the same images, while the multi-platform data have very different characteristics. In fact, while the WV3 image of the *Agnano* dataset has been acquired within a few days from the EO-1 data, the WV3 image of the *Capodichino* was collected more than 10 years earlier. Accordingly, the layout of the object present in the *Capodichino* scene is very different among the two passages, also because the area contains rapidly changing objects. A comparison of the two images can be achieved by having a look at **Figure 2(a)** and **(b)**. The latter scene refers to Naples Airport and contains a plane on the runway that is not detectable in the corresponding WV3 MS image shown in **Figure 3(d)**. Furthermore, different man-made objects are present in the illuminated area at the two acquisition times.

The results related to the *Agnano* dataset (see **Table 2**) confirm the conclusions drawn from the analysis of the *Harlem* dataset. They correspond to the most typical situation in which the images to fuse are ordered to a data provider, minimizing as

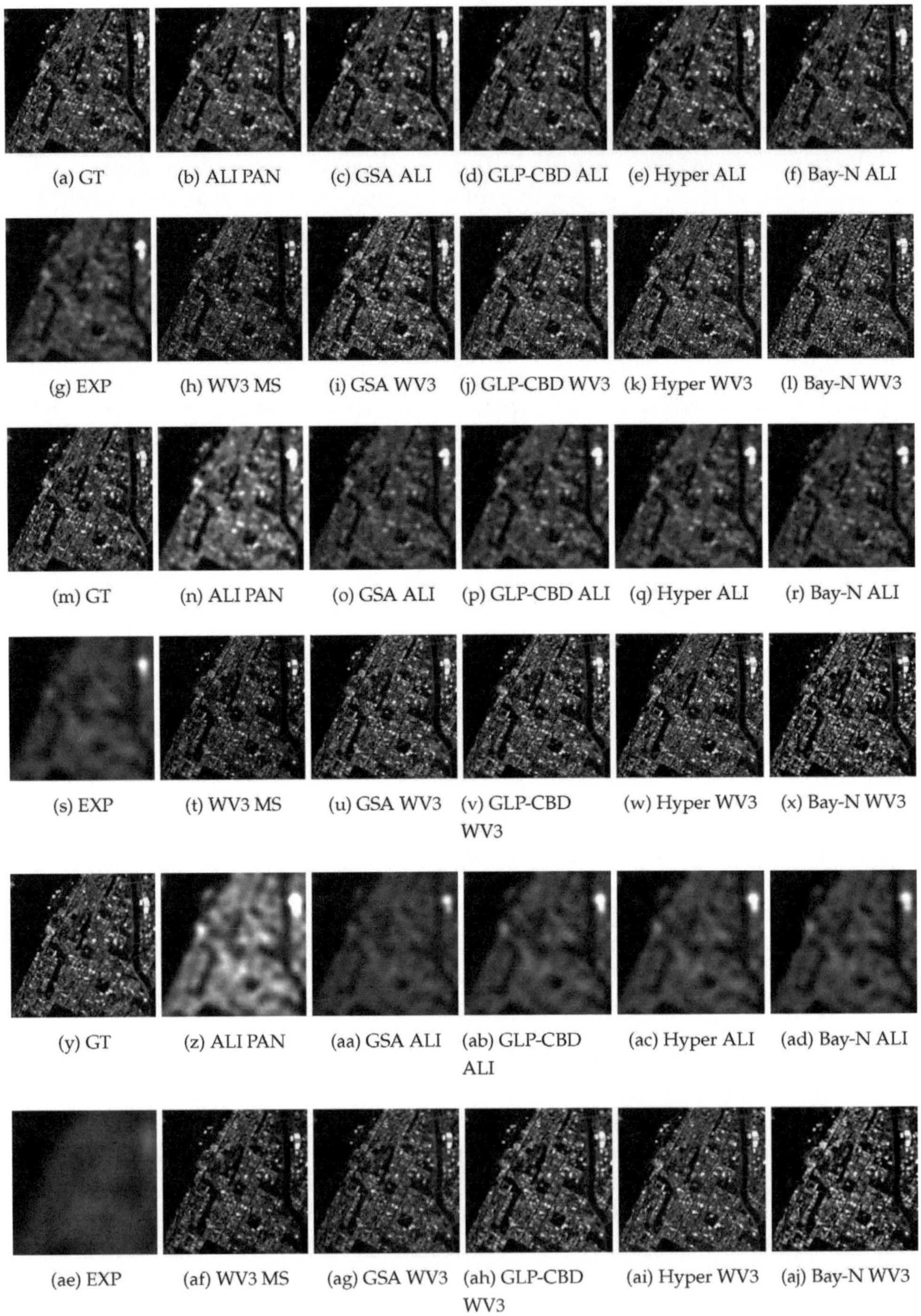

Figure 1.
Close-ups of the products achieved by applying the pansharpening algorithms to the RR Harlem *dataset (red, green, and blue bands). The resolution enhancement factor is R = 3 (first two rows), 6 (3rd and 4th rows), 12 (5th and 6th rows). (WorldView-3 satellite images courtesy of the DigitalGlobe Foundation). The figure labels indicate the fusion algorithm (see Section 3.3) and the high resolution data utilized.*

much as possible the difference between the passage times of the two satellites. Accordingly, in both cases, the illuminated areas contain very similar features that make the multi-temporal data particularly valuable. However, both also represent

		$R = 3$			$R = 6$			$R = 12$		
		SAM	ERGAS	$Q2^n$	SAM	ERGAS	$Q2^n$	SAM	ERGAS	$Q2^n$
Optimum		0	0	1	0	0	1	0	0	1
EXP		3.5265	5.8326	0.7130	5.1319	3.8836	0.4504	6.5924	2.3097	0.1948
BT	PAN	3.5265	6.5102	0.7966	5.1319	3.9027	0.6722	6.5924	2.2775	0.4588
	MS-CEN	3.5803	5.2828	0.8226	4.2943	2.8664	0.7881	4.9775	1.6175	0.7234
	MS-CC	3.3063	5.1159	**0.8228**	**3.9316**	**2.7988**	**0.7893**	**4.6801**	**1.6036**	**0.7325**
	MS-SAM	**3.2360**	**5.1028**	0.8210	**3.9316**	**2.7988**	**0.7893**	**4.6801**	**1.6036**	**0.7325**
GS	PAN	5.3862	7.0484	0.8087	6.6416	4.1369	0.6680	7.7176	2.3742	0.4410
	MS-CEN	3.6328	5.2939	0.8230	4.3261	2.8723	0.7886	4.9842	1.6189	0.7235
	MS-CC	3.2752	5.1224	**0.8265**	**3.8607**	**2.7679**	**0.7929**	**4.5271**	**1.5734**	**0.7273**
	MS-SAM	**3.2524**	**5.1175**	0.8264	**3.8607**	**2.7679**	**0.7929**	**4.5271**	**1.5734**	**0.7273**
GSA	PAN	3.2214	**4.7124**	**0.8738**	4.8934	3.3652	0.6894	6.6072	2.2022	0.4087
	MS-CEN	3.5223	5.3652	0.8409	3.4018	2.5822	0.8428	3.8959	1.3216	**0.8294**
	MS-CC	**3.1317**	4.9960	0.8560	**2.9116**	**2.3978**	**0.8584**	**3.4708**	**1.2932**	0.8209
	MS-SAM	3.1743	4.9975	0.8561	**2.9116**	**2.3978**	**0.8584**	**3.4708**	**1.2932**	0.8209
AWLP	PAN	3.7616	5.4225	0.8676	5.2760	3.4602	0.6878	6.6735	2.2121	0.3316
	MS-CEN	2.8262	4.3152	0.8917	3.4476	2.5087	0.8453	4.6396	1.5423	0.7435
	MS-CC	2.5918	4.0802	**0.8964**	**3.1629**	**2.4025**	**0.8500**	**4.4146**	**1.5199**	**0.7475**
	MS-SAM	**2.5858**	**4.0637**	0.8957	**3.1629**	**2.4025**	**0.8500**	**4.4146**	**1.5199**	**0.7475**
GLP-HPM	PAN	3.8136	5.4635	0.8586	5.4884	3.7330	0.6855	6.9504	2.2929	0.4577
	MS-CEN	2.3843	3.8074	0.9040	3.1578	2.3075	0.8535	3.9734	1.3581	0.7813
	MS-CC	**2.1285**	**3.6578**	**0.9083**	**2.7886**	**2.2014**	**0.8592**	**3.5383**	**1.3000**	**0.7867**
	MS-SAM	2.1307	3.6586	0.9082	**2.7886**	**2.2014**	**0.8592**	**3.5383**	**1.3000**	**0.7867**
GLP-CBD	PAN	3.1941	4.5103	0.8809	4.9075	3.3653	0.7091	6.7263	2.2100	0.4833
	MS-CEN	2.4442	4.0778	0.8955	3.0302	2.3854	0.8653	3.3037	1.2603	0.8559
	MS-CC	2.1961	3.9109	**0.9007**	**2.6360**	**2.2524**	**0.8728**	**2.7772**	**1.1730**	**0.8643**
	MS-SAM	**2.1949**	**3.9103**	0.9007	**2.6360**	**2.2524**	**0.8728**	**2.7772**	**1.1730**	**0.8643**
Hyper	PAN	3.1925	4.5103	0.8809	4.8948	3.3646	0.7091	6.5771	2.2062	0.4840
	MS	**2.1810**	**4.1296**	**0.8901**	**2.5145**	**2.3331**	**0.8631**	**2.4683**	**1.1685**	**0.8584**
CNMF	PAN	3.6166	**4.9517**	**0.8486**	5.1629	3.4878	0.6767	6.5140	2.1778	0.4502
	MS	**2.7434**	5.0313	0.8244	**3.0144**	**2.5666**	**0.8161**	**3.1548**	**1.2958**	**0.8152**
Bay-N	PAN	3.0726	**4.1725**	**0.8832**	5.5648	3.6632	0.6391	7.3189	2.2828	0.4263
	MS	**2.4412**	4.2739	0.8741	**3.7782**	**2.8095**	**0.8122**	**4.1716**	**1.4252**	**0.8083**
Bay-S	PAN	2.9726	**4.1264**	**0.8857**	5.4515	3.6479	0.6328	7.3540	2.2766	0.4241
	MS	**2.4381**	4.2740	0.8741	**3.7800**	**2.8104**	**0.8122**	**4.1295**	**1.4233**	**0.8085**
HySure	PAN	2.9758	**4.2484**	**0.8864**	6.6141	4.3498	0.6034	7.7052	2.3314	0.4497
	MS	**2.3304**	4.5347	0.8634	**3.7736**	**2.8694**	**0.8068**	**3.4966**	**1.3647**	**0.8187**

For each algorithm, the best result among the HR options is in boldface.

Table 1.
Values of the quality indexes, related to the reduced resolution assessment procedure, using the Harlem *dataset, for resolution enhancement ratio* $R = 3, 6, 12$.

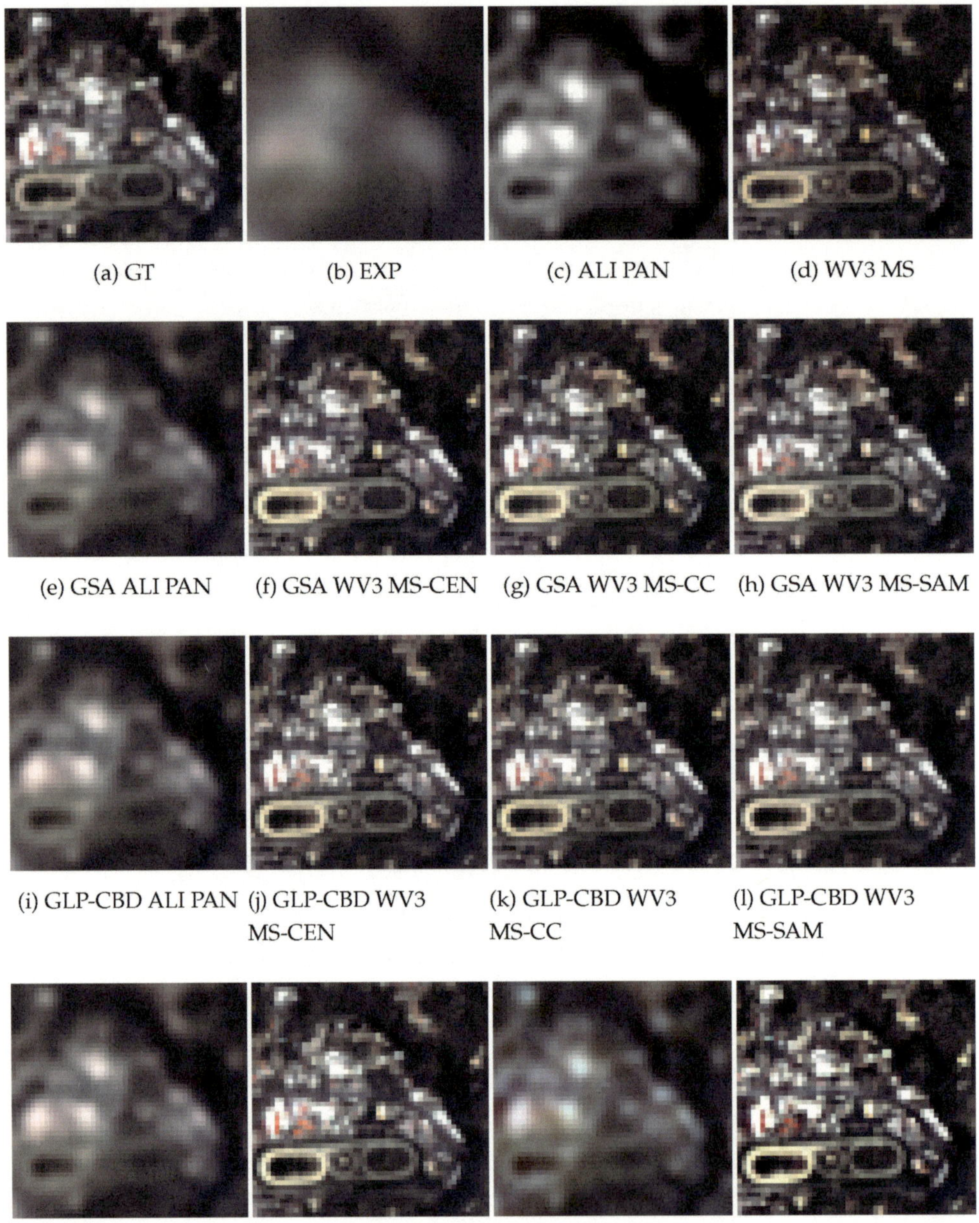

(a) GT (b) EXP (c) ALI PAN (d) WV3 MS

(e) GSA ALI PAN (f) GSA WV3 MS-CEN (g) GSA WV3 MS-CC (h) GSA WV3 MS-SAM

(i) GLP-CBD ALI PAN (j) GLP-CBD WV3 MS-CEN (k) GLP-CBD WV3 MS-CC (l) GLP-CBD WV3 MS-SAM

(m) Hyper ALI PAN (n) Hyper WV3 MS (o) Bayes N ALI PAN (p) Bayes N WV3 MS

Figure 2.
Close-ups of the products achieved by applying the pansharpening algorithms to the RR Agnano *dataset (red, green, and blue bands). The resolution enhancement factor is $R = 6$ (WorldView-3 satellite images courtesy of the DigitalGlobe Foundation). The figure labels indicate the fusion method (see Section 3.3), the high resolution data and the assignation algorithm (see Section 2.1.2), utilized.*

almost ideal cases, since the presence of rapidly changing objects, for example, the aircrafts present in the *Capodichino* dataset, can vary also within very close passages. Accordingly, particularly interesting is the case of the *Capodichino* dataset, which gives rise to somewhat unalike results, which are reported in **Table 3**. In fact, in most cases, the single-platform setting almost always yields better results, even if the visual appearance of the images related to the multi-platform approach is often preferable in terms of quantity of injected details (see **Figure 3**). Actually, a more accurate analysis evidences that multi-platform products yield a sharpened image in

(a) GT (b) EXP (c) ALI PAN (d) WV3 MS

(e) GSA ALI PAN (f) GSA WV3 MS-CEN (g) GSA WV3 MS-CC (h) GSA WV3 MS-SAM

(i) GLP-CBD ALI PAN (j) GLP-CBD WV3 MS-CEN (k) GLP-CBD WV3 MS-CC (l) GLP-CBD WV3 MS-SAM

(m) Hyper ALI PAN (n) Hyper WV3 MS (o) Bayes N ALI PAN (p) Bayes N WV3 MS

Figure 3.
Close-ups of the products achieved by applying the pansharpening algorithms to the RR Capodichino *dataset (red, green, and blue bands). The resolution enhancement factor is $R = 6$ (WorldView-3 satellite images courtesy of the DigitalGlobe Foundation). The figure labels indicate the fusion method (see Section 3.3), the high resolution data and the assignation algorithm (see Section 2.1.2), utilized.*

which the plane is absent (especially in CS methods). Moreover, the spectral quality of the final products is significantly compromised if the WV3 MS images are used.

The spatial quality differences among the various algorithms can be further investigated by resorting to a quality index that allows a band-by-band analysis of the quality of the algorithms output. To this aim, we report in **Figures 4** and **5** the behavior of the Q-index as a function of the HS band. The two images reveal both similarities and discrepancies in the algorithms' performance. In particular, we can note that for the HS channels with support contained in the frequency range

		$R = 3$			$R = 6$			$R = 12$		
		SAM	ERGAS	$Q2^n$	SAM	ERGAS	$Q2^n$	SAM	ERGAS	$Q2^n$
Optimum		0	0	1	0	0	1	0	0	1
EXP		2.6173	2.5563	0.8068	3.7601	1.7890	0.5523	4.6496	1.0807	0.2831
BT	PAN	**2.6173**	3.0548	0.8058	3.7601	1.8723	0.6009	4.6496	1.0984	0.3604
	MS-CEN	3.2295	2.8406	0.8228	3.6738	1.5425	0.7624	4.2802	0.9126	0.6314
	MS-CC	2.8772	**2.7482**	**0.8259**	**3.3037**	**1.4760**	**0.7778**	3.9821	**0.8829**	**0.6574**
	MS-SAM	2.8785	2.7545	0.8246	3.3167	1.4778	0.7771	**3.9799**	0.8831	0.6573
GS	PAN	**2.5586**	2.9906	0.8245	3.5826	1.8154	0.6350	4.4993	1.0752	0.3833
	MS-CEN	3.3566	2.9027	0.8164	3.7937	1.5864	0.7551	4.3747	0.9302	0.6257
	MS-CC	2.8725	**2.7552**	**0.8289**	**3.2766**	**1.4747**	**0.7795**	3.9470	0.8804	0.6553
	MS-SAM	2.8751	2.7627	0.8279	3.2827	1.4756	0.7792	**3.9423**	**0.8803**	**0.6554**
GSA	PAN	**2.0386**	**1.9146**	**0.9131**	2.9847	1.4490	0.7389	4.0761	0.9754	0.4544
	MS-CEN	3.5162	3.3626	0.8386	3.4506	1.5113	0.8447	3.5818	0.7576	0.8114
	MS-CC	3.1628	3.2125	0.8467	2.6754	**1.3571**	**0.8631**	**2.7824**	**0.6787**	0.8335
	MS-SAM	3.1205	3.2341	0.8434	**2.6582**	1.3579	0.8625	2.7882	0.6801	**0.8343**
AWLP	PAN	2.8338	2.5814	0.8813	3.8646	1.6842	0.6804	4.7083	1.0524	0.3699
	MS-CEN	2.7408	2.3775	0.9046	3.3902	1.3975	0.8461	4.2634	0.8638	0.7295
	MS-CC	2.0621	**1.9661**	**0.9277**	**2.4336**	**1.1492**	**0.8788**	**3.1755**	**0.7410**	**0.7617**
	MS-SAM	**2.0383**	1.9784	0.9257	2.4348	1.1512	0.8779	3.1781	0.7414	0.7613
HPM	PAN	2.6258	2.3637	0.8801	3.7500	1.6695	0.6946	4.6745	1.0314	0.4644
	MS-CEN	2.0732	1.8683	0.9279	2.7382	1.1754	0.8645	3.4479	0.7399	0.7318
	MS-CC	1.6181	**1.6259**	**0.9404**	**2.2147**	**1.0522**	**0.8808**	3.0151	**0.6926**	0.7478
	MS-SAM	**1.6025**	1.6284	0.9401	2.2211	1.0528	0.8806	**3.0126**	0.6927	**0.7478**
GLP-CBD	PAN	1.9534	1.8586	0.9140	2.9661	1.4434	0.7528	3.7656	0.9312	0.5485
	MS-CEN	2.1162	1.9590	0.9251	2.8919	1.2444	0.8807	3.5286	0.7418	0.8378
	MS-CC	1.7546	**1.8129**	**0.9340**	2.1960	**1.1043**	**0.9003**	**2.4993**	0.6279	0.8699
	MS-SAM	**1.7344**	1.8256	0.9323	**2.1917**	1.1067	0.8994	2.5042	**0.6276**	**0.8699**
Hyper	PAN	1.9543	1.8586	0.9140	2.9688	1.4419	0.7530	3.7703	0.9171	0.5490
	MS	**1.5897**	**1.7214**	**0.9382**	**2.0229**	**1.0444**	**0.9080**	**2.6430**	**0.6815**	**0.8437**
CNMF	PAN	2.7720	**2.6075**	**0.8584**	3.8859	1.7337	0.7138	4.6329	1.0405	0.5231
	MS	**2.5088**	2.7525	0.8413	**2.6865**	**1.3843**	**0.8302**	**3.0105**	**0.7685**	**0.7988**
Bay-N	PAN	2.2560	**2.1131**	**0.9017**	3.8832	1.7313	0.6794	5.0346	1.1319	0.5224
	MS	**2.2126**	2.3448	0.8934	**3.4757**	**1.6422**	**0.8013**	**3.9694**	**0.9266**	**0.7793**
Bay-S	PAN	**1.9858**	**1.8416**	**0.9190**	3.7604	1.6862	0.6807	4.9424	1.1049	0.5233
	MS	2.2130	2.3451	0.8934	**3.4818**	**1.6433**	**0.8010**	**4.1745**	**0.9468**	**0.7705**
HySure	PAN	**2.3509**	**2.2174**	**0.8922**	4.5235	2.0695	0.6128	5.3742	1.2250	0.5362
	MS	2.5649	2.7776	0.8513	**3.1989**	**1.5863**	**0.7770**	**3.2956**	**0.8437**	**0.7707**

For each algorithm, the best result among the HR options is in boldface.

Table 2.
Values of the quality indexes, related to the reduced resolution assessment procedure, using the Agnano *dataset, for resolution enhancement ratio* $R = 3, 6, 12$.

		$R = 3$			$R = 6$			$R = 12$		
		SAM	ERGAS	$Q2^n$	SAM	ERGAS	$Q2^n$	SAM	ERGAS	$Q2^n$
Optimum		0	0	1	0	0	1	0	0	1
EXP		2.9041	3.4640	0.7607	4.0809	2.3556	0.4930	5.1271	1.4488	0.2097
BT	PAN	**2.9041**	**4.1628**	**0.7804**	**4.0809**	**2.4750**	**0.6310**	5.1271	**1.4643**	0.3702
	MS-CEN	4.6792	5.7317	0.5938	4.9025	2.8810	0.5576	5.2432	1.5154	0.4746
	MS-CC	4.4343	5.5489	0.5875	4.6256	2.8173	0.5608	**4.8858**	1.4960	0.4877
	MS-SAM	4.4509	5.6304	0.5926	4.5951	2.8322	0.5656	4.8969	1.4970	**0.4884**
GS	PAN	**3.2286**	**4.2133**	**0.7758**	4.6558	**2.5912**	**0.5960**	6.0683	1.5821	0.3326
	MS-CEN	4.7700	5.7476	0.5942	5.0022	2.8997	0.5559	5.3204	1.5280	0.4738
	MS-CC	4.4891	5.6363	0.6008	4.5862	2.8320	0.5674	4.8663	**1.4973**	0.4873
	MS-SAM	4.4772	5.6713	0.6002	**4.5710**	2.8401	0.5688	**4.8625**	1.4977	**0.4875**
GSA	PAN	**2.4807**	**2.5976**	**0.8833**	**3.4450**	**1.8687**	**0.6998**	4.7540	**1.2970**	0.3636
	MS-CEN	7.0619	8.2274	0.5357	6.4658	3.6062	0.5650	6.2811	1.6761	0.5705
	MS-CC	6.0976	6.8763	0.6001	5.1292	2.9285	0.6236	4.5374	1.3304	**0.6124**
	MS-SAM	6.3286	7.3363	0.5718	5.1970	3.0603	0.6081	**4.5366**	1.3311	0.6116
AWLP	PAN	**3.1491**	**3.3732**	**0.8598**	4.3651	**2.1254**	0.6899	5.3684	1.3789	0.3466
	MS-CEN	3.5341	3.9606	0.7920	4.4168	2.4048	0.6799	5.3696	1.4223	0.5509
	MS-CC	3.2680	3.6163	0.8090	3.9660	2.2291	0.7016	4.6378	**1.3293**	0.5765
	MS-SAM	3.2595	3.6703	0.8095	**3.9215**	2.2381	**0.7044**	**4.6313**	1.3300	**0.5770**
HPM	PAN	3.0965	3.1605	**0.8526**	4.4371	2.2155	0.6823	5.6302	1.4059	0.4234
	MS-CEN	2.7198	3.1964	0.8373	3.5213	2.0407	0.7212	4.2637	1.2216	0.5688
	MS-CC	2.5362	**3.0548**	0.8462	3.2128	**1.9735**	0.7323	3.8668	**1.1926**	0.5824
	MS-SAM	**2.5133**	3.0672	0.8469	**3.1841**	1.9742	**0.7343**	**3.8640**	1.1927	**0.5827**
CBD	PAN	**2.4126**	**2.5037**	**0.8832**	**3.3688**	**1.8193**	0.7261	4.5275	**1.2246**	0.4657
	MS-CEN	2.6355	3.1271	0.8385	3.6260	2.1248	0.7234	4.7470	1.3681	0.6321
	MS-CC	2.5513	3.0624	0.8432	3.4488	2.0790	0.7322	4.2992	1.3201	**0.6488**
	MS-SAM	2.5421	3.0807	0.8436	3.4306	2.0895	**0.7336**	**4.2828**	1.3220	0.6487
Hyper	PAN	**2.4126**	**2.5037**	**0.8832**	**3.3684**	**1.8199**	**0.7259**	**4.5152**	**1.2254**	0.4652
	MS	2.7138	3.2570	0.8224	3.8293	2.2194	0.6966	4.6147	1.3181	**0.6051**
CNMF	PAN	**3.0309**	**3.2174**	**0.8361**	4.1597	**2.1199**	**0.7035**	5.0892	**1.3082**	0.4882
	MS	4.2695	5.4648	0.5984	**3.7804**	2.6307	0.6027	**4.3318**	1.4644	**0.5163**
Bay-N	PAN	**2.4809**	**2.5412**	**0.8897**	**4.2876**	**2.1478**	**0.6600**	5.7306	**1.4619**	0.4276
	MS	2.8266	3.3996	0.8173	4.3109	2.5638	0.6354	**4.9158**	1.5127	**0.5777**
Bay-S	PAN	**2.3080**	**2.3705**	**0.8981**	**4.1732**	**2.1120**	**0.6596**	5.7597	**1.4522**	0.4304
	MS	2.8267	3.3989	0.8173	4.3114	2.5637	0.6354	**4.9126**	1.5115	**0.5780**
HySure	PAN	**2.4928**	**2.7947**	**0.8754**	5.3229	**2.7732**	**0.6101**	5.7868	**1.4747**	0.4592
	MS	3.2759	4.3963	0.7367	**4.1931**	2.8471	0.5906	**4.5497**	1.5079	**0.5723**

For each algorithm, the best result among the HR options is in boldface.

Table 3.
Values of the quality indexes, related to the reduced resolution assessment procedure, using the Capodichino *dataset, for resolution enhancement ratio* $R = 3, 6, 12$.

covered by the ALI PAN, the use of single-platform data is always preferable, except for the case of the Hyper algorithm applied to the *Agnano* dataset with $R = 6$. Clearly, this consideration is all the more true in the experiment related to the *Capodichino* dataset. Instead, different trends are experienced for the near-infrared (NIR) bands. All the algorithms (except the GSA algorithm with $R = 3$) obtain better

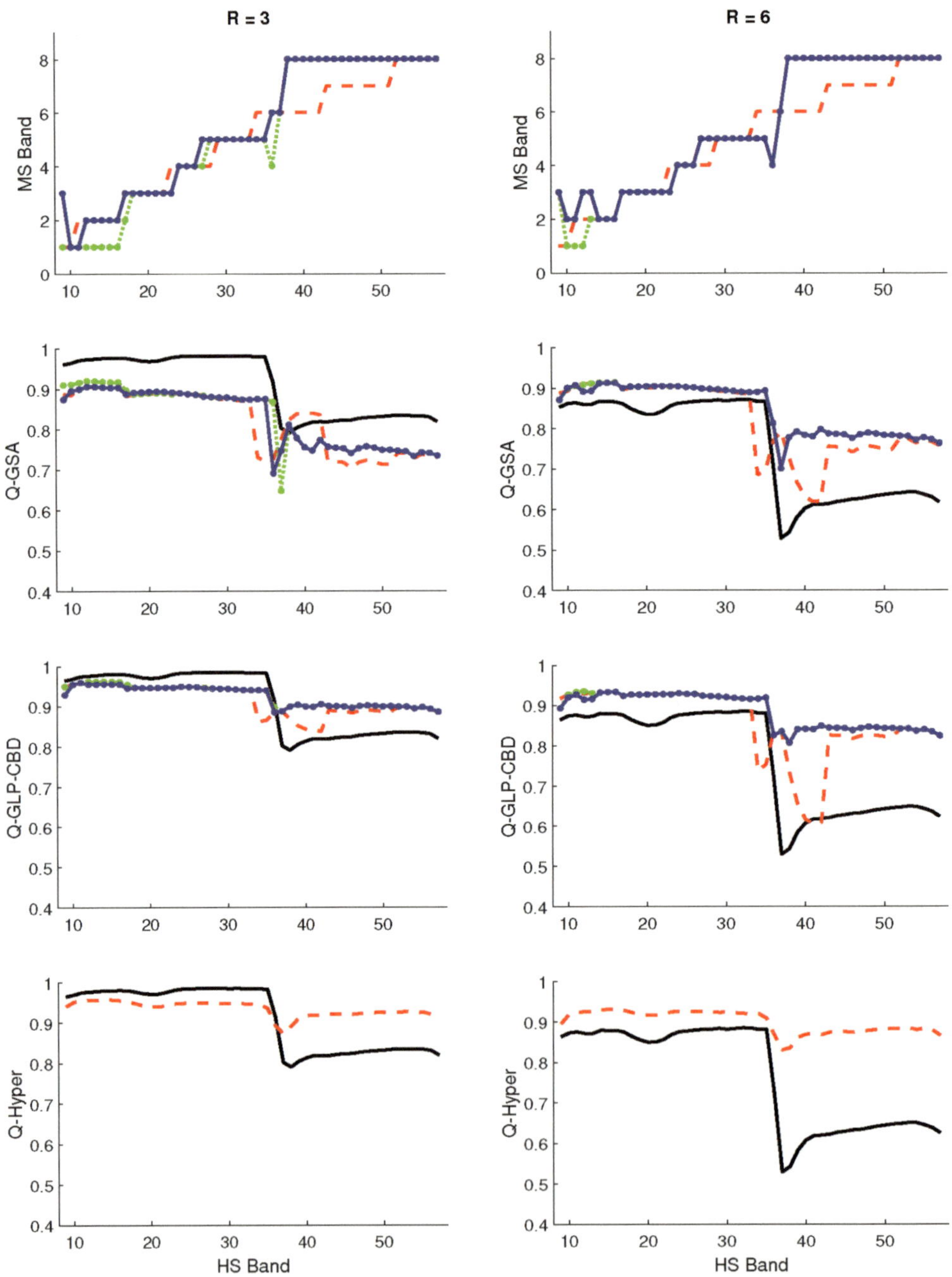

Figure 4.
Q-index as a function of the HS band for the Agnano *dataset. The curves refer to the data fusion of the Hyperion images with the ALI PAN (black continuous), the MS-CEN (red dashed curve), MS-CC (green dotted curve), and MS-SAM (blue continuous curve with circle marks).*

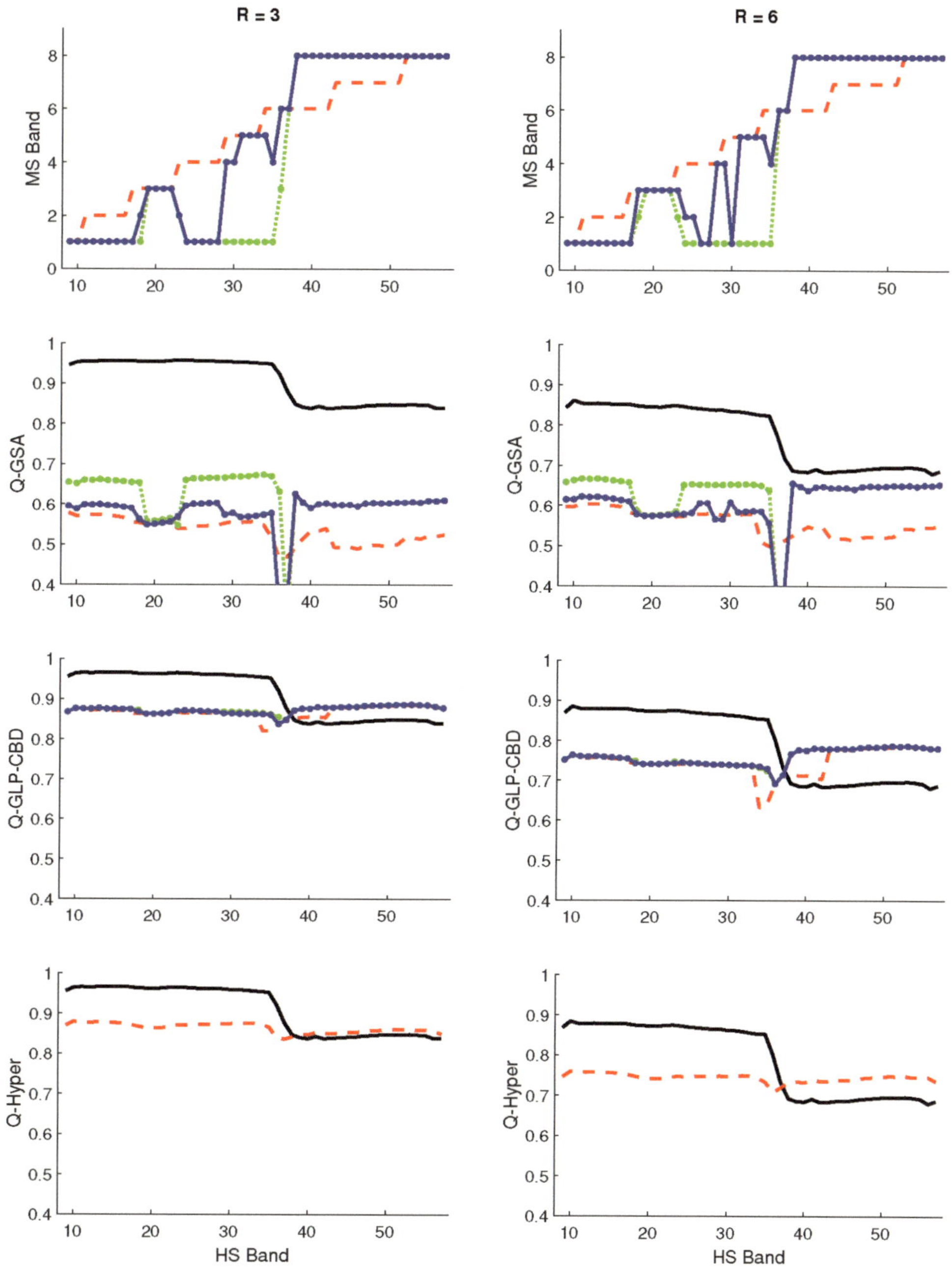

Figure 5.
Q-index as a function of the HS band for the Capodichino *dataset. The curves refer to the data fusion of the Hyperion images with the ALI PAN (black continuous), the MS-CEN (red dashed curve), MS-CC (green dotted curve), and MS-SAM (blue continuous curve with circle marks).*

performance by using multi-platform data working on the *Agnano* dataset. On the contrary, using the *Capodichino* dataset, the GSA algorithms always obtain superior results by using the ALI PAN image, while the other two methods obtain a slightly better performance in the NIR region that is not able to balance the scarce quality in the visible range, thus resulting in an inferior overall performance of the multi-platform approach. Finally, it is very clear from both **Figures 4** and **5** that the

CC-AA and the SAM-AA algorithms are able to obtain significant improvements with respect to CEN-CC, especially in the NIR frequencies.

5. Conclusions

The aim of this work was to illustrate the recent advances in the field of hyperspectral image sharpening through single-platform and multi-platform data. The study was conducted on real data acquired by the Earth Observing-1 and the WorldView-3 satellites in order to highlight the practical issues to be addressed when fusing images acquired by different platforms. We focused on well-known algorithms based on classical approaches borrowed from the pansharpening literature and on techniques developed on purpose. We evaluated the possibility of completing the fusion process, both in the absence and presence of temporal misalignments between the scenes illuminated by the sensors mounted on the two satellites. The study highlighted the suitability of the employment of multi-platform data especially in the presence of high-resolution enhancement factors. Actually, in some cases, the use of multispectral images was also proven to be useful at low-resolution enhancement factors, and this result can be easily justified by taking into consideration that the details contained in the MS channels are able to provide more specific spatial information for a given HS channel.

Author details

Rocco Restaino[1†], Gemine Vivone[2*†], Paolo Addesso[1†], Daniele Picone[3†] and Jocelyn Chanussot[3†]

1 Department of Information Engineering, Electrical Engineering and Applied Mathematics, University of Salerno, Fisciano, Italy

2 Institute of Methodologies for Environmental Analysis, CNR-IMAA, Tito Scalo, Italy

3 University Grenoble Alpes, CNRS, Grenoble INP, GIPSA-lab, Grenoble, France

*Address all correspondence to: gvivone@unisa.it; gemine.vivone@imaa.cnr.it

† These authors contributed equally.

References

[1] Camps-Valls G, Tuia D, Bruzzone L, Benediktsson JA. Advances in hyperspectral image classification: Earth monitoring with statistical learning methods. IEEE Signal Processing Magazine. 2014;**31**(1):45-54

[2] Yang J, Zhao Y-Q, Chan JC-W. Survey of hyperspectral earth observation applications from space in the Sentinel-2 context. Remote Sensing. 2018;**10**(2):157

[3] Gomez C, Viscarra Rossel RA, McBratney AB. Soil organic carbon prediction by hyperspectral remote sensing and field vis-NIR spectroscopy: An Australian case study. Geoderma. 2008;**146**(3):403-411

[4] Carter G, Lucas K, Blossom G, Lassitter C, Holiday D, Mooneyhan D, et al. Remote sensing and mapping of tamarisk along the Colorado river, USA: A comparative use of summer-acquired Hyperion, Thematic Mapper and QuickBird data. Remote Sensing. 2009; **1**(3):318-329

[5] Okujeni A, van der Linden S, Hostert P. Extending the vegetation-impervious-soil model using simulated EnMAP data and machine learning. Remote Sensing of Environment. 2015; **158**:69-80

[6] Walsh SJ, McCleary AL, Mena CF, Shao Y, Tuttle JP, González A, et al. Quickbird and Hyperion data analysis of an invasive plant species in the Galapagos islands of Ecuador: Implications for control and land use management. Remote Sensing of Environment. 2008;**112**(5): 1927-1941

[7] Siegmann B, Jarmer T, Beyer F, Ehlers M. The potential of pan-sharpened EnMAP data for the assessment of wheat LAI. Remote Sensing. 2015;**7**(10):12737-12762

[8] Yokoya N, Chan JC-W, Segl K. Potential of resolution-enhanced hyperspectral data for mineral mapping using simulated EnMAP and Sentinel-2 images. Remote Sensing. 2016;**8**(3):172

[9] Loncan L, Fabre S, Almeida LB, Bioucas-Dias JM, Wenzhi L, Briottet X, et al. Hyperspectral pansharpening: A review. IEEE Geoscience and Remote Sensing Magazine. 2015;**3**(3):27-46

[10] Yokoya N, Grohnfeldt C, Chanussot J. Hyperspectral and multispectral data fusion: A comparative review of the recent literature. IEEE Geoscience and Remote Sensing Magazine. 2017;**5**(2):29-56

[11] Marcello J, Ibarrola-Ulzurrun E, Gonzalo-Martn C, Chanussot J, Vivone G. Assessment of hyperspectral sharpening methods for the monitoring of natural areas using multiplatform remote sensing imagery. IEEE Transactions on Geoscience and Remote Sensing. 2019;**57**(10):8208-8222

[12] Vivone G, Restaino R, Licciardi G, Dalla Mura M, Chanussot J. Multiresolution analysis and component substitution techniques for hyperspectral pansharpening. In: Proc. IEEE IGARSS. 2014. pp. 2649-2652

[13] Licciardi GA, Khan MM, Chanussot J. Fusion of hyperspectral and panchromatic images: A hybrid use of indusion and nonlinear PCA. In: Proc. 2012 IEEE International Conference on Image Processing (ICIP). 2012. pp. 2133-2136

[14] Picone D, Restaino R, Vivone G, Addesso P, Dalla Mura M, Chanussot J. Band assignment approaches for hyperspectral sharpening. IEEE Geoscience and Remote Sensing Letters. 2017;**14**(5):739-743

[15] Aiazzi B, Alparone L, Baronti S, Santurri L, Selva M. Spatial resolution enhancement of ASTER thermal bands. Proceedings of SPIE. 2005;**5982**:59821G-59821G–10

[16] Selva M, Aiazzi B, Butera F, Chiarantini L, Baronti S. Hyper-sharpening: A first approach on SIM-GA data. IEEE Journal on Selected Topics in Signal Processing. 2015;**8**(6): 3008-3024

[17] Selva M, Santurri L, Baronti S. "Improving hypersharpening for WorldView-3 data." IEEE Geoscience and Remote Sensing Letters. 2019;**16**(6): 987-991

[18] Hardie RC, Eismann MT, Wilson GL. MAP estimation for hyperspectral image resolution enhancement using an auxiliary sensor. IEEE Transactions on Image Processing. 2004;**13**(9):1174-1184

[19] Zhang Y, De Backer S, Scheunders P. Noise-resistant wavelet-based Bayesian fusion of multispectral and hyperspectral images. IEEE Transactions on Geoscience and Remote Sensing. 2009;**47**(11):3834-3843

[20] Wei Q, Bioucas-Dias J, Dobigeon N, Tourneret J. Hyperspectral and multispectral image fusion based on a sparse representation. IEEE Geoscience and Remote Sensing Letters. 2015;**53**(7): 3658-3668

[21] Yokoya N, Yairi T, Iwasaki A. Coupled nonnegative matrix factorization unmixing for hyperspectral and multispectral data fusion. IEEE Transactions on Geoscience and Remote Sensing. 2012; **50**(2):528-537

[22] Simões M, Bioucas-Dias JM, Almeida LB, Chanussot J. A convex formulation for hyperspectral image superresolution via subspace-based regularization. IEEE Transactions on Geoscience and Remote Sensing. 2015; **53**(6):3373-3388

[23] Wald L, Ranchin T, Mangolini M. Fusion of satellite images of different spatial resolutions: Assessing the quality of resulting images. Photogrammetric Engineering and Remote Sensing. 1997; **63**(6):691-699

[24] Vivone G, Alparone L, Chanussot J, Dalla Mura M, Garzelli A, Licciardi G, et al. A critical comparison among pansharpening algorithms. IEEE Transactions on Geoscience and Remote Sensing. 2015;**53**(5):2565-2586

[25] Tu T-M, Su S-C, Shyu H-C, Huang PS. A new look at IHS-like image fusion methods. Information Fusion. 2001;**2**(3):177-186

[26] Gillespie AR, Kahle AB, Walker RE. Color enhancement of highly correlated images-II. Channel ratio and "chromaticity" transform techniques. Remote Sensing of Environment. 1987; **22**(3):343-365

[27] Carper W, Lillesand T, Kiefer R. The use of intensity-hue-saturation transformations for merging SPOT panchromatic and multispectral image data. Photogrammetric Engineering and Remote Sensing. 1990; **56**(4):459-467

[28] Chavez PS Jr, Sides SC, Anderson JA. Comparison of three different methods to merge multiresolution and multispectral data: Landsat TM and SPOT panchromatic. Photogrammetric Engineering and Remote Sensing. 1991;**57**(3):295-303

[29] Chavez PS Jr, Kwarteng AW. Extracting spectral contrast in Landsat Thematic Mapper image data using selective principal component analysis. Photogrammetric Engineering and Remote Sensing. 1989;**55**(3):339-348

[30] Shettigara VK. A generalized component substitution technique for spatial enhancement of multispectral images using a higher resolution data set. Photogrammetric Engineering and Remote Sensing. 1992;**58**(5):561-567

[31] Shah VP, Younan NH, King RL. An efficient pan-sharpening method via a combined adaptive-PCA approach and contourlets. IEEE Transactions on Geoscience and Remote Sensing. 2008; **46**(5):1323-1335

[32] Laben CA, Brower BV. Process for enhancing the spatial resolution of multispectral imagery using pan-sharpening. 2000, U.S. Patent # 6011875

[33] Aiazzi B, Baronti S, Selva M. Improving component substitution pansharpening through multivariate regression of MS + Pan data. IEEE Transactions on Geoscience and Remote Sensing. 2007;**45**(10):3230-3239

[34] Liu JG. Smoothing filter based intensity modulation: A spectral preserve image fusion technique for improving spatial details. International Journal of Remote Sensing. 2000;**21**(18): 3461-3472

[35] Wald L, Ranchin T. Comments on the paper by Liu "smoothing filter based intensity modulation: A spectral preserve image fusion technique for improving spatial details". International Journal of Remote Sensing. 2002;**23**(3): 593-597

[36] Burt PJ, Adelson EH. The Laplacian pyramid as a compact image code. IEEE Transactions on Communications. 1983; **31**(4):532-540

[37] Otazu X, González-Audícana M, Fors O, Núñez J. Introduction of sensor spectral response into image fusion methods. Application to wavelet-based methods. IEEE Transactions on Geoscience and Remote Sensing. 2005; **43**(10):2376-2385

[38] Restaino R, Vivone G, Dalla Mura M, Chanussot J. Fusion of multispectral and panchromatic images based on morphological operators. IEEE Transactions on Image Processing. 2016; **25**(6):2882-2895

[39] Baronti S, Aiazzi B, Selva M, Garzelli A, Alparone L. A theoretical analysis of the effects of aliasing and misregistration on pansharpened imagery. IEEE Journal on Selected Topics in Signal Processing. 2011;**5**(3): 446-453

[40] Aiazzi B, Alparone L, Baronti S, Carlà R, Garzelli A, Santurri L. Sensitivity of pansharpening methods to temporal and instrumental changes between multispectral and panchromatic data sets. IEEE Transactions on Geoscience and Remote Sensing. 2017;**55**(1):308-319

[41] Picone D, Restaino R, Vivone G, Addesso P, Chanussot J. Pansharpening of hyperspectral images: Exploiting data acquired by multiple platforms. Proc. IEEE IGARSS. 2016:7220-7223

[42] Yuhas RH, Goetz AFH, Boardman JW. Discrimination among semi-arid landscape endmembers using the Spectral Angle Mapper (SAM) algorithm. In: Proc. Summaries of the Third Annual JPL Airborne Geoscience Workshop. 1992. pp. 147-149

[43] Wei Q, Dobigeon N, Tourneret J. Fast fusion of multi-band images based on solving a Sylvester equation. IEEE Transactions on Image Processing. 2015; **24**(11):4109-4121

[44] Wei Q, Dobigeon N, Tourneret J. Bayesian fusion of multi1193 band images. IEEE Journal on Selected Topics in Signal Processing. 2015;**9**(6): 1117-1127

[45] Wald L. Data Fusion: Definitions and Architectures—Fusion of Images of Different Spatial Resolutions. Paris,

France: Les Presses de l'École des Mines; 2002

[46] Garzelli A, Nencini F. Hypercomplex quality assessment of multi-/hyper-spectral images. IEEE Transactions on Geoscience and Remote Sensing. 2009;**6**(4):662-665

[47] Wang Z, Bovik AC. A universal image quality index. IEEE Signal Processing Letters. 2002;**9**(3):81-84

[48] Aiazzi B, Alparone L, Baronti S, Garzelli A. Context-driven fusion of high spatial and spectral resolution images based on oversampled multiresolution analysis. IEEE Transactions on Geoscience and Remote Sensing. 2002;**40**(10):2300-2312

[49] Aiazzi B, Alparone L, Baronti S, Garzelli A, Selva M. MTF-tailored multiscale fusion of high-resolution MS and Pan imagery. Photogrammetric Engineering and Remote Sensing. 2006; **72**(5):591-596

[50] Aiazzi B, Alparone L, Baronti S, Garzelli A, Selva M. An MTF-based spectral distortion minimizing model for Pan-sharpening of very high resolution multispectral images of urban areas. In: Proc. 2nd GRSS/ISPRS Joint Workshop on Remote Sensing and Data Fusion over Urban Areas. 2003. pp. 90-94

[51] Alparone L, Wald L, Chanussot J, Thomas C, Gamba P, Bruce LM. Comparison of pansharpening algorithms: Outcome of the 2006 GRS-S data fusion contest. IEEE Transactions on Geoscience and Remote Sensing. 2007;**45**(10):3012-3021

Chapter 3

Application of Deep Learning Approaches for Enhancing Mastcam Images

Ying Qu, Hairong Qi and Chiman Kwan

Abstract

There are two mast cameras (Mastcam) onboard the Mars rover Curiosity. Both Mastcams are multispectral imagers with nine bands in each. The right Mastcam has three times higher resolution than the left. In this chapter, we apply some recently developed deep neural network models to enhance the left Mastcam images with help from the right Mastcam images. Actual Mastcam images were used to demonstrate the performance of the proposed algorithms.

Keywords: Mastcam, Curiosity rover, image fusion, pansharpening, deep learning, Dirichlet-net, U-net, transition learning

1. Introduction

The Curiosity rover (**Figure 1**) has several instruments that are used to characterize the Mars surface. For example, the Alpha Particle X-Ray Spectrometer (APXS) [1] can analyze rock samples collected from the robotic arm and extract compositions of rocks; the Laser Induced Breakdown Spectroscopy (LIBS) [2] can extract spectral features from the vaporized fumes and deduce the rock compositions at a distance of 7 m; and the Mastcam imagers [3] can perform surface characterization from 1 km away.

The two Mastcam multispectral imagers are separated by 24.2 cm [3]. As shown in **Figure 2**, the left Mastcam (34 mm focal length) has three times the field of view of the right Mastcam (100 mm focal length). In other words, the right imager has three times higher resolution than that of the left. To generate stereo image or construct a 12-band image cube by fusing bands from the multispectral imagers from the left and right Mastcams [4–6], a practical solution is to downsample the resolution of the right images to that of the left images, which would avoid the artifacts caused by Bayer pattern [7] or the JPEG compression loss [8]. Although this approach has practical merits, it may restrict the potential ability of Mastcams. First, downsampling the right images will throw away those high spatial resolution pixels in the right bands. Second, the lower resolution of the current stereo images may degrade the augmented reality or virtual reality experience of users. If one can apply some advanced pansharpening algorithms to the left bands, then one can have 12 bands of high-resolution image cube for the purpose of stereo vision and image fusion.

In the past two decades, there have been many papers discussing the fusion of a high resolution panchromatic (pan) image with a low-resolution multispectral image

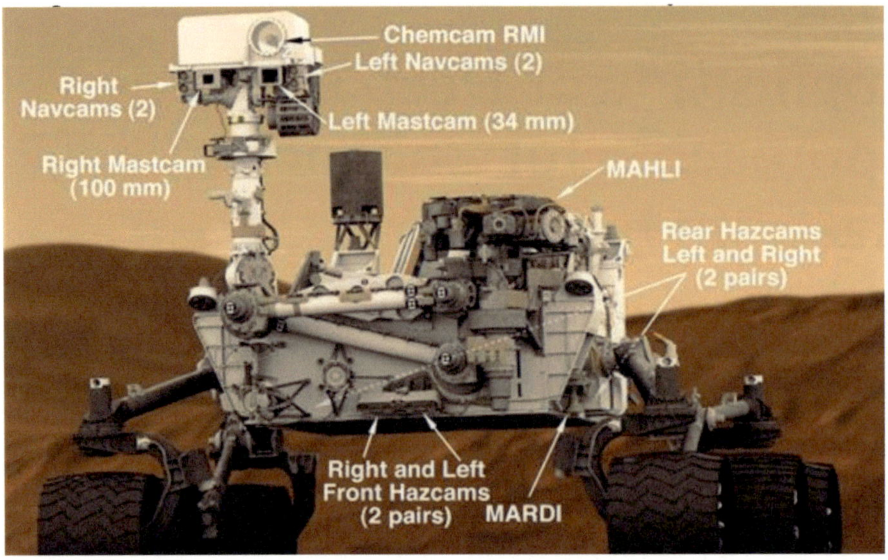

Figure 1.
Curiosity rover and its onboard instruments [7].

Figure 2.
The two Mastcam imagers [9]. (a) Left Mastcam (b) Right Mastcam.

(MSI) [10–14]. This is known as pansharpening. In our recent papers [15, 16], we proposed an unsupervised network structure to address the image fusion/super-resolution (SR) problem for hyperspectral image (HSI), referred to as HSI-SR, where a low-resolution (LR) HSI with high spectral resolution and a high-resolution (HR) MSI with low spectral resolution are fused to generate an HSI with high-resolution in both spatial and spectral dimensions. Similar to MSI, HSI has found extensive applications [17–21]. In this chapter, we adopt the innovative approaches designed in [15, 16], referred to as unsupervised sparse Dirichlet Network (uSDN), to enhance Mastcam images, where we treat the right Mastcam image as MSI with higher spatial resolution and the left Mastcam image as HSI with low spatial resolution.

In this chapter, we focus on the application of uSDN to enhance Mastcam images. In Section 2, we first introduce the problem of HSI-SR and then briefly summarize the key ideas of uSDN. In Section 3, we apply uSDN on actual Mastcam images. In Section 4, we include some further enhancements of uSDN and experiments. In Section 5, we introduce a transition learning concept, which is a natural extension of uSDN. Some preliminary results are also included. Finally, we conclude the chapter with some remarks.

2. The uSDN algorithm for HSI-SR

In this section, we describe the uSDN algorithm developed in [15, 16]. For more details, please refer to the reference. First of all, we will formulate the problem of HSI-SR to facilitate the discussion of Mastcam enhancement. **Table 1** summarizes the mathematical symbols used in this chapter.

The basic idea of uSDN is illustrated in **Figure 3**. First, the LR HSI, $\overline{Y_h} \in R^{m \times n \times L}$ with its width, height, and number of spectral bands denoted as m, n, and L, respectively, is unfolded into a 2D matrix, $Y_h \in R^{mn \times L}$. Similarly, the HR MSI, $\overline{Y_m} \in R^{M \times N \times l}$ with its width, height, and number of spectral bands denoted as M, N, and l, respectively, is unfolded into a 2D matrix $Y_m \in R^{MN \times l}$. And the SR HSI, $\bar{X} \in R^{M \times N \times L}$, is unfolded into a 2D matrix $X \in R^{MN \times L}$. Note that, generally, the spatial resolution of the MSI is much higher than that of the HSI, that is, $M \gg m$, $N \gg n$, and the spectral resolution of HSI is much higher than that of the MSI, that is, $L \gg l$. The objective is to reconstruct the high spatial and spectral resolution HSI, $\bar{X} \in R^{M \times N \times L}$, with LR HSI and HR MSI.

Due to the limitation of hardware, each pixel in an HSI or MSI may cover more than one constituent materials, leading to mixed pixels. These mixtures can be assumed to be a linear combination of a few basis vectors (or source signatures). Both LR HSI Y_h and HR MSI Y_m can be assumed to be a linear combination of c

HSI	Hyperspectral image
MSI	Multispectral image
HSI-SR	HSI super-resolution
HR	High-resolution
LR	Low-resolution
$\overline{Y_h} / Y_h$	3D/2D LR HSI
$\overline{Y_m} / Y_m$	3D/2D HR MSI
$\bar{X} / X$	3D/2D Reconstructed HR MSI
Φ_h	Spectral bases of HSI
Φ_m	Spectral bases of MSI
S_h	Coefficients/Representations of HSI
S_m	Coefficients/Representations of MSI
R	Transformation matrix
$\dot{Y}_h$	Reconstructed 2D HSI
W,b	Network weights and bias
$E_m(\theta_{he}) / E_m(\theta_{me})$	Encoder of the HIS/MSI
$D_h(\theta_{hd})$	Decoder of the HIS and MSI
$\theta_{he} / \theta_{me}$	Encoder weights of HIS/MSI
θ_{hd}	Decoder weights of HSI and MSI
s	Representations vector of a single pixel
v,u,β	Stick-breaking parameters
$H_p(s)$	Entropy function
$A(\tilde{S}_h, S_m)$	Angular difference

Table 1.
Symbols and abbreviations.

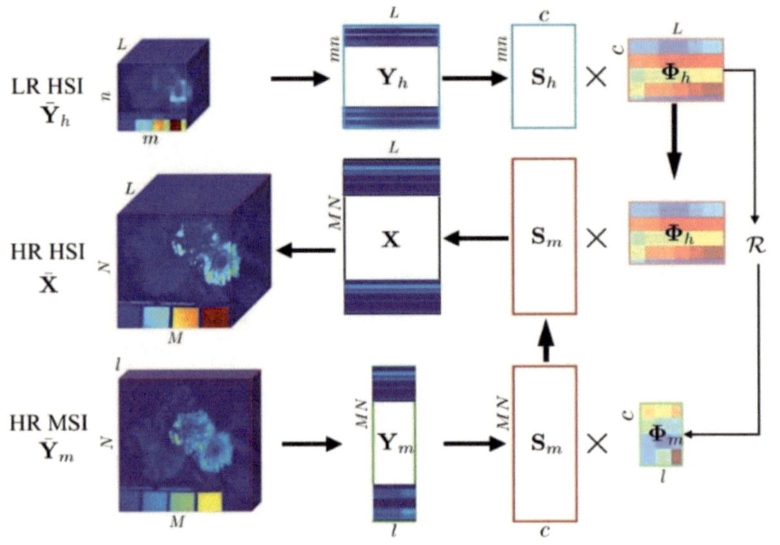

Figure 3.
General procedure of HSI-SR [15].

basis vectors with their corresponding proportional coefficients (referred to as representations in deep learning), as expressed in Eqs. (1) and (2), where $\Phi_h \in R^{c\times L}$ and $\Phi_m \in R^{c\times l}$ denote the spectral basis of Y_h and Y_m, respectively. They preserve the spectral information of the images. $S_h \in R^{mn\times c}$ and $S_m \in R^{MN\times c}$ are the proportional coefficients of Y_h and Y_m, respectively. Since the coefficients indicate how much each spectral basis has in constructing the mixed pixel at specific spatial locations, they preserve the spatial structure of HSI. The relationship between HSI and MSI bases can be expressed in the right part of Eq. (2), where $R \in R^{L\times l}$ is the transformation matrix given as a prior from the sensor [22–29].

$$Y_h = S_h \Phi_h, \tag{1}$$

$$Y_m = S_m \Phi_m, \; \Phi_m = \Phi_h R, \tag{2}$$

$$X = S_m \Phi_h. \tag{3}$$

With $\Phi_h \in R^{c\times L}$ carrying the high spectral information and $S_m \in R^{MN\times c}$ carrying the high spatial information, the desired HR HSI, X, is generated by Eq. (3). See **Figure 3**. Since the ground truth X is not available, the problem has to be solved in an unsupervised fashion. In addition, the linear combination assumption enforces the representation vectors of HSI or MSI to be non-negative and sum-to-one, that is, $\sum_{j=1}^{c} s_{ij} = 1$, where s_i is the row vector of either S_m *or* S_h [24, 29].

The uSDN unsupervised architecture is shown in **Figure 4**. It has three unique structures. First, the network consists of two encoder-decoder networks, to extract the representations of the LR HSI and HR MSI, respectively. The two networks share the same decoder, such that both the spectral and spatial information from multi-modalities can be extracted with unsupervised settings. Second, the representations of both modalities, S_h and S_m, are enforced to follow a Dirichlet distribution where

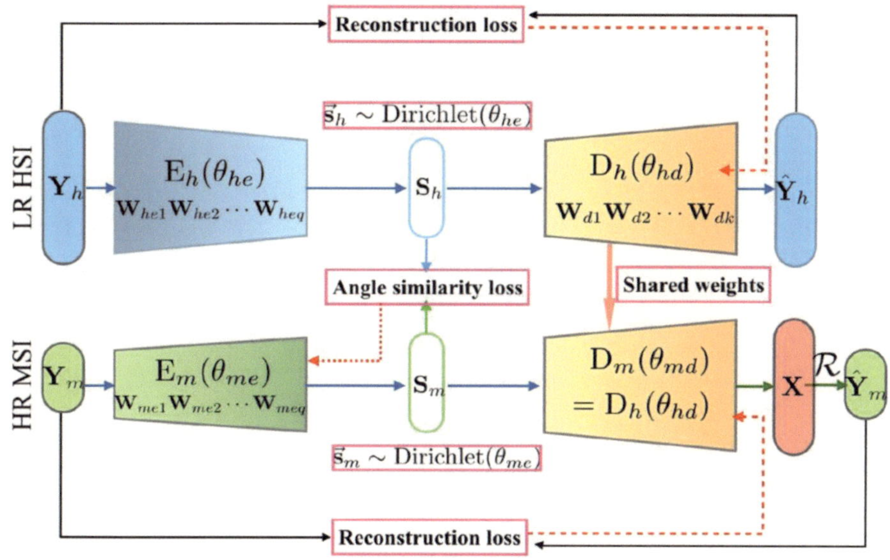

Figure 4.
Simplified architecture of uSDN [15].

the sum-to-one and non-negative properties are naturally incorporated into the network [30–34]. The solution space is further regularized with a sparsity constraint. Third, the angular difference of the representations from two modalities is minimized to preserve the spectral information of the reconstructed HR HSI.

3. Mastcam image enhancement using uSDN with improvements

3.1 Applying uSDN for Mastcam enhancement

uSDN has been thoroughly evaluated with two widely used benchmark datasets, CAVE [35] and Harvard [36]. Details can be found in [15, 16]. Here, we adopt uDSN to enhance the resolution of Mastcam images. As mentioned earlier, the right Mastcam has high resolution than the left. Hence, we treat the right Mastcam images are HR MSI and the left images as LR HSI. Although uSDN was introduced to deal with the general HSI super-resolution problem, we can treat the Mastcam image enhancement simply as a special case of HSI-SR.

For quantitative comparison, the root mean squared error (RMSE) and spectral angle mapper (SAM) are applied to evaluate the reconstruction error and the amount of spectral distortion, respectively.

The results are shown in **Figure 5**. The reconstructed image is very close to the ground truth. Most methods require that the size of high-resolution image should be equal to an integer multiplication of the size of low-resolution image. Thus, we only compare the method with CNMF [29] which works for arbitrary image size. The results are shown in **Table 2**. We observe that uSDN is able to outperform the CNMF.

3.2 Improvement based on uSDN

In this section, we summarize some further improvement of uDSN by fine-tuning the existing network structure in uSDN in order to further enhance the fusion performance.

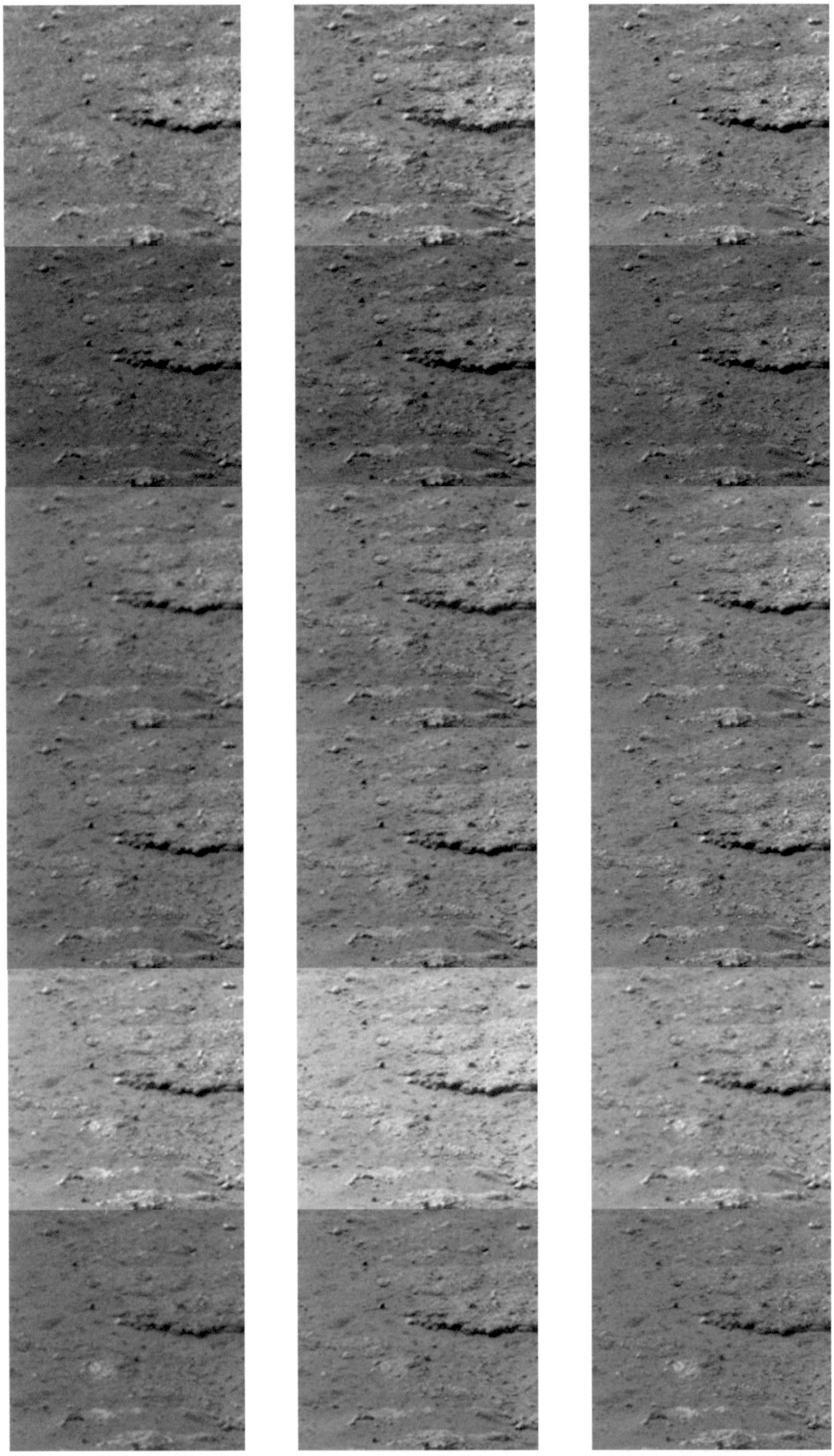

Figure 5.
Results of Mastcam image enhancement using uSDN. The left column shows the six bands from the left camera. The middle column shows the corresponding reconstructed results. The right column shows the six bands from the right camera.

Approaches	RMSE	SAM
CNMF	0.056	2.48
uSDN	0.033	2.09

Table 2.
Evaluations for image enhancement from Mastcam.

The existing structure of uDSN described in Section 3.1 is improved in two ways. First, in Section 3.1, the architecture consists of two deep networks, for the representation learning of the LR HSI and HR MSI, respectively. And only the decoders of the LR HSI and HR HSI networks are shared. The spectral information (i.e., the decoder of the LR HSI network) is extracted through the LR HSI network. Then the representation layer of the HR HSI is optimized by enforcing the spectral angle similarity. However, this introduces additional cost function, that is, angular difference minimization, and the optimization procedure is time consuming. In the improved uDSN, for the HR HSI network, most of the encoder weights are shared with the weights of the LR HSI encoder. Only a couple of encoder weights are updated during the HR HSI optimization. In this way, both the representations of the LR HSI and HR HSI networks are reinforced to follow Dirichlet distributions with parameters following the same trends. And the representations extracted from the LR HSI matches the patterns of that extracted from the HR HSI as shown in **Figure 6**.

Second, to further reduce the spectral distortion of the estimated HR HSI, instead of using l_2 loss, we adopt the l_{21} loss, which encourages the network to reduce the spectral loss of each pixel. Compared to the network with l_2 loss, the network with l_{21} loss is able to extract spectral information of images more accurately. The l_{21} loss can not only reduce the spectral distortion of the estimated HR HSI, but also improve the convergence speed of the network.

The result of the proposed method on individual HSI is visualized in **Figure 7**. When we optimize the network with l_{21} loss, we can observe that the difference between the estimated MSI and the ground truth MSI is very small, with RMSE of 1.7428 and SAM of 0.25615.

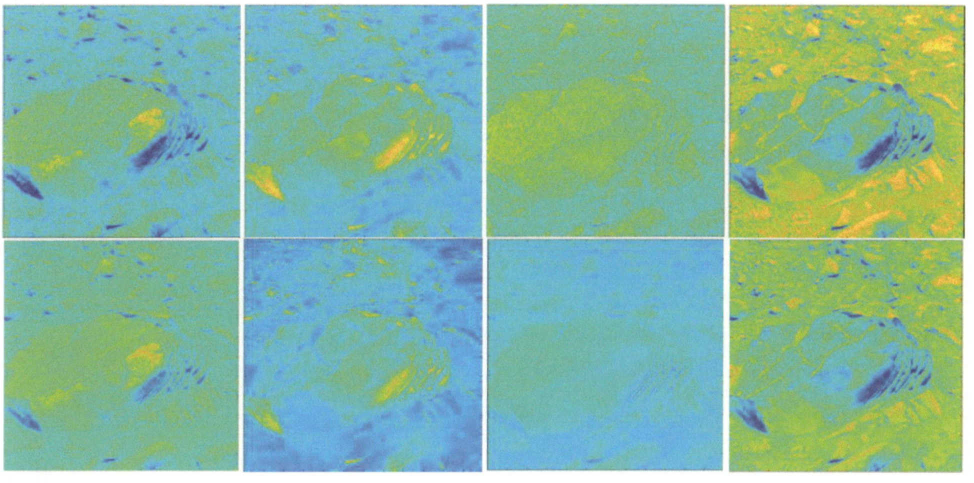

Figure 6.
Representations extracted from the LR HSI (top row) and the HR HSI (bottom row).

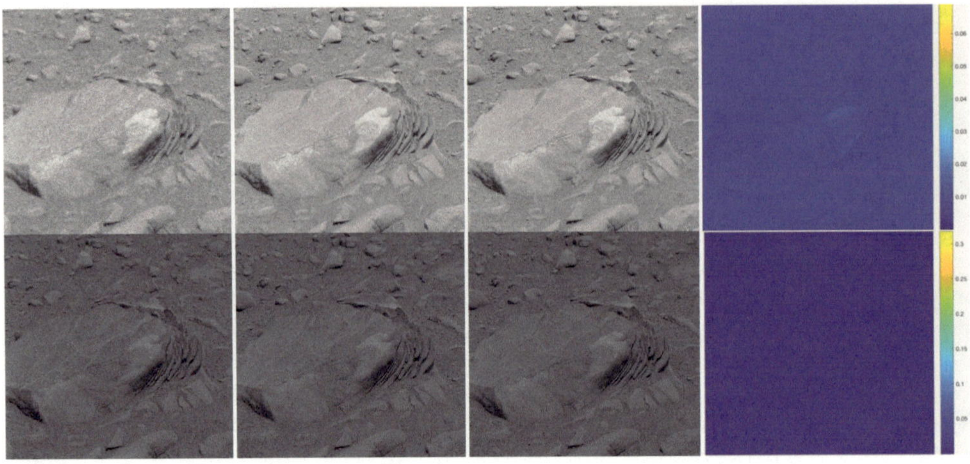

Figure 7.
The results using improved uSDN. The left column shows the first two bands from the left camera. The second column shows the corresponding reconstructed images from the improved uSDN. The third column shows the reference images from the right camera. The right column shows the absolute difference between the reconstructed images and the reference images.

4. Combination of Dirichlet-Net and U-Net

In this section, we propose to combine Dirichlet-Net with U-Net [37] to mitigate the mis-registration issue in the left and right Mastcam images.

Since in real scenarios, the images from the left and right cameras may not match each other perfectly even after registration, we propose a combination of Dirichlet-Net and U-Net to further improve the fusion performance using non-perfectly registered patches. We propose an unsupervised architecture as shown in **Figure 8**, which consists of two deep networks, an improved Dirichlet-Net for the representation learning of the MSI, and a U-Net for switching the low-resolution spatial information patches with high-resolution spatial information patches. Then the HR MSI of the left Mastcam image is generated by combining its spectral information with the spatial information of improved resolution.

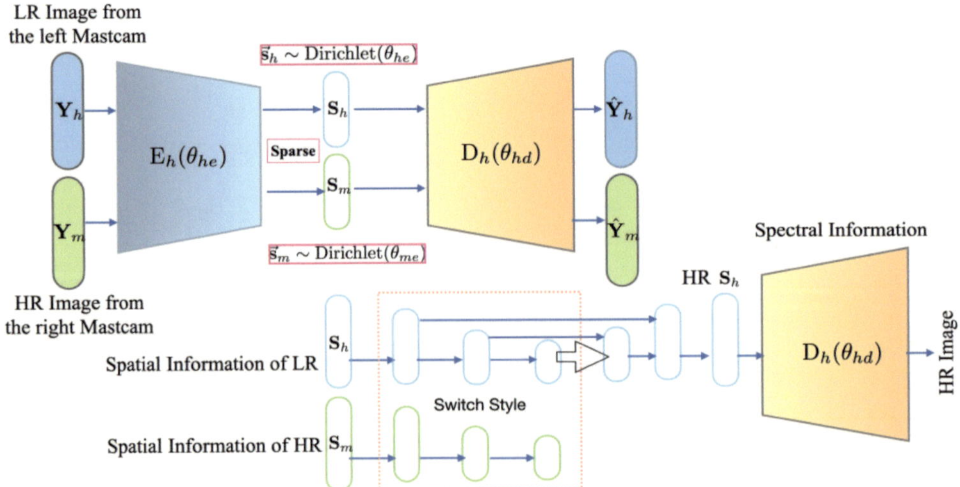

Figure 8.
The architecture of the proposed approach that combines Dirichlet-net with U-Net.

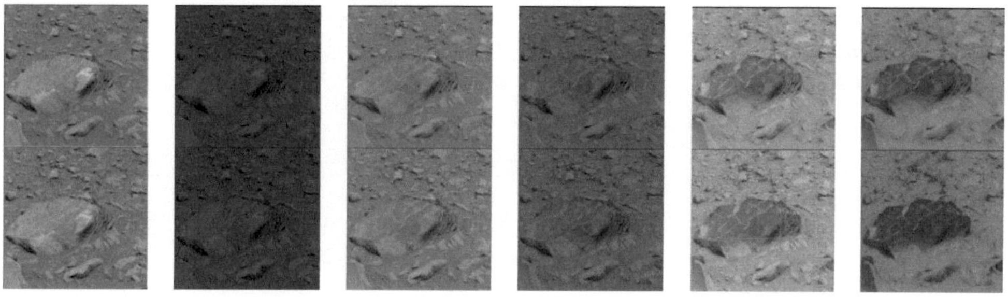

Figure 9.
The results of test image MSL_0002_0114_M1. The top row shows the six bands of raw images from the left camera. The bottom row shows the corresponding reconstructed images from the proposed method.

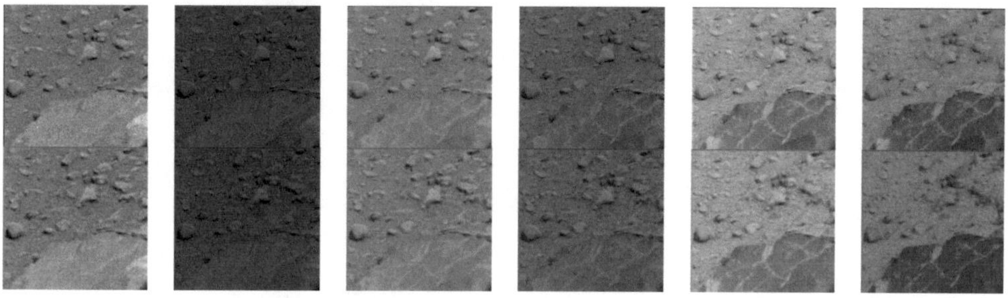

Figure 10.
The cropped results of test image MSL_0002_0114_M1. The top row shows the six bands of raw images from the left camera. The bottom row shows the corresponding reconstructed images from the proposed method.

From the last step in **Figure 8**, we are able to extract both the spectral and spatial information from LR MSI (left Mastcam) and HR MSI (right Mastcam). Although the scenes from the left and right camera are not the same, we assume they share the same group of spectral bases. And if we could improve the spatial information of the LR MSI using HR MSI, the quality of the LR MSI can be enhanced.

The architecture of the U-Net is illustrated in the lower part of **Figure 8**. We first learn a U-Net to recover the extracted spatial information, S_m, of HR MSI, Y_m, by convolution and deconvolution layers. The convolution layers extract HR spatial features from S_m, and the de-convolutional layers take these extracted features to rebuild the spatial information of S_m. Then we extract features from the spatial patches S_h of the LR HSI Y_h with the same convolution layers and switch these feature patches with their most similar feature patches in the HR spatial features [38]. Finally, the left Mastcam image with enhanced resolution, X, is generated by feeding the switching patches into de-convolutional layers of U-Net and the decoder of the Dirichlet-Net.

Here, we show experimental results from the proposed combination (Dirichlet-Net and U-Net) approach in **Figures 9** and **10**. We can observe that the reconstructed left Mastcam image is sharper than the raw MSI captured from the left camera directly and the spectral distortion of the recovered MSI is small, although only part of the high resolution MSI (right Mastcam image) is given from the right camera. Note that, due to the memory constraint, only a small patch can be recovered every time, thus there exist some disconnected parts in the results. This issue will be addressed in Section 5.

5. Spatial representation improvement with transition learning

High spatial resolution images have one natural property, that is, the transitions among pixel values are smooth. The patch-based method aims to replace the LR

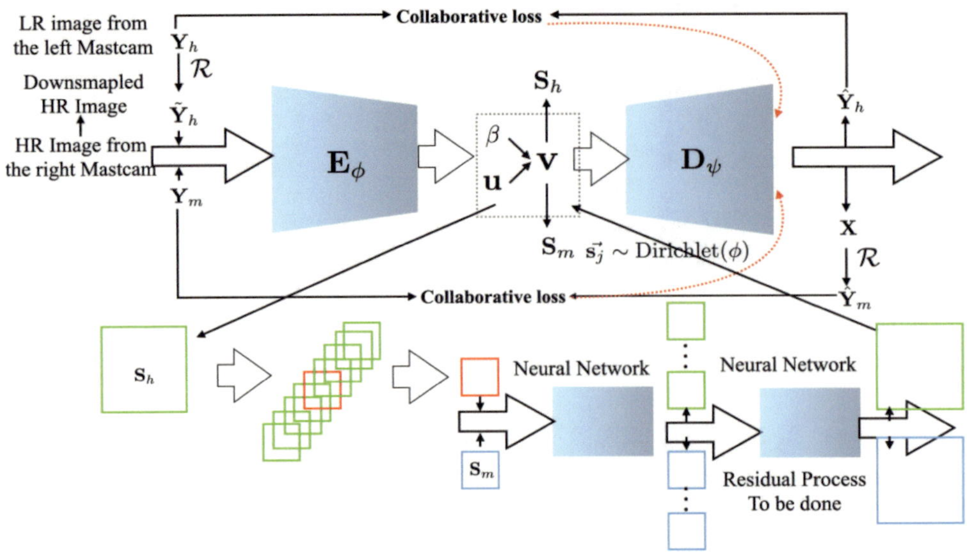

Figure 11.
The architecture of the proposed transition learning approach.

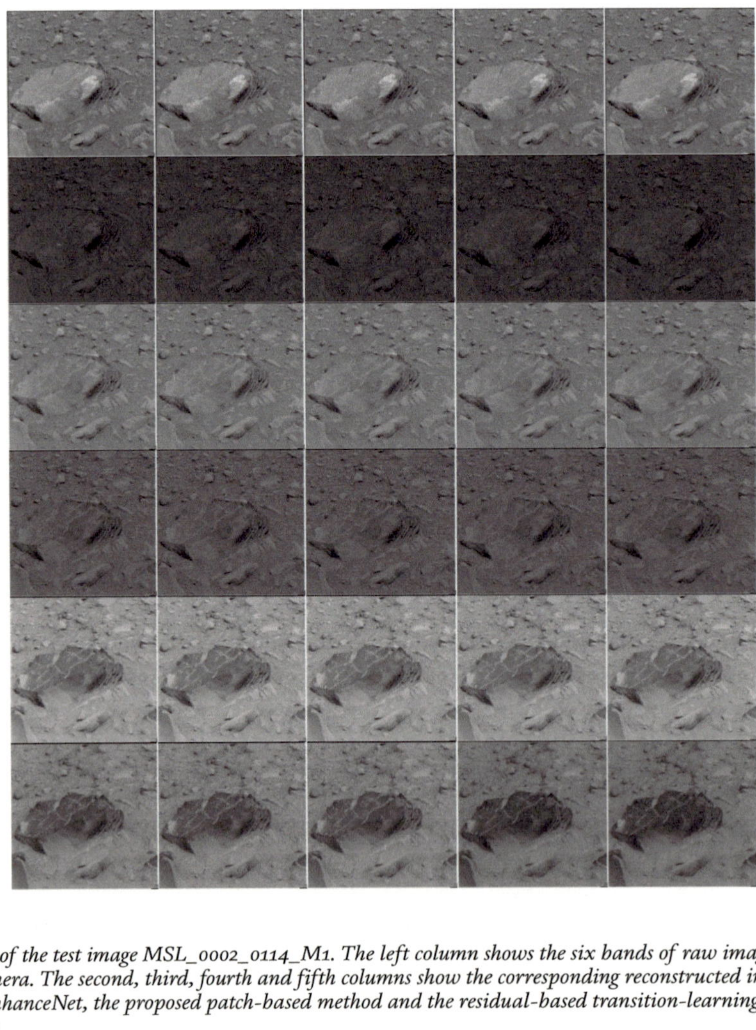

Figure 12.
The results of the test image MSL_0002_0114_M1. The left column shows the six bands of raw images from the left camera. The second, third, fourth and fifth columns show the corresponding reconstructed images from Bicubic, EnhanceNet, the proposed patch-based method and the residual-based transition-learning method, respectively.

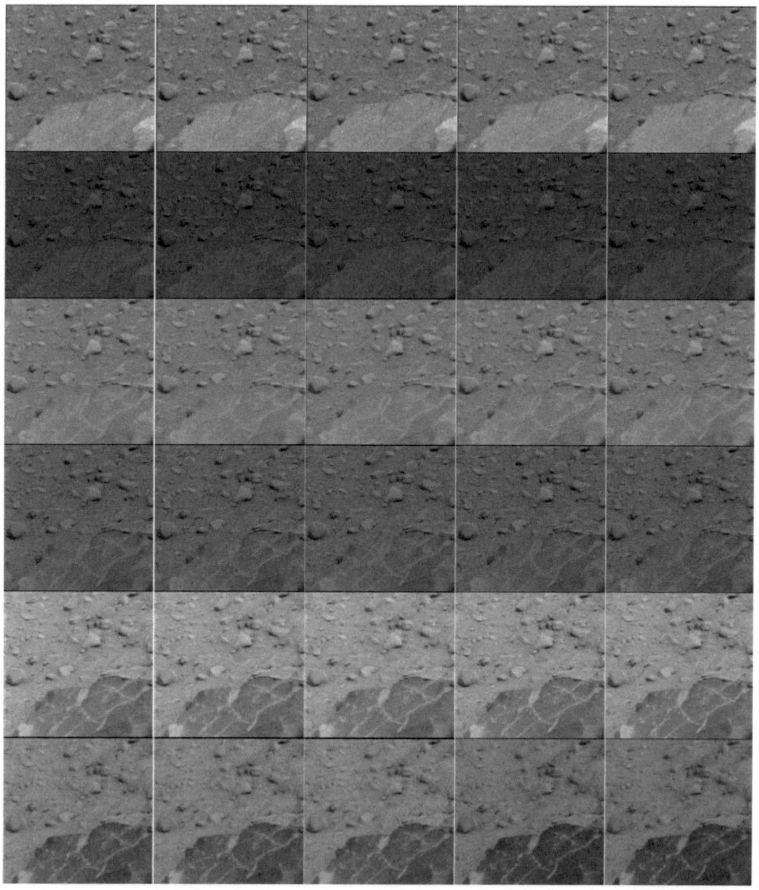

Figure 13.
The cropped results of the test image MSL_0002_0114_M1. The left column shows the six bands of raw images from the left camera. The second, third, fourth, and fifth columns show the corresponding reconstructed images from Bicubic, EnhanceNet, the proposed patch-based method and the residual-based transition-learning method, respectively.

patches from the LR MSI representations S_h with the most similar HR patches from the HR MSI representation, S_m. Since the LR MSI and HR MSI are unregistered and there is no ground truth of enhanced MSI, the patch-based improvement could not guarantee the smooth transitions in the reconstructed images, that is, the replaced patches may not match their neighbors. Therefore, in this section, we propose another structure based on transition-learning, to further improve the spatial resolution of LR HSI. The main structure is shown in **Figure 11**.

To learn smooth transitions between pixels, we first extract sub-images from the representations S_m, of HR MSI with stride 3, as shown in the lower part of **Figure 11**. For example, since the super-resolution factor is 3, we extract 9 sub-images from S_m. Then the network learns the transitions between the center sub-image with the other 8 sub-images. Since the LR MSI and HR MSI have similar statistic distributions, we assume that the transitions among pixels in both modalities are the same. Therefore, the representations S_h of LR MSI can be treated as the center sub-image of enhanced MSI and the other 8 sub-images of enhanced MSI can be estimated by feeding the representations S_h of LR MSI into the network trained by S_m. There are still residuals between the reconstructed and the ideal representations of S_m. This time, we adopt the principle described earlier to add high frequency residuals on the enhanced MSI.

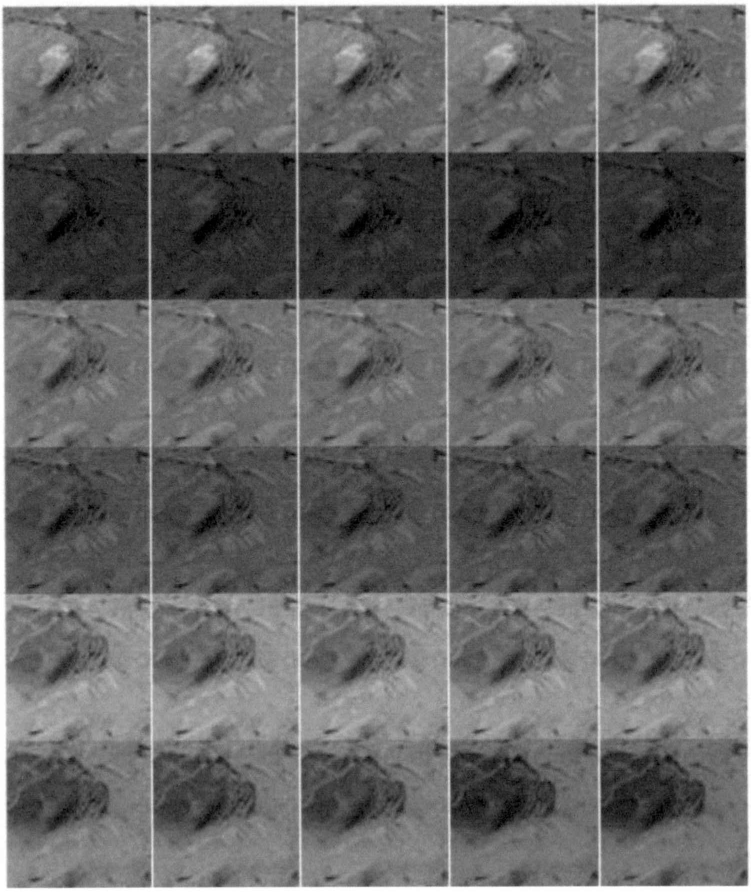

Figure 14.
The cropped results of the test image MSL_0002_0114_M1. The left column shows the six bands of raw images from the left camera. The second, third, fourth, and fifth columns show the corresponding reconstructed images from Bicubic, EnhanceNet, the proposed patch-based method and the residual-based transition-learning method, respectively.

Here, the experimental results of the proposed approaches are compared with the results from Bicubic and the state-of-the-art single image super-resolution method EnhanceNet [39], as shown in **Figures 12–14**. Note that, since the EnhanceNet only offers the 4X pre-trained weights, we show its 4X reconstruction results for fair comparison, in case the down-sampling procedure reduces the quality of the reconstructed images. The Bicubic does not improve the resolution much. The EnhanceNet was trained on natural image dataset; thus it works poorly on remote sensing images. Compared to the bicubic or EnhanceNet methods, we can observe that the proposed methods can not only improve the spatial resolution of LR MSI, but also preserve the spectral information well, even though the images from the left and right camera are not registered. The transition-based approach works better than the patch-based one, because it learns the relationship between the reconstructed pixels.

6. Conclusions

In this chapter, we summarize the application of several deep learning-based image fusion algorithms to enhance Mastcam images from Mars rover. The first algorithm termed as uDSN is based on the Dirichlet-Net, which incorporates the sum-to-one and sparsity constraints. Two improvements of the uDSN were then investigated. Finally, a transition learning-based approach was developed. Promising results using actual Mastcam images are presented. More research will be carried out in the future to continue the above investigations.

Acknowledgements

This work was supported in part by NASA NNX12CB05C and NNX16CP38P.

Author details

Ying Qu[1], Hairong Qi[1] and Chiman Kwan[2]*

1 University of Tennessee Knoxville, Knoxville, Tennessee, USA

2 Applied Research LLC, Rockville, Maryland, USA

*Address all correspondence to: chiman.kwan@arllc.net

References

[1] Ayhan B, Kwan C, Vance S. On the Use of a Linear Spectral Unmixing Technique for Concentration Estimation of APXS Spectrum. Journal of Multidisciplinary Engineering Science and Technology. 2015;**2**(9):2469-2474

[2] Wang W, Li S, Qi H, Ayhan B, Kwan C, Vance S. Revisiting the preprocessing procedures for elemental concentration estimation based on CHEMCAM LIBS on MARS Rover. In: 6th Workshop on Hyperspectral Image and Signal Processing: Evolution in Remote Sensing (WHISPERS). Lausanne, Switzerland; 2014

[3] Bell JF et al. The Mars Science Laboratory Curiosity Rover Mast Camera (Mastcam) Instruments: Pre-flight and in-flight calibration, validation, and data archiving. Earth and Space Science. July 2017;**4**(7): 396-452

[4] Ayhan B, Kwan C. Mastcam image resolution enhancement with application to disparity map generation for stereo images with different resolutions. Sensors. 2019;**19**:3526

[5] Kwan C, Chou B, Ayhan B. Enhancing stereo image formation and depth map estimation for Mastcam images. In: IEEE Ubiquitous Computing, Electronics & Mobile Communication Conference. New York City; 2018

[6] Ayhan B, Dao M, Kwan C, Chen H, Bell JF III, Kidd R. A novel utilization of image registration techniques to process Mastcam images in Mars rover with applications to image fusion, pixel clustering, and anomaly detection. IEEE Journal of Selected Topics in Applied Earth Observations and Remote Sensing. 2017;**10**(10):4553-4564

[7] Kwan C, Chou B, Bell JF III. Comparison of deep learning and conventional demosaicing algorithms for Mastcam images. Electronics. 2019;**8**:308

[8] Kwan C, Larkin J, Budavari B, Chou B. Compression algorithm selection for multispectral Mastcam images. Signal & Image Processing: An International Journal. 2019;**10**(1)

[9] Available from: https://msl-scicorner.jpl.nasa.gov/Instruments/Mastcam/

[10] Aiazzi B, Alparone L, Baronti S, Garzelli A, Selva M. Mtf-tailored multiscale fusion of high-resolution ms and pan imagery. Photogrammetric Engineering & Remote Sensing. 2006;**72**(5):591-596

[11] Aiazzi B, Baronti S, Selva M. Improving component substitution pansharpening through multivariate regression of ms+ pan data. IEEE Transactions on Geoscience and Remote Sensing. 2007;**45**(10)

[12] Akhtar N, Shafait F, Mian A. Bayesian sparse representation for hyperspectral image super resolution. In: Proceedings of the IEEE Conference on Computer Vision and Pattern Recognition. 2015. pp. 3631-3640

[13] Akhtar N, Shafait F, Mian A. Hierarchical beta process with Gaussian process prior for hyperspectral image super resolution. In: European Conference on Computer Vision. 2016. pp. 103-120

[14] Borengasser M, Hungate WS, Watkins R. Hyperspectral Remote Sensing: Principles and Applications. Boca Raton, Florida, USA: CRC Press; 2007

[15] Qu Y, Qi H, Kwan C. Unsupervised sparse Dirichlet-Net for hyperspectral image super-resolution. In: The IEEE Conference on Computer Vision and Pattern Recognition (CVPR). 2018. pp. 2511-2520

[16] Qu Y, Qi H, Kwan C. Unsupervised and Unregistered Hyperspectral Image Super-Resolution with Mutual Dirichlet-Net, arXiv preprint arXiv:1904.12175; 2019

[17] Zhou J, Kwan C, Ayhan B, Eismann MT. A novel cluster kernel RX algorithm for anomaly and change detection using hyperspectral images. IEEE Transactions on Geoscience and Remote Sensing. 2016;**54**(11):6497-6504

[18] Li S, Wang W, Qi H, Ayhan B, Kwan C, Vance S. Low-rank tensor decomposition based anomaly detection for hyperspectral imagery. In: IEEE International Conference on Image Processing (ICIP). 2015

[19] Kwan C, Budavari B, Bovik AC, Marchisio G. Blind quality assessment of fused WorldView-3 images by using the combinations of pansharpening and hypersharpening paradigms. IEEE Geoscience and Remote Sensing Letters. 2017;**14**(10):1835-1839

[20] Zhou J, Kwan C, Budavari B. Hyperspectral image super-resolution: A hybrid color mapping approach. Journal of Applied Remote Sensing. 2016;**10**(3):035024

[21] Kwan C, Ayhan B, Chen G, Wang J, Ji B, Chang C-I. A novel approach for spectral unmixing, classification, and concentration estimation of chemical and biological agents. IEEE Transactions on Geoscience and Remote Sensing. 2006;**44**(2):409-419

[22] Dian R, Fang L, Li S. Hyperspectral image super-resolution via non-local sparse tensor factorization. In: Proceedings of the IEEE Conference on Computer Vision and Pattern Recognition. 2017. pp. 5344-5353

[23] Kawakami R, Matsushita Y, Wright J, Ben-Ezra M, Tai Y-W, Ikeuchi K. High-resolution hyperspectral imaging via matrix factorization. In: 2011 IEEE Conference on Computer Vision and Pattern Recognition (CVPR). 2011. pp. 2329-2336

[24] Lanaras C, Baltsavias E, Schindler K. Hyperspectral super-resolution by coupled spectral unmixing. In: Proceedings of the IEEE International Conference on Computer Vision. 2015. pp. 3586-3594

[25] Loncan L, de Almeida LB, Bioucas-Dias JM, Briottet X, Chanussot J, Dobigeon N, et al. Hyperspectral pansharpening: A review. IEEE Geoscience and Remote Sensing Magazine. 2015;**3**(3):27-46

[26] Simoes M, Bioucas-Dias J, Almeida LB, Chanussot J. A convex formulation for hyperspectral image superresolution via subspace-based regularization. IEEE Transactions on Geoscience and Remote Sensing. 2015;**53**(6):3373-3388

[27] Vivone G, Alparone L, Chanussot J, Dalla Mura M, Garzelli A, Licciardi GA, et al. A critical comparison among pansharpening algorithms. IEEE Transactions on Geoscience and Remote Sensing. 2015;**53**(5):2565-2586

[28] Wei Q, Bioucas-Dias J, Dobigeon N, Tourneret J-Y. Hyperspectral and multispectral image fusion based on a sparse representation. IEEE Transactions on Geoscience and Remote Sensing. 2015;**53**(7):3658-3668

[29] Yokoya N, Yairi T, Iwasaki A. Coupled nonnegative matrix factorization unmixing for hyperspectral and multispectral data fusion. IEEE Transactions on Geoscience and Remote Sensing. 2012;**50**(2):528-537

[30] Wycoff E, Chan T-H, Jia K, Ma W-K, Ma Y. A non-negative sparse promoting algorithm for high resolution hyperspectral imaging. In: 2013 IEEE International Conference on Acoustics,

Speech and Signal Processing (ICASSP). 2013. pp. 1409-1413

[31] Sethuraman J. A constructive definition of Dirichlet priors. Statistica Sinica. 1994;**4**:639-650

[32] Ozkan S, Kaya B, Esen E, Akar G. EndNet: Sparse AutoEncoder Network for Endmember Extraction and Hyperspectral Unmixing, 08; arXiv:1708.01894; 2017

[33] Yokoya N, Grohnfeldt C, Chanussot J. Hyperspectral and multispectral data fusion: A comparative review of the recent literature. IEEE Geoscience and Remote Sensing Magazine. 2017;**5**(2):29-56

[34] Huang S, Tran TD. Sparse signal recovery via generalized entropy functions minimization. arXiv preprint arXiv:1703.10556; 2017

[35] Yasuma F, Mitsunaga T, Iso D, Nayar SK. Generalized assorted pixel camera: postcapture control of resolution, dynamic range, and spectrum. IEEE Transactions on Image Processing. 2010;**19**(9):2241-2253

[36] Chakrabarti A, Zickler T. Statistics of real-world hyperspectral images. In: The IEEE Conference on Computer Vision and Pattern Recognition (CVPR). 2011. pp. 193-200

[37] Isola P, Zhu J-Y, Zhou T, Efros AA. Image-to-image translation with conditional adversarial networks. In: Proceedings of the IEEE Conference on Computer Vision and Pattern Recognition. 2017. pp. 1125-1134

[38] Chen TQ, Schmidt M. Fast Patch-Based Style Transfer of Arbitrary Style. arXiv preprint arXiv:1612.04337; 2016

[39] Sajjadi M, Scholkopf B, Hirsch M. EnhanceNet: Single image super-resolution through automated texture synthesis. In: The IEEE Conference on Computer Vision and Pattern Recognition (CVPR). 2017

Section 3

Application of Generative Adversarial Network

Chapter 4

Generative Adversarial Networks for Visible to Infrared Video Conversion

Mohammad Shahab Uddin and Jiang Li

Abstract

Deep learning models are data driven. For example, the most popular convolutional neural network (CNN) model used for image classification or object detection requires large labeled databases for training to achieve competitive performances. This requirement is not difficult to be satisfied in the visible domain since there are lots of labeled video and image databases available nowadays. However, given the less popularity of infrared (IR) camera, the availability of labeled infrared videos or image databases is limited. Therefore, training deep learning models in infrared domain is still challenging. In this chapter, we applied the pix2pix generative adversarial network (Pix2Pix GAN) and cycle-consistent GAN (Cycle GAN) models to convert visible videos to infrared videos. The Pix2Pix GAN model requires visible-infrared image pairs for training while the Cycle GAN relaxes this constraint and requires only unpaired images from both domains. We applied the two models to an open-source database where visible and infrared videos provided by the signal multimedia and telecommunications laboratory at the Federal University of Rio de Janeiro. We evaluated conversion results by performance metrics including Inception Score (IS), Frechet Inception Distance (FID) and Kernel Inception Distance (KID). Our experiments suggest that cycle-consistent GAN is more effective than pix2pix GAN for generating IR images from optical images.

Keywords: image conversion, generative adversarial network, cycle-consistent loss, IR image, Pix2Pix, cycle GAN

1. Introduction

Image-to-image conversion, such as data augmentation [1] or style transfer [2], has been applied to recent computer vision applications. Traditional image conversion models had been investigated for specific applications [3–14]. Since the creation of the GAN model [15], it opened a new door to train generative models for image conversion. For example, computer vision researchers have successfully developed GAN models for day-to-night and sketch-to-photograph image conversions [16]. Two recent popular models that can perform image-to-image translations are Pix2Pix GAN [2] and Cycle GAN [16]. Pix2Pix GAN needs paired images for training whereas Cycle GAN relaxes this constraint and can be trained with unpaired images. In practice, paired images from different domains are often difficult to obtain. Therefore, Cycle GAN is a better choice for image to image translation where paired images are not available.

IR image datasets are not largely available as compared to optical images. As a result, we face the shortage of data when we train models for object detection in IR domain. This problem can be mitigated by using the Cycle GAN model to covert labeled optical images to IR images. In this chapter, we evaluate two models, Pix2Pix GAN and Cycle GAN, for image conversion from optical domain to IR domain. We used four different datasets to perform the conversion and three metrics including Inception Score (IS), Frechet Inception Distance (FID) and Kernel Inception Distance (KID) to assess quality of the converted IR images.

2. Image to image conversion models

2.1 Generative adversarial network

GAN consists of one generative model and one discriminative model to generate images from noise as shown in **Figure 1**. The generator "G" tries to generate images from the input noise "z" as realistic as possible to misguide the discriminator "D" whereas "D" is trained to discriminate the fake image "$G(z)$" from the real one "x." During training, errors at output "D" are backpropagated to update parameters in "G" and "D," and the following loss function is optimized [15]:

$$\min_{G} \max_{D} V(D; G) = E_{x \sim p_{data}(x)}[\log D(x)] + E_{z \sim p_z(z)}[\log(1 - D(G(z)))] \tag{1}$$

where x and z represent training data and input noise, respectively. $p_{data}(x)$ and $p_z(z)$ are distributions of training data and input noise. The discriminator "D" is trained to minimize the probability of the generated fake image to be real so that it can correctly assign labels to "$G(z)$" and "x" in **Figure 1**. The generator "G" is trained to maximize $D(G(z))$ or equivalently to minimize $\log(1 - D(G(z)))]$ in equ (1), generating realistic images. Essentially, the generator learns to generate real data's distribution given by the training dataset. Once the goal is achieved, the generator can be used to generate realistic images by sampling from the learned probability distribution.

2.2 Conditional GAN

GAN can be converted into a conditional model with auxiliary information that is used to impose condition on generator and discriminator [17]. In the conditional GAN model, additional data are fed into the generator and discriminator so that data generation can be controlled. The loss function in conditional GAN becomes [17].

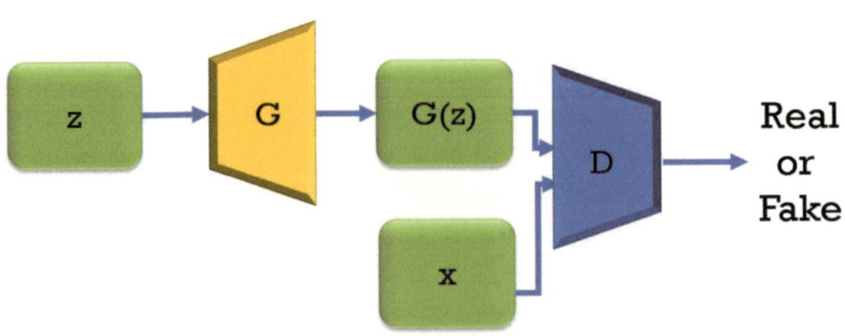

Figure 1.
Structure of generative adversarial network.

$$\min_G \max_D V(D;G) = E_{y\sim p_{data}(y)}[\log D(y|x)] + E_{z\sim p_z(z)}[\log(1 - D(G(z|x)))] \quad (2)$$

where y and z are training data and input noise, respectively. The input noise z combined with extra information x generate the output $G(z|x)$. **Figure 2** shows the diagram of conditional GAN.

2.3 Pix2Pix GAN

The Pix2Pix GAN model is built upon the concept of conditional GAN and it has been a common platform for various image conversion tasks. The diagram of Pix2Pix GAN model is given in **Figure 3**. Pix2Pix GAN consists of a "U-Net" [18] based generator and a "PatchGAN" discriminator [2]. The "U-Net" generator passes low level information of input image to output image, and the "PatchGAN" discriminator helps capture statistics of local styles. The loss function of pix2pix GAN is:

$$\min_G \max_D V(D;G) = E_{x,y}[\log D(x,y)] + E_{x,z}[\log(1 - D(x, G(x,z)))] + E_{x,y,z}[\|y - G(x,z)\|_1] \quad (3)$$

Pix2Pix GAN learns to map input image x and random noise z to output image y. The generator tries to minimize the loss function while the discriminator tries to

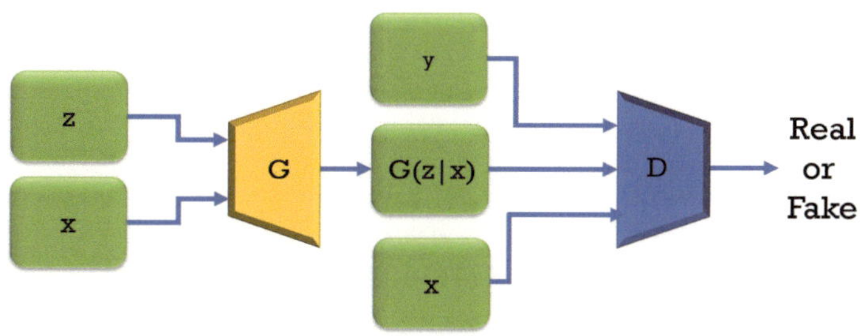

Figure 2.
Architecture of conditional GAN. Extra information x *is given to both* G *and* D*. the discriminator trains itself to distinguish between real and fake image. The generator trains itself to fool discriminator by generating images similar to real images. Here both* G *and* D *get* x *as input.*

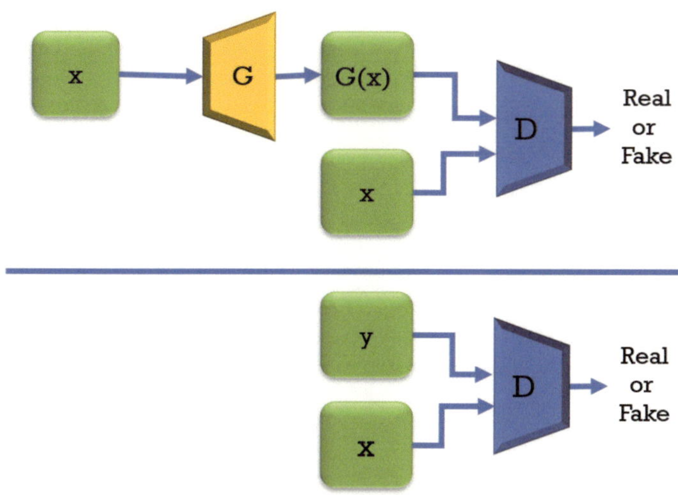

Figure 3.
Block diagram of Pix2Pix GAN.

maximize the loss function. The L_1 loss between real image and fake one is included to achieve pixel level matching. Pix2Pix GAN had been applied to many applications including edges-to-photo conversion, sketch-to-photo conversion, map-to-aerial photo conversion etc. The main drawback of Pix2Pix GAN is that it needs paired images in both domains for training, which is not always possible in practice.

2.4 Cycle GAN

In many cases, it is difficult to get paired images from different domains. Cycle GAN [16] addressed this challenge by introducing the cycle-consistent loss function as shown in **Figure 4**. There are two generator G and F in Cycle GAN along with two adversarial discriminator D_x and D_y. X and Y are input domain and target domain, respectively. While D_x helps G to generate images from X domain to Y domain, F is trained to generate images from Y domain to X domain. G: X → Y and F: Y → X are two mappings that are trained in Cycle GAN and these are kept consistent by two cycle-consistency losses. The total loss function of Cycle GAN is given by:

$$\min_{G,F} \max_{D_x, D_y} L(G, F, D_x, D_y) = L_{GAN}(G, D_Y, X, Y) + L_{GAN}(F, D_x, Y, X) + \lambda L_{cyc}(G, F) \tag{4}$$

where

$$L_{GAN}(G, D_Y, X, Y) = E_{y\sim pdata(y)}[\log D_Y(y)] + E_{x\sim pdata(x)}[\log(1 - D_Y(G(x)))] \tag{5}$$

$$L_{GAN}(F, D_x, Y, X) = E_{x\sim pdata(x)}[\log D_X(x)] + E_{y\sim pdata(y)}[\log(1 - D_X(G(y)))] \tag{6}$$

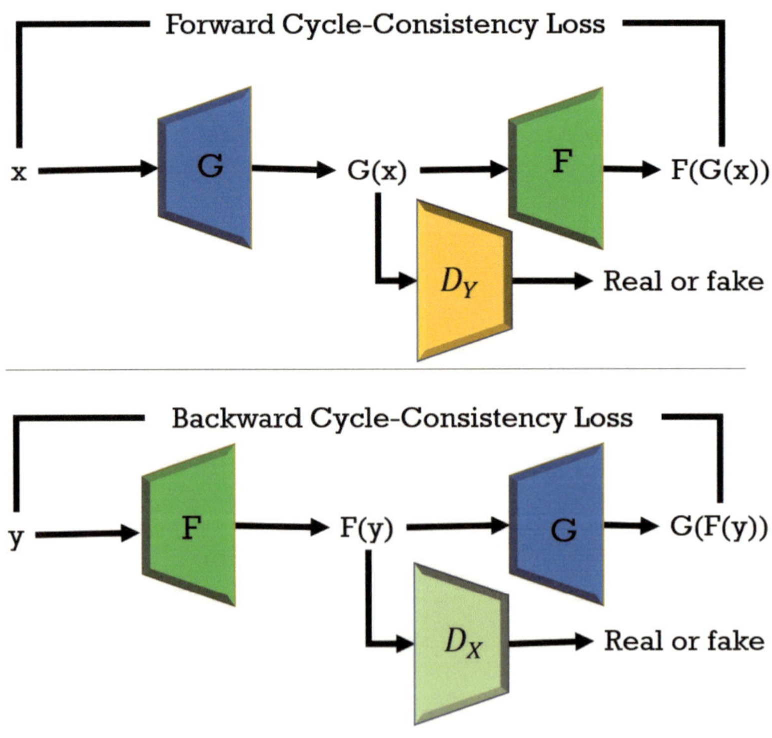

Figure 4.
Overall architecture of cycle GAN.

$$L_{cyc}(G, F) = E_{x\sim pdata(x)}\left[\left[\|G(F(x)) - x\|_1\right] + E_{y\sim pdata(y)}\left[\|G(F(y)) - y\|_1\right]\right. \tag{7}$$

There are two terms in the loss function of Cycle GAN: adversarial losses and cycle-consistency losses. $L_{GAN}(G, D_Y, X, Y)$ and $L_{GAN}(F, D_X, Y, X)$ are the adversarial losses for G: X→Y and F: Y→X mapping, respectively, which ensure that target images' distribution and generated images' distribution are close. The cycle-consistency loss, $L_{cyc}(G, F)$, ensures that the two mappings have no contradictions. λ is a weight controlling balance between the two categories of losses.

Cycle GAN has been used in different applications including season transfer, style transfer, etc. [16]. In addition, Cycle GAN has resolved the mode collapse problem in training if only the adversarial loss is used [19]. Mode collapse happens when the generator outputs the same image for different inputs. Though other methods [2–10, 20–24] can also offer image-to-image translation with unpaired images, Cycle GAN has become a common platform for many image translation related tasks.

3. Experimental setups

3.1 Datasets

For training Pix2Pix GAN and Cycle GAN, we have used images pairs from the open-source visible and infrared video database from the signal multimedia and telecommunications laboratory at the Federal University of Rio de Janeiro [25]. IR and visible-light video pairs in the database are synchronized and registered. We utilized 80% of frames in the "Guanabara Bay_take_1" video pair for training and the remaining 20% frames for testing. In addition, we evaluated the trained model on other three image pairs named "Guanabara Bay_take_2", "Camouflage_take_1" and "Camouflage_take_2". Detailed information of the four video pairs are listed in **Table 1** and some example pairs are shown in **Figure 5**.

Dataset Name	Description [25]
Guanabara Bay_take_1	• Contains scenes of "the Guanabara Bay and the Rio de Janeiro-Niteroi bridge". • Taken during Nighttime. • Contains 1 scene plane at approximately 500 m distance.
Guanabara Bay_take_2	• Contains scenes of "the Guanabara Bay and the Rio de Janeiro-Niteroi bridge". • Taken during nighttime. • Contains 1 scene plane at approximately 500 m distance.
Camouflage_take_1	• Contains outdoor scenes. • Taken during bright sunlight. • Contains 2 scene planes at approximately 10 m and 300 m distances. • Contains people who are hiding behind vegetation.
Camouflage_take_2	• Contains outdoor scenes. • Taken during bright sunlight. • Contains 2 scene planes at approximately 10 m and 300 m distances. • Contains people who are hiding behind vegetation.

Table 1.
Detailed information of video pairs used in our experiments.

(a) (b)

Figure 5.
Visible-IR images from Guanabara Bay_take_1 video pair used for training Pix2Pix GAN and cycle GAN models. (a) Visible images. (b) IR images.

3.2 Performance metrics

3.2.1 Inception score

Inception score (IS) is widely used for evaluating GANs [26]. IS considers quality and diversity of generated images by evaluating the entropy of probability distribution outputted created by the pre-trained "Inception v3" model on the generated data [27]. A large inception score represents high quality of the generated images. One drawback of the inception score is that it does not consider information in the real images used for training the GAN model. Therefore, it is not clear how the generated images compare to the real training images.

3.2.2 Frechet inception distance

Frechet Inception Distance (FID) indicates the similarity between two sets of datasets and is often used for evaluating GANs [28, 29]. FID is the Wasserstein-2 distance between feature representations of real and fake images computed by the

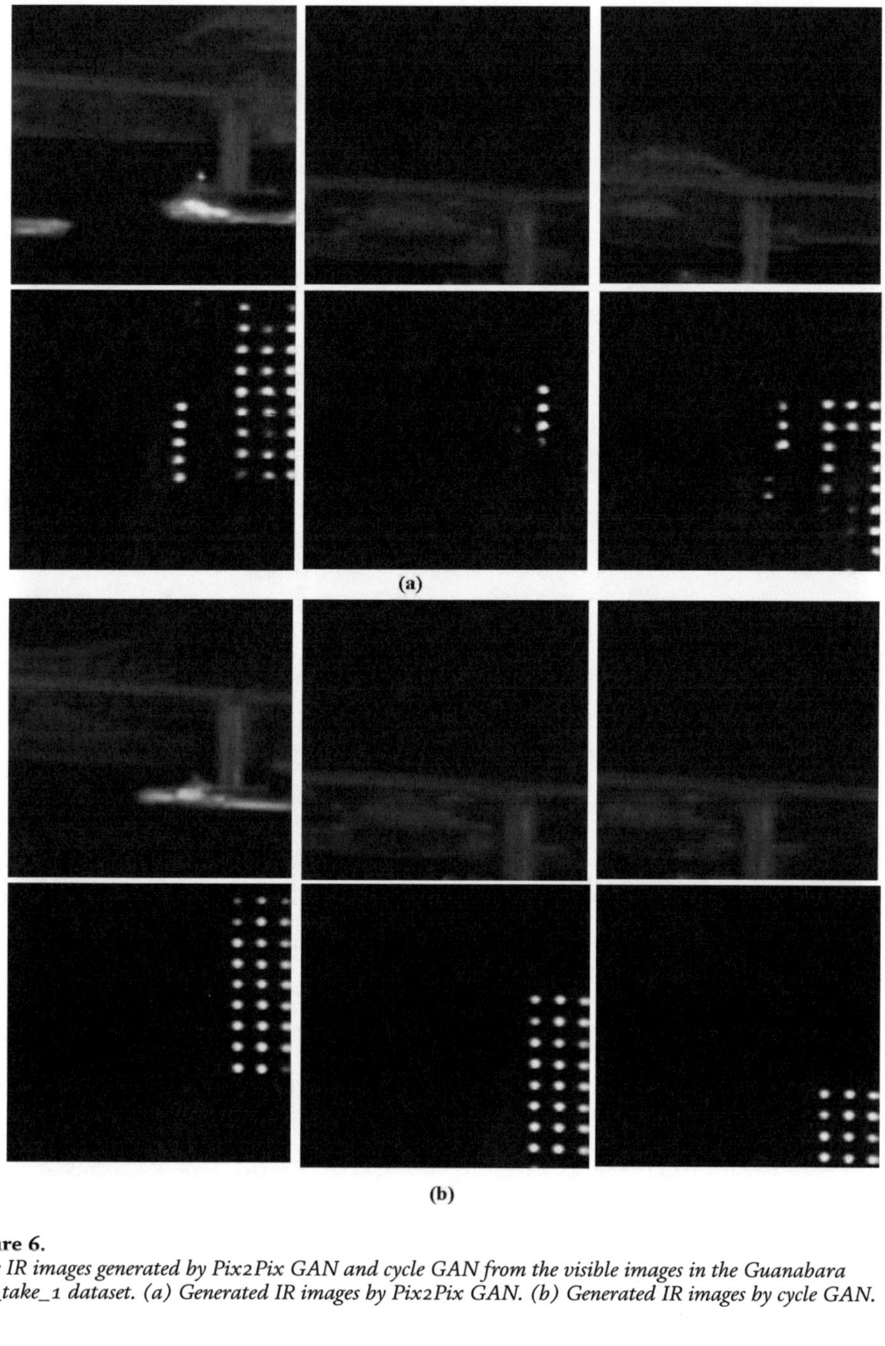

Figure 6.
Fake IR images generated by Pix2Pix GAN and cycle GAN from the visible images in the Guanabara Bay_take_1 dataset. (a) Generated IR images by Pix2Pix GAN. (b) Generated IR images by cycle GAN.

Metrics	Datasets							
	Guanabara Bay_take_1		Guanabara Bay_take_2	Camouflage take_1			Camouflage take_2	
IS Score	PixPix GAN	Cycle GAN	PixPix GAN	Cycle GAN	PixPix GAN	Cycle GAN	PixPix GAN	Cycle GAN
	2.70	2.88	1.85	3.61	1.02	2.72	1.02	2.66
FID	0.90	0.84	2.33	1.12	3.64	1.51	3.35	1.52
KID	4.24	2.42	24.00	7.10	48.61	9.13	43.55	9.15

Table 2.
Evaluation metrics on generated IR images of different datasets using Pix2Pix GAN and cycle GAN.

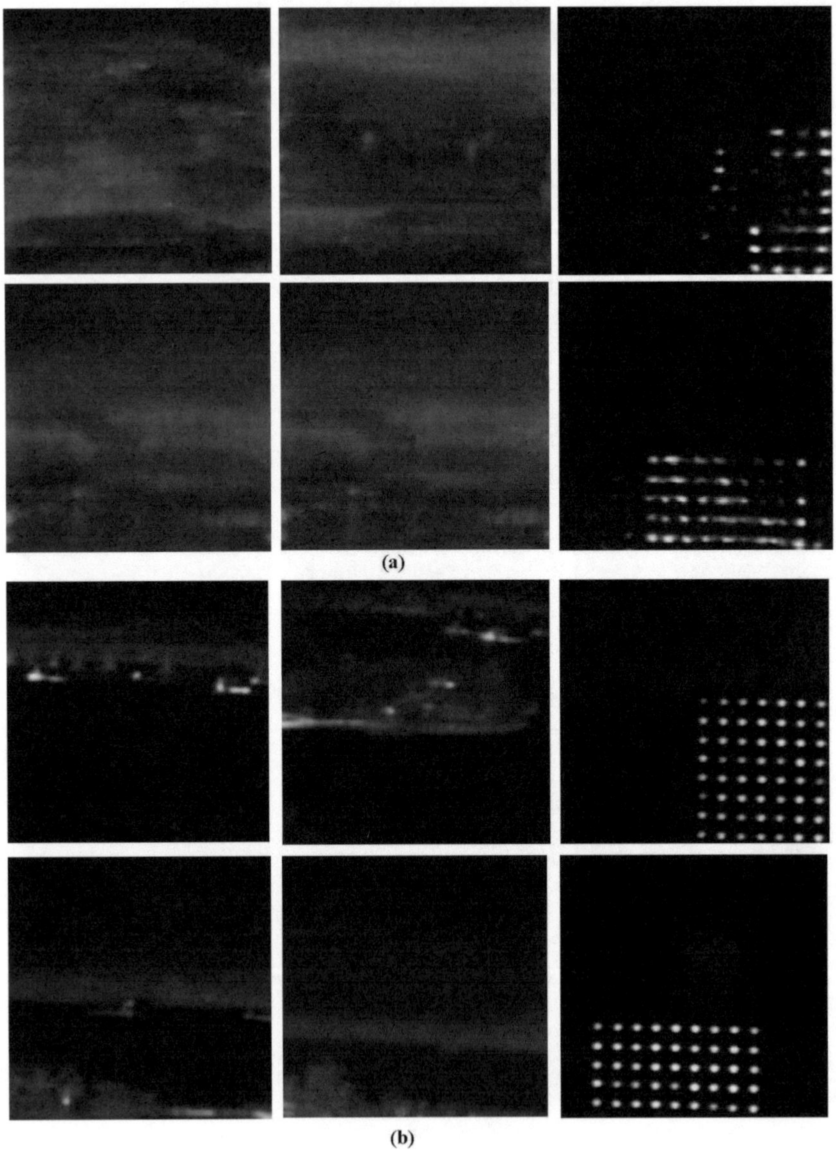

Figure 7.
Fake IR images generated by Pix2Pix GAN and cycle GAN from the visible images of Guanabara Bay_take_2 dataset. (a) Generated IR images by Pix2Pix GAN cycle GAN. (b) Generated IR images by cycle GAN.

Inception v3 model [27]. We used the coding layer of the Inception model to obtain feature representation of each image. FID is consistent with the human-judgment of image quality and it can also detect intra-class mode collapse. A lower FID score indicates that the two groups of images are similar so that the generated fake images are of high quality.

3.2.3 Kernel inception distance

Kernel Inception Distance (KID) is another metric often used to assess quality of GAN generated images relative to real images [30]. KID first uses the Inception v3 model to obtain representations of generated images. It then calculates the squared

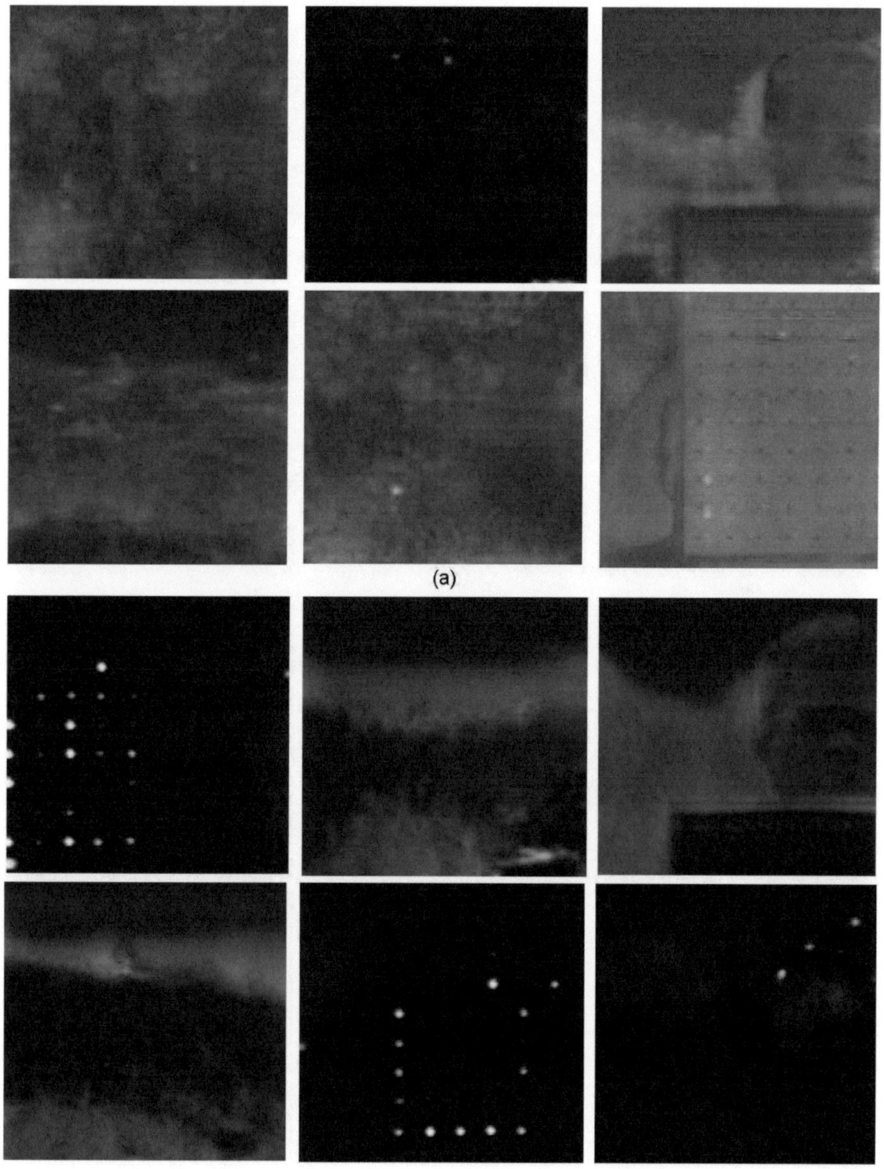

Figure 8.
Fake IR images generated by Pix2Pix GAN and cycle GAN from the visible images of Camouflage_take_1 dataset. (a) Generated IR images by Pix2Pix GAN. (b) Generated IR images by cycle GAN.

maximum mean discrepancy (MMD) between the representations of real training images and generated images. KID score is also consistent with human judgment of image quality. A small KID value indicates high quality of the generated images.

4. Results

4.1 Testing results on "Guanabara Bay_take_1" and "Guanabara Bay_take_2"

We trained the Pix2Pix GAN and Cycle GAN on 80% of the frames in "Guanabara Bay_take_1" video pair and tested the trained models on the remaining

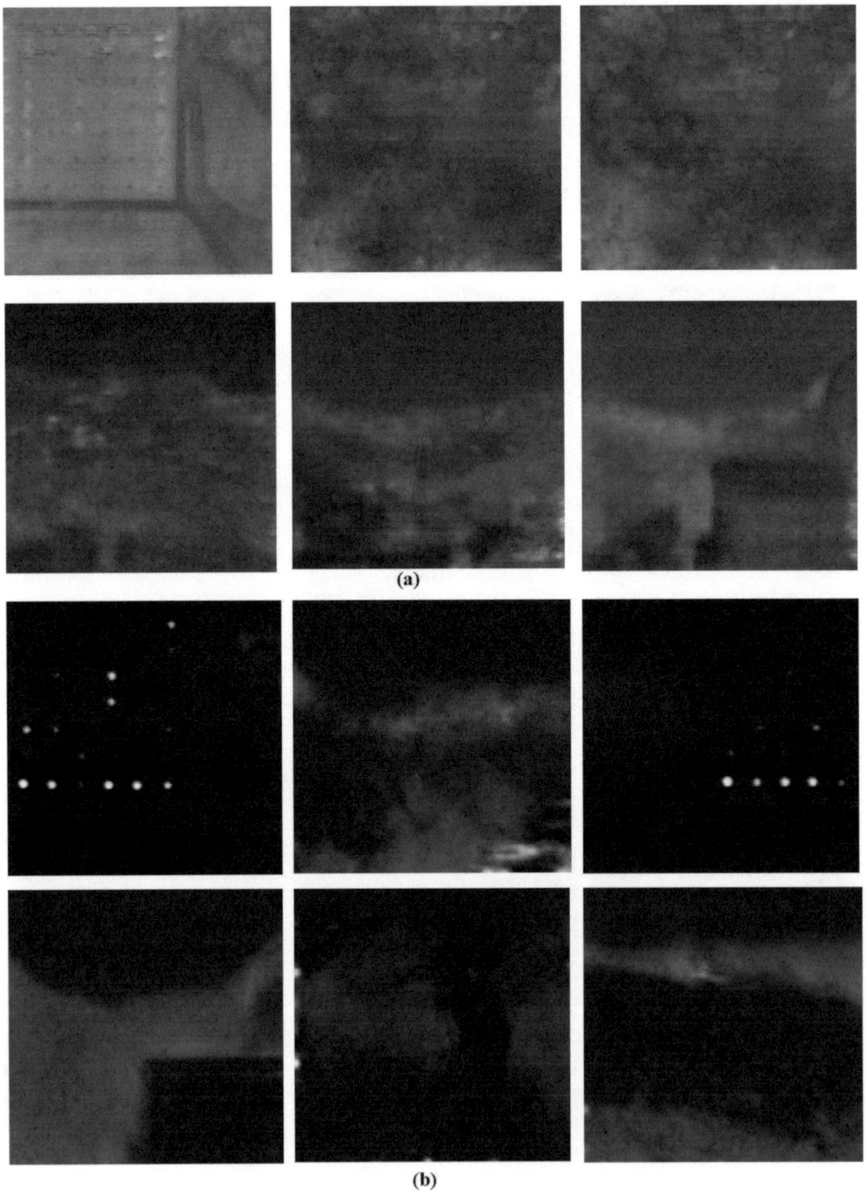

Figure 9.
Fake IR images generated by Pix2Pix GAN and cycle GAN from the visible images of Camouflage_take_2 dataset. (a) Generated IR images by Pix2Pix GAN. (b) Generated IR images by cycle GAN.

20% frames. Some visible and IR images that we have used for training are shown in **Figure 5**. After training, we also applied both models to the "Guanabara Bay_take_2" dataset. **Figures 6** and **7** show some generated IR images. By visual inspection, Cycle GAN can generate better results than Pix2Pix GAN does. In addition, we observe that IR images generated by Cycle GAN are similar to the real IR images. **Table 2** lists the quantitative performance metrics of the generated images by the two models. Cycle GAN outperforms Pix2Pix GAN in terms of all the metrics including IS, FID and KID on this dataset.

4.2 Testing results on "Camouflage_take_1" and "Camouflage_take_2"

We have applied the trained models to "Camouflage_take_1" and "Camouflage_take_2" datasets and results are shown in **Figures 8** and **9**. Both models did not generate good quality IR images though the quantitative metrics as shown in **Table 2**. Cycle GAN is slightly better than Pix2Pix GAN. One possible reason is that the data in the two sets have different distributions as those in the training data, making both models failed.

5. Conclusion

In this chapter, we have investigated visible-to-IR image conversion using Pix2Pix GAN and Cycle GAN. Cycle GAN is a better model than Pix2Pix GAN and both can generate good visual quality IR images based on visible images, if training data and test data are similar. Overall, IR images generated by Cycle GAN have sharper appearances and better quantitative performance metrics than those by Pix2Pix GAN. However, if testing data have significant distribution shift as compared to training data, both models cannot generate quality IR images. Therefore, our recommendations are 1). Cycle GAN appears to be a better tool to convert optical images to IR images if training and testing datasets have similar distributions and 2) Both models are sensitive to distribution shift and additional techniques are needed to address the challenge.

Author details

Mohammad Shahab Uddin and Jiang Li*
Department of ECE, Old Dominion University, Norfolk, VA, United States

*Address all correspondence to: jli@odu.eduas

References

[1] Fahimi F, Dosen S, Ang KK, Mrachacz-Kersting N, Guan C. Generative adversarial networks-based data augmentation for brain–computer Interface. IEEE transactions on neural networks and learning systems. 2020

[2] Isola P, Zhu JY, Zhou T, Efros AA. Image-to-image translation with conditional adversarial networks. In Proceedings of the IEEE conference on computer vision and pattern recognition. 2017:1125-1134

[3] Zhao H, Yang H, Su H, Zheng S. Natural image Deblurring based on ringing artifacts removal via knowledge-driven gradient distribution priors. IEEE Access. 2020 Jul 8;**8**: 129975-129991

[4] Su JW, Chu HK, Huang JB. Instance-aware image colorization. In: InProceedings of the IEEE/CVF Conference on Computer Vision and Pattern Recognition 2020. pp. 7968-7977

[5] Park B, Yu S, Jeong J. Densely connected hierarchical network for image denoising. In: InProceedings of the IEEE Conference on Computer Vision and Pattern Recognition Workshops 2019. (pp. 0-0)

[6] Chen T, Cheng MM, Tan P, Shamir A, Hu SM. Sketch2photo: Internet image montage. ACM transactions on graphics (TOG). 2009 Dec 1;**28**(5):1-0

[7] Shi W, Qiao Y. Fast texture synthesis via pseudo optimizer. In: InProceedings of the IEEE/CVF Conference on Computer Vision and Pattern Recognition 2020. pp. 5498-5507

[8] Anwar S, Barnes N. Real image denoising with feature attention. InProceedings of the IEEE International Conference on Computer Vision. 2019: 3155-3164

[9] Pan L, Dai Y, Liu M. Single image deblurring and camera motion estimation with depth map. In: In2019 IEEE Winter Conference on Applications of Computer Vision (WACV) 2019 Jan 7. IEEE. pp. 2116-2125

[10] Shih Y, Paris S, Durand F, Freeman WT. Data-driven hallucination of different times of day from a single outdoor photo. ACM Transactions on Graphics (TOG). 2013 Nov 1;**32**(6):1-1

[11] Laffont PY, Ren Z, Tao X, Qian C, Hays J. Transient attributes for high-level understanding and editing of outdoor scenes. ACM Transactions on graphics (TOG). 2014 Jul 27;**33**(4):1-1

[12] Long J, Shelhamer E, Darrell T. Fully convolutional networks for semantic segmentation. In Proceedings of the IEEE conference on computer vision and pattern recognition. 2015:3431-3440

[13] Eigen D, Fergus R. Predicting depth, surface normals and semantic labels with a common multi-scale convolutional architecture. In Proceedings of the IEEE international conference on computer vision. 2015: 2650-2658

[14] Fergus R, Singh B, Hertzmann A, Roweis ST, Freeman WT. Removing camera shake from a single photograph. In: ACM SIGGRAPH 2006 Papers 2006 Jul 1. pp. 787-794

[15] Goodfellow I, Pouget-Abadie J, Mirza M, Xu B, Warde-Farley D, Ozair S, et al. Generative adversarial nets. In: Advances in Neural Information Processing Systems 2014. pp. 2672-2680

[16] Zhu JY, Park T, Isola P, Efros AA. Unpaired image-to-image translation using cycle-consistent adversarial networks. In: Proceedings of the IEEE

International Conference on Computer Vision 2017. pp. 2223-2232

[17] Mirza M, Osindero S. Conditional Generative Adversarial Nets. arXiv Preprint arXiv:1411.1784. 2014 Nov 6.

[18] Ronneberger O, Fischer P, Brox T. U-net: Convolutional networks for biomedical image segmentation. In: International Conference on Medical Image Computing and Computer-Assisted Intervention 2015 Oct 5. Cham: Springer. pp. 234-241

[19] Goodfellow I. NIPS 2016 Tutorial: Generative Adversarial Networks. arXiv Preprint arXiv:1701.00160. 2016 Dec 31.

[20] Eigen D, Fergus R. Predicting depth, surface normals and semantic labels with a common multi-scale convolutional architecture. In Proceedings of the IEEE international conference on computer vision. 2015: 2650-2658

[21] Johnson J, Alahi A, Fei-Fei L. Perceptual losses for real-time style transfer and super-resolution. In: European Conference on Computer Vision 2016 Oct. Vol. 8. Cham: Springer. pp. 694-711

[22] Wang X, Gupta A. Generative image modeling using style and structure adversarial networks. In: European Conference on Computer Vision 2016 Oct. Vol. 8. Cham: Springer. pp. 318-335

[23] Xie S, Tu Z. Holistically-nested edge detection. In Proceedings of the IEEE international conference on computer vision. 2015:1395-1403

[24] Zhang R, Isola P, Efros AA. Colorful image colorization. In: European Conference on Computer Vision 2016 Oct. Vol. 8. Cham: Springer. pp. 649-666

[25] Ellmauthaler A, Pagliari CL, da Silva EA, Gois JN, Neves SR. A visible-light and infrared video database for performance evaluation of video/image fusion methods. Multidimensional Systems and Signal Processing. 2019 Jan 15;**30**(1):119-143

[26] Salimans T, Goodfellow I, Zaremba W, Cheung V, Radford A, Chen X. Improved techniques for training gans. In: Advances in Neural Information Processing Systems 2016. pp. 2234-2242

[27] Szegedy C, Vanhoucke V, Ioffe S, Shlens J, Wojna Z. Rethinking the inception architecture for computer vision. In Proceedings of the IEEE conference on computer vision and pattern recognition. 2016:2818-2826

[28] Heusel M, Ramsauer H, Unterthiner T, Nessler B, Hochreiter S. Gans trained by a two time-scale update rule converge to a local Nash equilibrium. InAdvances in neural information processing systems. 2017: 6626-6637

[29] Fréchet M. Sur la distance de deux lois de probabilité. COMPTES RENDUS HEBDOMADAIRES DES SEANCES DE L ACADEMIE DES. Sciences. 1957 Jan 1; **244**(6):689-692

[30] Bińkowski M, Sutherland DJ, Arbel M, Gretton A. Demystifying mmd gans. arXiv preprint arXiv:1801.01401. 2018 Jan 4.

Chapter 5

Style-Based Unsupervised Learning for Real-World Face Image Super-Resolution

Ahmed Cheikh Sidiya and Xin Li

Abstract

Face image synthesis has advanced rapidly in recent years. However, similar success has not been witnessed in related areas such as face single image super-resolution (SISR). The performance of SISR on real-world low-quality face images remains unsatisfactory. In this paper, we demonstrate how to advance the state-of-the-art in face SISR by leveraging style-based generator in unsupervised settings. For real-world low-resolution (LR) face images, we propose a novel unsupervised learning approach by combining style-based generator with relativistic discriminator. With a carefully designed training strategy, we demonstrate our converges faster and better suppresses artifacts than Bulat's approach. When trained on an ensemble of high-quality datasets (CelebA, AFLW, LS3D-W, and VGGFace2), we report significant visual quality improvements over other competing methods especially for real-world low-quality face images such as those in Widerface. Additionally, we have verified that both our unsupervised approaches are capable of improving the matching performance of widely used face recognition systems such as OpenFace.

Keywords: single image super-resolution (SISR), unsupervised learning, degradation modeling, real-world face images

1. Introduction

With recent advancements in deep learning algorithms [1], Single Image Superresolution (SISR) has seen a significant advance in performance in terms of objective metrics like peak signal-to-noise-ratio (PSNR). With generative adversarial networks (GAN) such as improvements of objective quality metric have been extended to the visual quality of super-resolved images [2]. However, most of the existing deep learning algorithms for solving SISR problems are categorized as supervised; in that they rely on paired high-resolution (HR) and low-resolution (LR) images to optimize the neural network weights. The HR images are downsampled using algorithms (like bicubic downsampling) to create the corresponding LR ones. These artificially created LR data deviate significantly from the complex real word degradation model and with that a rapid decrease in performance is observed when neural networks trained on artificial LR that are tested on real-world LR images [3].

In this chapter, we will focus on solving the problem of image superresolution for face images. Super-resolving low resolution face images can help solve crucial tasks such as person identification and recognition in the real world. To make our solution work for real-world LR face images, we borrow ideas from recent advances in style transfer [4] and image synthesis [5]. Style transfer refers to the task of transforming one image from one style to another (e.g., photo to painting, daytime to nighttime, and summer to winter). An important motivation behind our approach is to treat SISR as a style transfer problem which does not require pairing the HR-LR training data. In our unsupervised learning approach, we only assume two uncorrelated datasets: one is a collection of real-world LR images and the other HR images.

In the next sections, we will first review some related works including convolutional neural network (CNN), generative adversarial networks (GAN), image synthesis, and style transfer. We will then present an unsupervised approach that works for real-world LR face images. The key idea is to combine style-based generator [5] with relativistic discriminator [6] within a recently developed cycle-consistent GAN (CycleGAN) framework [4]. We will show that both our approaches outperform previous state-of-the-art ones.

2. Related works

In this section, we will first present to the reader the convolution neural networks and go through the different types of functions used in such networks. Our focus will be on the main convolution operation. We will talk about the first paper that showed that convolution neural networks can outperform model-based approaches in the task of image super-resolution [7]. We will talk about generative adversarial networks (GAN) and show that adding a discriminator can significantly improve the visual quality of the superresolved image [2]. We will define image synthesis task and present the latest advancements in the field. Finally, we will talk about the style transfer problem and different architectures used to solve it; our focus will be on the most popular one: CycleGAN [4].

2.1 Convolutional neural networks

2.1.1 Definition

Neural networks are a class of machine learning algorithms that are modeled loosely on the mechanism of human brain (e.g., neocognitron [8]). It consists of thousands or even millions of simple processing units that are densely interconnected. Most existing neural networks are organized into layers of nodes (simple processing units). They usually feed-forward information from input data to the output in one direction. An individual node might be connected to several nodes in the layer beneath it from which it receives data and several nodes in the layer above it for which it sends data. **Figure 1** shows an example of feed-forward neural network. To each of its incoming connections, some nodes will assign a number called "weight," multiply the input coming from the connection with its corresponding weights; other nodes will sum the results and add a value called bias. In other nodes, a non-linearity called activation function is included which models the biological firing of neurons in human brains [9].

The Convolutional Neural Network (CNN) are a type of neural networks that are often designed to work on two-dimensional data such as image signals. In CNN, the most basic operation is called "convolution" implementing a linear filter and

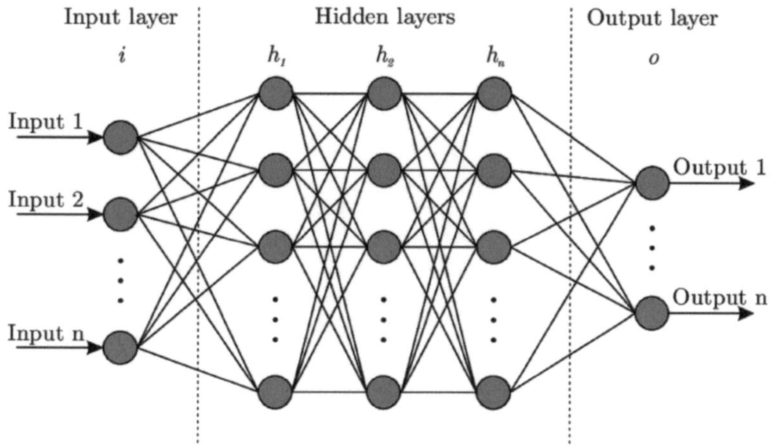

Figure 1.
Graphical representation of feed-forward neural network.

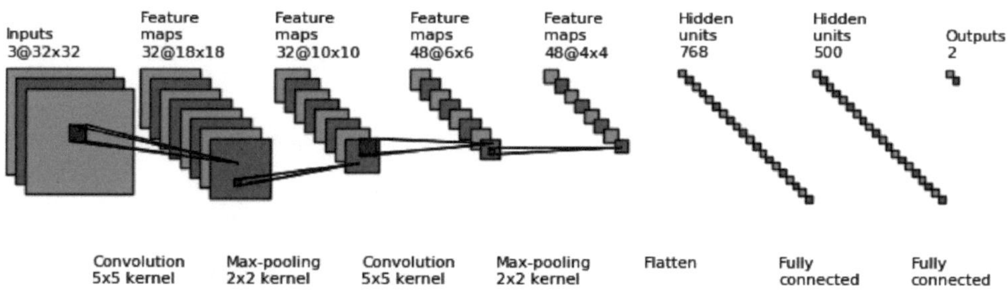

Figure 2.
Example of convolution neural network.

modeling simple cells in human brains [10]. In the context of convolutional neural networks, a convolution is a linear filtering operation that involves multiplying the input with the weights similar to the traditional neural network. Given the nature of 2D inputs, the multiplication is done between an array of data and 2D array of weights (often called filter or kernel).

The filter is smaller than the data and the multiplication operation between the filter and the data is the dot product. The dot product is the element-wise multiplication and summation resulting in one value. Having a filter or a kernel smaller than the input data enables the sliding of the kernel over the whole input, therefore giving the trained weights of the filter the ability to detect features anywhere in the image. Convolutional neural networks might also consist of max-pooling operations, used to down-sample the input (modeling complex cells in human brain [10]). **Figure 2** shows a graphical representation of neural network.

2.1.2 Image super-resolution using convolutional neural networks

In [7], the authors present the first convolutional neural network called SRCNN that outperforms traditional model-based approaches for the task of single image super-resolution (SISR). The key idea underlying SRCNN is to learn a nonlinear mapping from the space of LR images to that of HR ones. The work of SRCNN is under the framework of supervised learning with the assumption of paired training data (artificial LR images are generated by down-sampling of HR images). Their

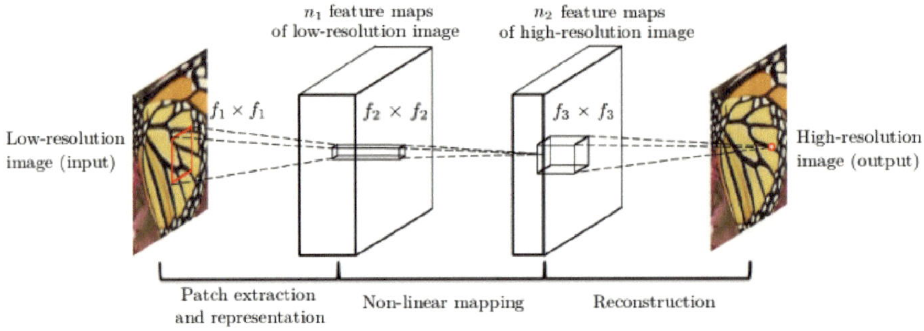

Figure 3.
Convolution neural network architecture for [7].

Figure 4.
Comparisons between [7] and state-of-the-art model based methods.

convolution neural network as shown in **Figure 3** consists of two layers. **Figure 4** shows the comparison between [7] and traditional model-based SR methods such as sparse coding [11].

With advancements in deep neural networks, deeper architectures powered by residual learning [12] has led to FSRCNN [13], DRCN [14], VDSR [15], EDSR [16] and LapSRN [17], RDN [18], and RCAN [19]. With deeper and densely connected networks, the performance of SISR has increased steadily at the price of higher computational complexity. With millions of parameters, EDSR and RCAN have advanced the state-of-the-art in supervised learning-based SISR. For face images, SISR has also been studied in recent works (e.g., Super-FAN [20] and FSRNet [21]).

2.2 Generative adversarial networks (GAN)

2.2.1 Definition

In [22], Ian Goodfellow presented a novel system for the task of data generation. This system is called generative adversarial network (GAN) consists of two interacting subnetworks (generator and discriminator) as shown in **Figure 5**. A generator subnetwork is responsible for generating synthetic data capturing the

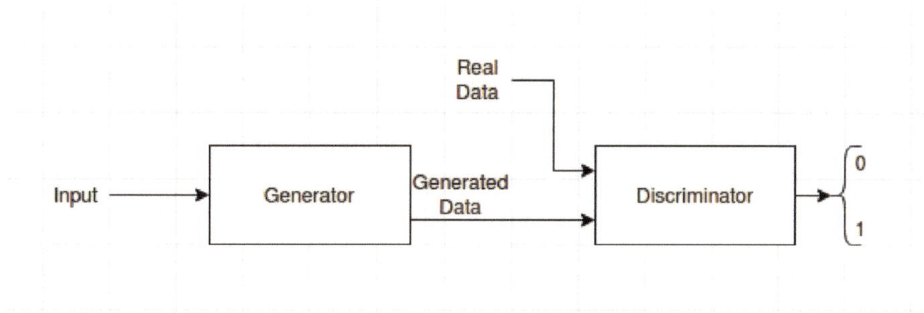

Figure 5.
Architecture of GANs.

Figure 6.
Comparison between SRGAN and SRResnet.

data distribution and a discriminator subnetwork for estimating the probability that a sample comes from the real training data rather than synthetic. Through the interplay between two subnetworks, the generator and discriminator networks can be trained together by a minimax two-player game. The invention of GAN opens the door to construct a whole new class of powerful generative models which have found numerous applications in low-level vision including SISR, face image synthesis, and style transfer.

2.2.2 Single image super-resolution using generative adversarial networks

In SRGAN [2], the authors showed that using a GAN-based architecture for the task of single image super-resolution leads to noticeable improvements in terms of subjective visual quality despite the sacrifice on traditional objective quality metric such as PSNR. In the construction of SRGAN, residue network for SR-called SRResnet is used as the generator; a separated discriminator inspired by Deep Convolutional GAN (DCGAN) [23] is constructed to tell apart real SR from fake SR. **Figure 6** shows the visual quality improvement when using a GAN-based architecture compared to using a generator without a discriminator.

2.3 Face image synthesis

Another successful application of GAN [2] is to generate high-fidelity face images that do not even exist in the real world. Radford et al. designed a variation of GAN architecture called Deep Convolutional GAN (DCGAN) [23] to generate face images; however, their results suffered from noticeable artifacts in synthesized images. More recently, self-attention (SAGAN) [24] used an attention mechanism to help minimize undesirable artifacts in generated images. Cleverly, designing loss functions for both discriminator and generator has shown impressive improvements in terms of convergence and artifacts suppression for the GAN networks.

Before 2017, most generated faces were still of low resolution, with the highest resolution equal to 128 × 128. In [5, 25], it was shown that progressively training the generator network helped generate face images up to 1024 × 1024 resolution. **Figure 7** shows an example of visual quality improvements in face image synthesis in the past 5 years, for example, from Progressive GAN [25] to StyleGAN [5] and its enhancement version StyleGAN2 [26].

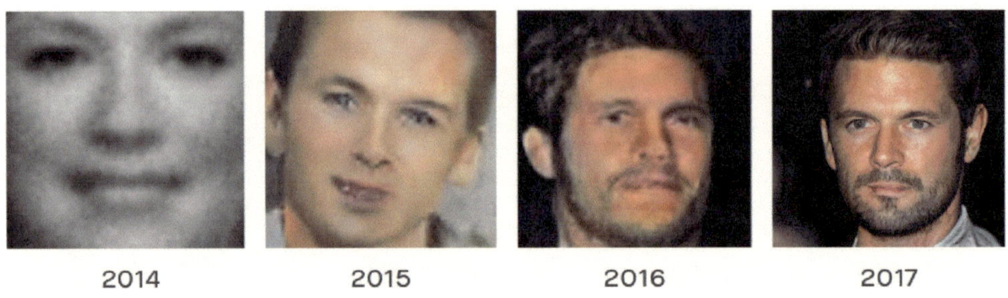

Figure 7.
Example of the progression made in GAN-based face synthesis from 2014 to 2017 (cited from [27]).

Figure 8.
Results from pix2pix [28].

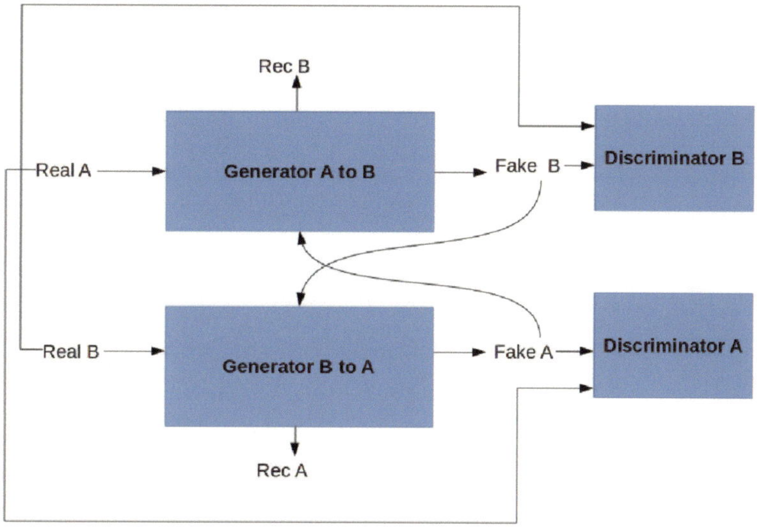

Figure 9.
CycleGAN [29] architecture.

2.4 Style transfer (CycleGAN)

Recently, GAN-based architectures were used for the task of style transfer, that is, translating one image from one style to another style (e.g., from sketch to real image). In [28], another GAN-based architecture called pix2pix was developed to transfer images from one style into another. **Figure 8** shows the example of translating sketch images of hand bags into real images. These works are based on an architecture called conditional GAN (cGAN) [30] in which the data instead of random noise are fed to (provided as the condition) both the generator and discriminator. However, pix2pix [28] is a supervised learning technique, and it requires the existence of groundtruth data.

To extend the style transfer to the domain where groundtruth is unavailable, an unsupervised architecture called cycle-consistent GAN (CycleGAN) was proposed in [29]. In CycleGAN [29], two parallel GAN architectures are trained concurrently: the first one to map from source domain to target domain and the second one to map from target domain back to source domain. The new insight brought by CycleGAN [29] is the enforcement of cycle-consistency, that is, when an image X is translated from source domain to target domain via forward mapping f and then translated back to the original domain via background mapping g, the result should approach the original image ($x \approx g(f(x))$). **Figure 9** shows an example of the CycleGAN [29] architecture with two generators and two discriminators.

3. Unsupervised approach

3.1 Overview of the method

We are interested in solving the problem of image face super-resolution for real world LR data. Unlike artificial LR data, the ground-truth is unavailable for real-world LR data. For such blind SR problem, we propose to tackle it as style transfer, that is, the transfer between LR and HR image data. We mainly focus on an asymmetrical formulation of style transfer problem in one direction: from LR to HR.

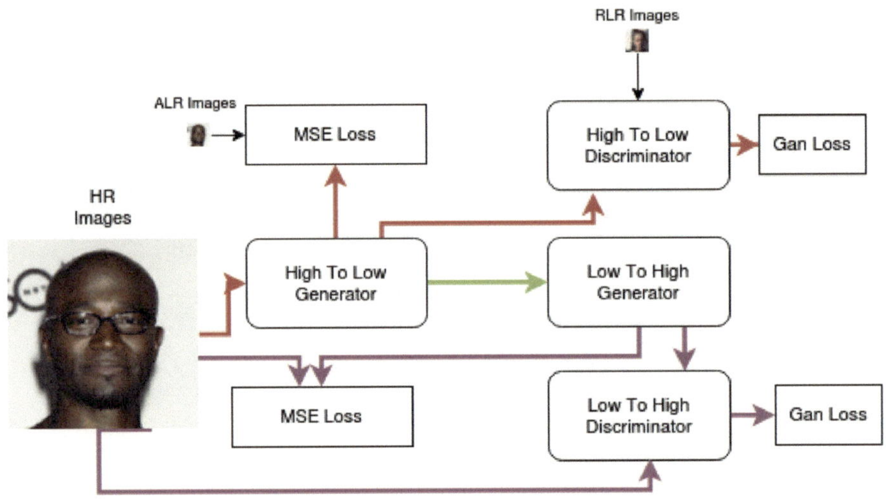

Figure 10.
Architecture of our unsupervised approach for real-world face superresolution.

Based on this observation, we do not need to enforce the cycle consistency for the direction of low-to-high transfer. Our overall network architecture is shown in **Figure 10**, consisting of two generative adversarial networks called high-to-low and low-to-high, respectively. The high-to-low GAN takes a HR face as the input and project it into the style of the real world LR faces. The low-to-high GAN takes the output of high-to-low generator as the input and try to reconstruct the original HR faces.

3.2 Dataset collection

High Resolution (HR) data: We have created our HR dataset by combining several publicly available HR face datasets: CelebA [31], AFLW [32], LS3D-W [33], and VGGFace2 [34]. For the reason of consistency, we have used S^3fd [35] to crop the face region in each image. We ended up with a total of 229,041 training images and 8892 testing images. All images are resized to 128 × 128. **Real Low Resolution Data (RLR):** We created our real LR dataset from Widerface [36] and we crop the face region using [35]. We have ended up with a total of 156,557 LR training images and 8241 LR testing images. All images have been resized to 16 × 16 (i.e., a scaling factor of 8).

Artificial Low Resolution (ALR) data: To create this dataset, we downsample our HR images by a factor of 8 using the "bilinear" method provided by Matlab. Note that the use of ALR is only for supervised learning experiences which require paired HR-LR training data.

3.3 Details of network architecture

In this section, we go through the detailed of the convolution neural networks that form our unsupervised architecture in **Figure 10**. We have two generators and two discriminators.

3.3.1 Building blocks

Our generators are made up of a number of blocks that we call residual + attention [37] (**Figure 11**). We use self attention layers as defined in [38] as part of both low-to-high and high-to-low discriminators. The details of self-attention layer are shown in **Figure 12**.

3.3.2 High-to-low generator

High-to-low generator has an encoder-decoder type architecture [39]: with the encoder consisting of five residual + attention blocks each followed by average

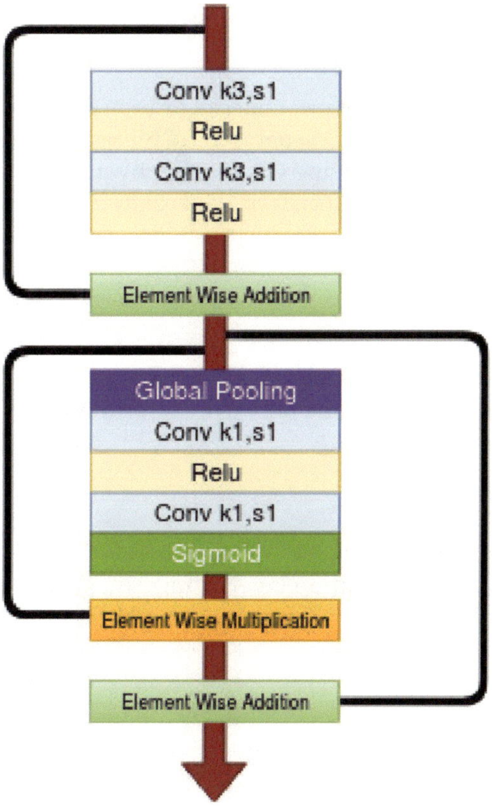

Figure 11.
Residual + attention block.

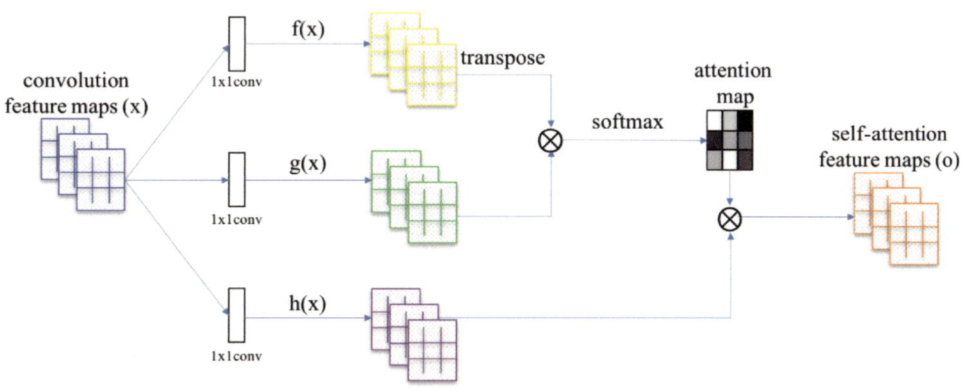

Figure 12.
Self-attention layer.

pooling layer and the decoder consisting of four residual + attention blocks where the first two are followed by bilinear upsampling layer. Therefore, the input is downsampled by a factor of 32 and upsampled by a factor of 4, which produces a down-sampled image by a factor of 8 but with more flexibility of modeling degradation (e.g., unknown blur [40]). We also concatenate a noise vector to the input image of the network using a fully connected layer, which contributes to the robustness of the proposed degradation modeling. The details of the high-to-low generator architecture is shown in **Figure 13**.

3.3.3 Low-to-high generator

Low to high generator subnetwork consists of four sections of 6, 3, 2, and 1 successive residual attention blocks separated by bilinear upsampling of 2 (similar to the strategy of progressive growing GAN [25]); overall the input 16 × 16 patch is up-sampled by a factor of 8. The details of the architecture are shown in **Figure 14**.

3.3.4 High-to-low discriminator

High-to-low discriminator subnetwork consists of three convolution layers followed by a leaky relu layer and a last convolutional layer. We have added two self-attention layers at the end of the network (refer to **Figure 15**).

3.3.5 Low-to-high discriminator

Low-to-high discriminator consists of four convolution layers followed by a leaky relu layer and a last convolution layer. Similarly, we have also added two self-attention layers. The details of the architecture are in **Figure 16**.

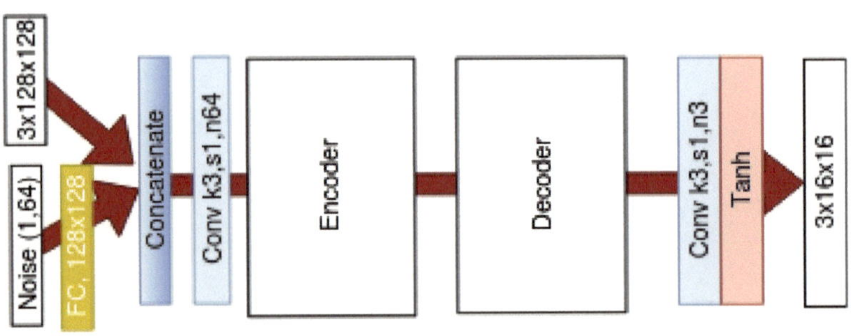

Figure 13.
Architecture of the high to low generator.

Figure 14.
Architecture of the low to high generator.

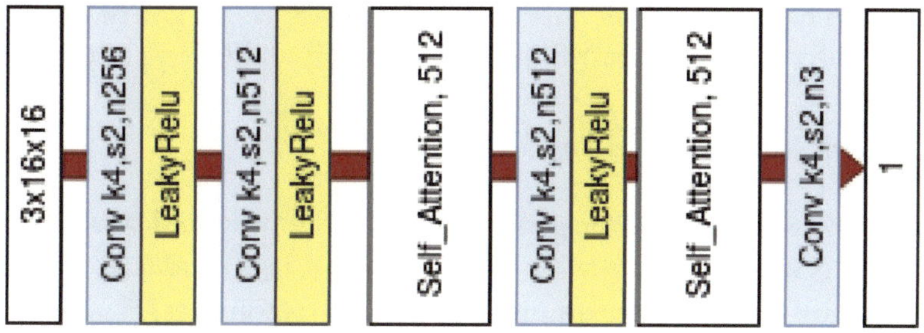

Figure 15.
Architecture of the high to low discriminator.

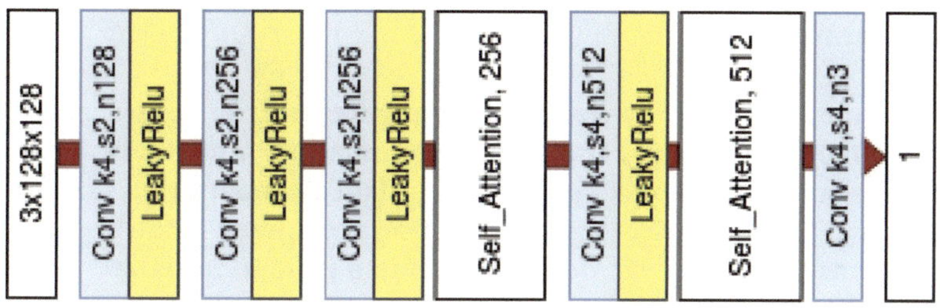

Figure 16.
Architecture of the low-to-high discriminator.

3.4 Loss functions

The generator loss, in both high-to-low and low-to-high GANs, is the weighted sum of the content loss and the GAN loss, as shown in Eq. (1) where $\alpha = 1$ and $\beta = 0.001$.

$$L_G = \alpha L_{pixel} + \beta L_{GAN}^{G} \tag{1}$$

The GAN losses and the pixel loss function follow the formula in Eqs. (2) and (3).

$$\begin{aligned} f(u,v) &= \frac{1}{2}\left\{ \mathop{\mathbb{E}}_{u\sim P_u}\left[\max\left(0, 1 - \left(D(u) - \mathop{\mathbb{E}}_{v\sim P_v}[D(v)]\right)\right)\right] + \right. \\ &\left. \mathop{\mathbb{E}}_{v\sim P_v}\left[\max\left(0, 1 + \left(D(v) - \mathop{\mathbb{E}}_{u\sim P_u}[D(u)]\right)\right)\right]\right\} \end{aligned} \tag{2}$$

$$g(u,v) = \frac{1}{WH}\sum_{i=1}^{W}\sum_{j=1}^{H}\left(u_{i,j} - v_{i,j}\right)^2 \tag{3}$$

3.4.1 High-to-low GAN loss functions

Generator loss: As mentioned above, the generator loss is the weighted sum of the content loss and the GAN loss, Eq. (1), where $L_{GAN}^{G} = f(I_{RLR}, I_{FLR})$ and $L_{pixel} = g(I_{ALR}, I_{FLR})$.

Discriminator loss: The discriminator is defined as follows: $L_{GAN}^{D} = f(I_{FLR}, I_{RLR})$. I_{ALR} is the artificial low resolution image, I_{FLR} the fake low resolution image generated by the high to low generator, and I_{RLR} the real world low resolution images. Functions f and g are defined, respectively, in Eqs. (2) and (3).

3.4.2 Low-to-high GAN loss functions

Generator Loss: Similarly, the generator loss is the weighted sum of the content loss and the GAN loss in Eq. (1), where $L^G_{GAN} = f(I_{HR}, I_{FHR})$ and $L_{pixel} = g(I_{HR}, I_{FHR})$.

Discriminator loss: The discriminator is defined as follows: $L^D_{GAN} = f(I_{FHR}, I_{HR})$. I_{FHR} is the fake high resolution image generated by the low to high generator and I_{HR} the real world high resolution image. Functions f and g are defined, respectively, in Eqs. (2) and (3).

3.5 Training strategy

It is worth mentioning that we have not augmented the data during training by standard techniques such as image flipping, scaling, and rotation. Our experience suggests that for unsupervised learning, data augmentation does not help improve the accuracy of face SR reconstruction but increase the computational burden as well as the risk of introducing artifacts (due to unpaired LR-HR training data). We have also found that the popular normalization tricks (e.g., batch normalization [41] and spectral normalization [42]) do not help in the unsupervised scenario but have the tendency of introducing artifacts to super-resolved images.

We have used a batch of size 32, and the total training requires about 20 epochs or ~143,000 generators and discriminators updates. The learning rate is kept at 0.001 throughout the training process, and the overall architecture is trained in an end-to-end manner. We also use Adam optimizer [43] with $\beta_1 = 0$ and $\beta_2 = 0.9$ and adopt a PyTorch-based implementation [44].

4. Experimental results

In this section, we present a comparison between our style-based approaches toward SISR of face images and state-of-the-art supervised (FSRNET [21]) and unsupervised ones (Bulat's [3]). First, we use extensive ablation studies to show the effect of removing the low-to-high discriminator (**Figure 16**) from the architecture and demonstrate the output of our degradation model. As an extension of our ablation study, we also present a supervised approach for ALR face images based on using GAN composed of our low-to-high generator (**Figure 14**) and low-to-high discriminator (**Figure 16**) but without any cycle involved. Finally, we will report our unsupervised learning results on real-world LR face images and compare them against other competing approaches.

4.1 Ablation study

4.1.1 Importance of the discriminator

We have compared the outputs of our unsupervised architecture with and without the high-to-low discriminator. The image comparison results are shown in **Figure 17**. It is obvious that discriminator plays a significant role in improving the visual quality of super-resolved images.

4.1.2 Degradation modeling

We next show the capability of high-to-low network on learning real-world degradation models. **Figure 18** includes several typical examples of learned LR images from HR inputs. It is important to note that our high-to-low network has managed to learn a variety of degradation models including varyimg poses and severe blurs.

4.1.3 Deep features visualization

We also visualize the feature maps of the low-to-high generator in **Figure 14**. In this visualization experiment, we have plotted the output from Sections 2, 3, and 4 as shown in **Figure 19**. It can be observed that as section/layer number increases, the learned feature representations have a larger field of view as well as more sophisticated semantic information related to faces.

4.2 Supervised approach

We have experimented with a GAN-based supervised approach toward SISR as an extension of our ablation study. Such experiment is included to demonstrate a degeneration of network architecture from unsupervised (**Figure 10**) to supervised (**Figure 20**) setting. We have used the same architecture for the low-to-high

Figure 17.
Comparison between our unsupervised method with and without the discriminator on Widerface dataset [36]. First row without discriminator; second row with discriminator. Please zoom in for better visualization.

Figure 18.
Effectiveness of degradation model learning: exemplar synthetic LR images from the high-to-low network (note the rich variability and similarity to the real-world Widerface dataset [36]).

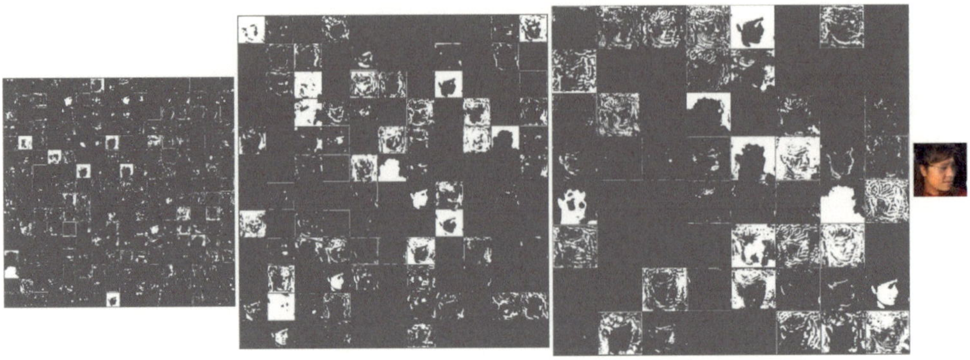

Figure 19.
Feature maps for low-to-high generator. From left to right: ×2-upsampling, ×4-upsampling, ×8-upsampling, and the output image.

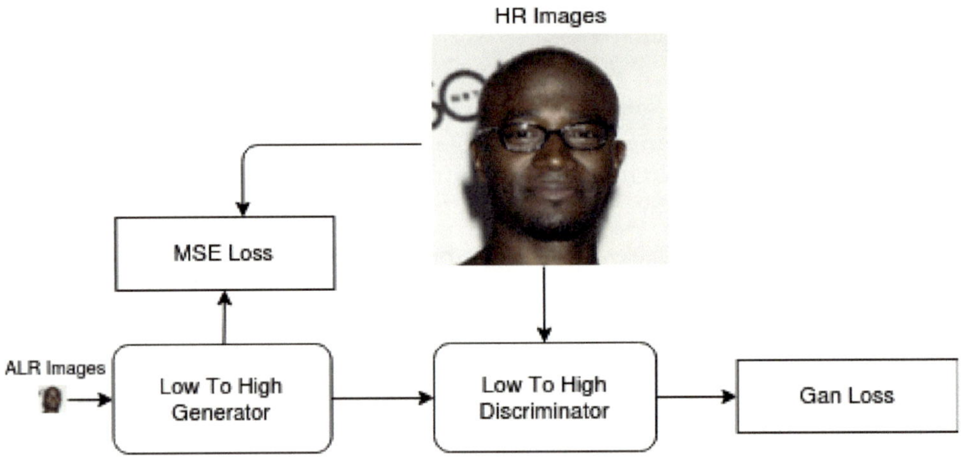

Figure 20.
Architecture of the supervised approach.

generator and discriminator as in **Figures 14** and **16**. To get paired LR and HR images; we downsample the original high resolution faces by a scaling factor of 8 to create artificial low resolution (ALR) images as explained in Section 3.2. The overall architecture of this reduced supervised approach is detailed in **Figure 20**.

4.2.1 Loss functions

Similar to Section 3.4, the loss functions for our supervised approach are defined as follows:

Generator loss: the generator loss is the weighted sum of the content loss and the GAN loss, Eq. (1) where $L^G_{GAN} = f(I_{FHR}, I_{HR})$ and $L_{pixel} = g(I_{HR}, I_{FHR})$.

Discriminator loss: $L^D_{GAN} = f(I_{HR}, I_{FHR})$ where I_{HR} denotes the high resolution image and I_{FHR} is the reconstructed high resolution one generated by our network. Functions f and g are defined, respectively, in Eqs. (2) and (3).

4.2.2 Training strategy

We have used a batch of size 32 and trained for 20 epochs or ~143,000 updates of generator and discriminator. The learning rate is kept at $1e-4$ throughout the training process. We have used Adam optimizer [43] with $\beta_1 = 0$ and $\beta_2 = 0.9$ and implemented our supervised learning SR using Pytorch [44].

4.3 Comparison with other supervised approaches

We compare our unsupervised face super-resolution approach with two supervised approaches; FSRNET [21] and our own approach outlined in Section 4.2. FSRNET [21] uses geometric priors to estimate (e.g., facial landmark heat maps and parsing maps) to facilitate the procedure of supervised learning.

4.3.1 Performance on artificial low resolution test data

We report our experimental results for ALR data and compare them against the current state-of-the-art FSRNet/FSRGAN [22]. Despite being synthetic, ALR images are still useful because they have ground-truth (HR) available and appropriate for gauging the performance of supervised learning (with paired HR-LR training data).

Subjective quality comparisons: Figure 21 shows the qualitative comparisons between our supervised/unsupervised approaches and state-of-the-art supervised method FSRGAN [21]. It can be easily verified that ours can produce visually more convincing and pleasant HR results than FSRGAN (e.g., sharper contrast, more natural hair, and fewer artifacts around earrings).

Figure 21.
Visual quality comparisons among competing methods on artificial low resolution face images. Rows top-down: bicubic, FSRGAN [21], ours (supervised), ours (unsupervised) and groundtruth. Please zoom in for better visualization.

Method	PSNR
FSRGAN [21]	22.840
Ours (Supervised)	**23.65**
Ours (Unsupervised)	21.97

Table 1.
Objective quality results of different methods on ALR images in terms of PSNR (dB) (highest PSNR is highlighted by bold-face).

Objective quality comparisons: We report the comparison results in terms of peak signal-to-noise ratio (PSNR) in **Table 1**. Our supervised learning outperforms FSRGAN [21] by as much as $0.8dB$.

4.3.2 Performance on real world wider test data

We tested both our supervised and unsupervised methods on the popular real-world LR dataset Widerface [36]. This dataset is particularly challenging for face detection and SR because its 393,703 faces contain a high degree of variability in scale, pose, and occlusion. Due to lack of groundtruth images (HR counterparts) for this dataset, we have to count on visual quality comparison alone for performance evaluation (without PSNR comparisons). We report our visual quality comparison between our methods and current state-of-the-art supervised (FSRGAN [22]). **Figure 22** shows the results; we can see that the unsupervised approach outperforms supervised ones in case of real world low resolution images.

4.4 Comparison with state-of-the-art unsupervised approach

We compare our unsupervised method with Bulat's [45]. We show that our methods are able to better preserve facial features **Figure 23**.

One can observe that the SR image produced by Bulat's [45] method has the following problems: age variation (third), gender swapping (fourth and seventh), and artifacts (second and seventh).

4.5 Performance in term of receiver operating curve (ROC)

Using Openface [46] matching algorithm, we plot the ROC curve for three types of degradation models: artificial degradation (or ALR), jpeg compression, and our high-to-low degradation model. We show that our proposed supervised approach outperform all previous ones in case of artificial degradation and our unsupervised approach performs the best when it comes to the other two degradation models.

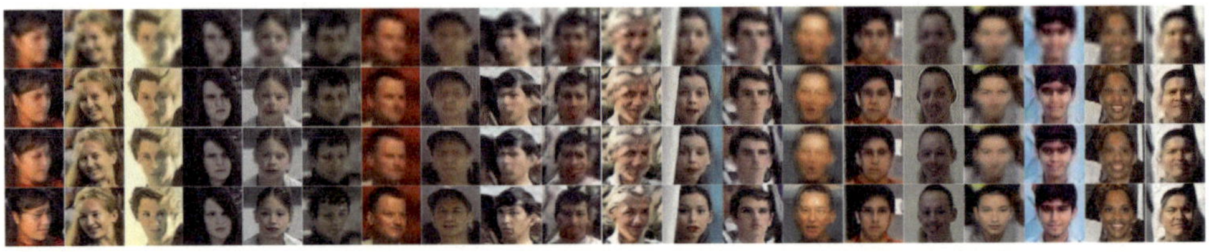

Figure 22.
Qualitative comparisons with FSRGAN on Widerface test data. Rows are respectively: Bicubic, FSRGAN, ours (supervised), and ours (unsupervised). Please zoom in for better visualization.

Figure 23.
Qualitative comparisons with Bulat's method [3] on Widerface test data. Rows are respectively: Bicubic, Bulat's method, and ours (unsupervised). Please zoom in for better visualization.

4.5.1 Performance on artificial low resolution data

We have compared our supervised and unsupervised approach with FSRNET [21] and Bulat's [45] in terms of ROC curve results. We use our Artificial Low Resolution (ALR) test data. **Figure 24** shows that our supervised method outperforms all other methods. On the other hand, our unsupervised method performs worse than FSRNET [21] but still performs significantly better than previous unsupervised state-of-the-art approach Bulat's [45].

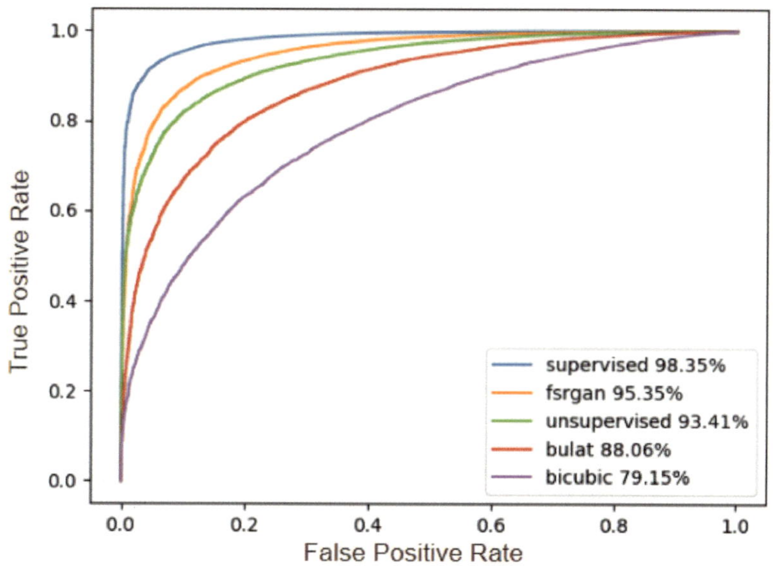

Figure 24.
ROC curve for ALR test data.

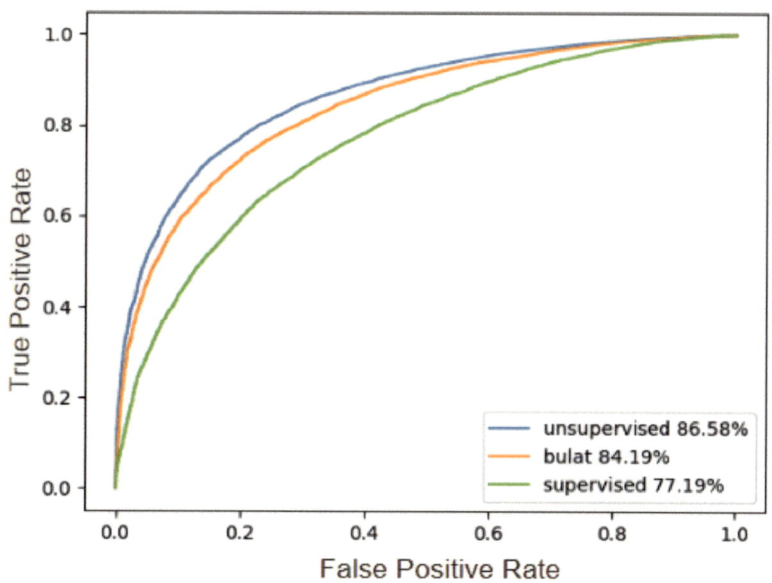

Figure 25.
ROC curve for compressed test data.

4.5.2 Performance on compressed data

We compressed our Artificial Low Resolution (ALR) test data using JPEG lossy compression. We used this compressed data to plot the ROC curve for our supervised and unsupervised approach as well as Bulat's [3]. Our unsupervised approach outperforms better than the other ones, as shown in **Figure 25**.

4.5.3 Performance on generated low resolution data

We also plotted the ROC curve using the data generated by passing high resolution test data to our trained high-to-low generator. We show here that our unsupervised approach performs better than our supervised one; **Figure 26**.

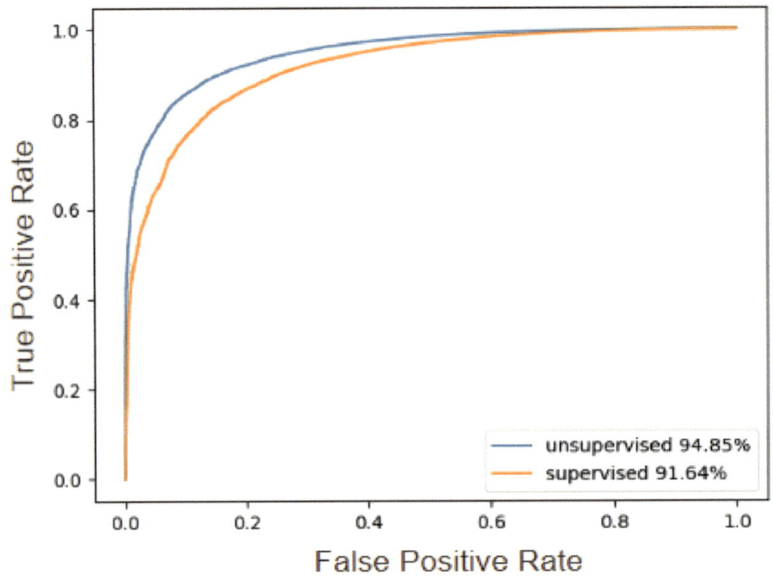

Figure 26.
ROC curve for our high-to-low degradation model.

Figure 27.
Exemplar failure cases of our unsupervised method on Widerface test data. Top-row: Input LR; bottom-row: our SR result (unsupervised).

4.6 Failure cases

As mentioned above, our approach intentionally skips the step of data augmentation. It turns out that our method is still sensitive to extreme variations of face pose such as as those shown in **Figure 27**. Due to severe occlusions and large pose variations, those LR examples are often rare even among Widerface dataset. This is within our expectation because high-to-low network simply does not have sufficient training data to learn the challenging degradation model. Note that similar findings have been reported for Bulat's method in [3] (refer to **Figure 9** in that paper).

5. Conclusions

We have studied the problem of SISR for real-world face images in this chapter and presented an unsupervised learning approach toward such blind reconstruction of SR images. The challenging scenario of real-world LR low-quality images defies conventional approaches based on paired HR-LR training data because groundtruth HR images are generally unavailable for real-world LR images. By pairing style-based generator with relativistic discriminator, we demonstrate an unsupervised learning approach with GAN-based end-to-end optimization that is capable of advancing the state-of-the-art in blind SR reconstruction of real-world LR face images. We have compared our degradation modeling against previous Bulat's method as well as their ROC performance on artificial LR dataset. Extensive experimental results have shown favorable performance for the proposed method over Bulat's method.

Author details

Ahmed Cheikh Sidiya and Xin Li*
Lane Department of Computer Science and Electrical Engineering, Morgantown, USA

*Address all correspondence to: xin.li@ieee.org

References

[1] Goodfellow I, Bengio Y, Courville A. Deep Learning. Cambridge, Massachusetts: MIT Press; 2016

[2] Christian L, Lucas T, Ferenc H, Jose C, Andrew C, Alejandro A, et al. Photo-realistic single image super-resolution using a generative adversarial network. In: Proceedings of the IEEE Conference on Computer Vision and Pattern Recognition. pp. 4681-4690

[3] Adrian B, Jing Y, Georgios T. To learn image super-resolution, use a gan to learn how to do image degradation first. In: Proceedings of the European Conference on Computer Vision (ECCV); 2018. pp. 185-200

[4] Zhu J-Y, Park T, Isola P, Efros AA. Unpaired image-to-image translation using cycle-consistent adversarial networks. In: Proceedings of the IEEE Conference on Computer Vision and Pattern Recognition. 2017. pp. 2223-2232

[5] Karras T, Laine S, Aila T. A style-based generator architecture for generative adversarial networks. In: Proceedings of the IEEE Conference on Computer Vision and Pattern Recognition. 2019. pp. 4401-4410

[6] Jolicoeur-Martineau A. The relativistic discriminator: a key element missing from standard gan. In: International Conference on Learning Representations; 2019

[7] Dong C, Loy CC, He K, Tang X. Image super-resolution using deep convolutional networks. IEEE Transactions on Pattern Analysis and Machine Intelligence. 2015;**38**(2):295-307

[8] Fukushima K, Miyake S. Neocognitron: A self-organizing neural network model for a mechanism of visual pattern recognition. In: Competition and Cooperation in Neural Nets. Springer; 1982. pp. 267-285

[9] Vinod N, Geoffrey EH. Rectified linear units improve restricted boltzmann machines. In: Proceedings of the 27th International Conference on Machine Learning (ICML-10); 2010. pp. 807-814

[10] Dominik S, Andreas M, Sven B. Evaluation of pooling operations in convolutional architectures for object recognition. In: International Conference on Artificial Neural Networks. Springer; 2010. pp. 92-101

[11] Huang TS, Yang J, Wright J, Ma Y. Image super-resolution via sparse representation. IEEE Transactions on Image Processing. 2010;**19**(11): 2861-2873. abs/1501.00092

[12] He K, Zhang X, Ren S, Sun J. Deep residual learning for image recognition. In: Proceedings of the IEEE Conference on Computer Vision and Pattern Recognition. 2016. pp. 770-778

[13] Chao D, Chen CL, Xiaoou T. Accelerating the super-resolution convolutional neural network. In: European Conference on Computer Vision. Springer; 2016. pp. 391-407

[14] Kim J, Lee JK, Lee KM. Deeply-recursive convolutional network for image super-resolution. In: Proceedings of the IEEE Conference on Computer Vision and Pattern Recognition. 2016. pp. 1637-1645

[15] Kim J, Lee JK, Lee KM. Accurate image super-resolution using very deep convolutional networks. In Proceedings of the IEEE Conference on Computer Vision and Pattern Recognition. 2016. pp. 1646-1654

[16] Bee L, Sanghyun S, Heewon K, Seungjun N, Kyoung ML. Enhanced deep residual networks for single image super-resolution. In: Proceedings of the

IEEE Conference on Computer Vision and Pattern Recognition Workshops. 2017. pp. 136-144

[17] Wei-Sheng L, Jia-Bin H, Narendra A, Ming-Hsuan Y. Deep laplacian pyramid networks for fast and accurate super-resolution. In: Proceedings of the IEEE conference on computer vision and pattern recognition. 2017

[18] Yulun Z, Yapeng T, Yu K, Bineng Z, Yun F. Residual dense network for image super-resolution. CVPR; 2018

[19] Yulun Z, Kunpeng L, Kai L, Lichen W, Bineng Z, Yun F. Image super-resolution using very deep residual channel attention networks. ECCV; 2018

[20] Adrian B, Georgios T. Super-fan: Integrated facial landmark localization and super-resolution of real-world low resolution faces in arbitrary poses with gans. In: Proceedings of the IEEE Conference on Computer Vision and Pattern Recognition. 2018. pp. 109-117

[21] Yu C, Ying T, Xiaoming L, Chunhua S, Jian Y. Fsrnet: End-to-end learning face super-resolution with facial priors. In: Proceedings of the IEEE Conference on Computer Vision and Pattern Recognition. 2018. pp. 2492-2501

[22] Goodfellow IJ, Pouget-Abadie J, Mirza M, Xu B, Warde-Farley D, Ozair S, et al. Generative adversarial nets. In: Proceedings of the 27th International Conference on Neural Information Processing Systems - Volume 2, NIPS'14. Cambridge, MA, USA: MIT Press; 2014. pp. 2672-2680

[23] Alec R, Luke M, Soumith C. Unsupervised representation learning with deep convolutional generative adversarial networks. In: International Conference on Learning Representations (ICLR); 2015

[24] Han Z, Ian G, Dimitris M, Augustus O. Self-attention generative adversarial networks. arXiv preprint arXiv: 1805.08318; 2018

[25] Tero K, Timo A, Samuli L, Jaakko L. Progressive growing of gans for improved quality, stability, and variation. CoRR. abs/1710.10196; 2017

[26] Tero K, Samuli L, Miika A, Janne H, Jaakko L, Timo A. Analyzing and improving the image quality of stylegan. arXiv preprint arXiv:1912.04958; 2019

[27] Miles B, Shahar A, Jack C, Helen T, Peter E, Ben G, et al. The malicious use of artificial intelligence: Forecasting, prevention, and mitigation. ICLR; 2018

[28] Phillip I, Jun-Yan Z, Tinghui Z, Alexei AE. Image-to-image translation with conditional adversarial networks. In: Proceedings of the IEEE Conference on Computer Vision and Pattern Recognition. 2017. pp. 1125-1134

[29] Jun-Yan Z, Taesung P, Phillip I, Alexei AE. Unpaired image-to-image translation using cycle-consistent adversarial networks. In: Proceedings of the IEEE International Conference on Computer Vision. 2017. pp. 2223-2232

[30] Mehdi M, Simon O. Conditional generative adversarial nets. arXiv preprint arXiv:1411.1784; 2014

[31] Ziwei L, Ping L, Xiaogang W, Xiaoou T. Deep learning face attributes in the wild. In: Proceedings of International Conference on Computer Vision (ICCV); December 2015

[32] Roth Martin Koestinger PM, Paul W, Horst B. Annotated facial landmarks in the wild: A large-scale, real-world database for facial landmark localization. In: Proceedings of the First IEEE International Workshop on Benchmarking Facial Image Analysis Technologies; 2011

[33] Adrian B, Georgios T. How far are we from solving the 2d & 3d face

alignment problem? (and a dataset of 230,000 3d facial landmarks). In: International Conference on Computer Vision; 2017

[34] Cao Q, Shen L, Xie W, Parkhi OM, Zisserman A. Vggface2: A dataset for recognising faces across pose and age. In: International Conference on Automatic Face and Gesture Recognition. 2018

[35] Shifeng Z, Xiangyu Z, Zhen L, Hailin S, Xiaobo W, Stan ZL. S3 fd: Single shot scale-invariant face detector. In: Proceedings of the IEEE International Conference on Computer Vision. pp. 192-201

[36] Shuo Y, Ping L, Chen CL, Xiaoou T. Wider face: A face detection benchmark. In: IEEE Conference on Computer Vision and Pattern Recognition (CVPR). 2016

[37] Yulun Z, Kunpeng L, Kai L, Lichen W, Bineng Z, Yun F. Image super-resolution using very deep residual channel attention networks. In: Proceedings of the European Conference on Computer Vision (ECCV). pp. 286-301

[38] Zhang H, Goodfellow I, Metaxas D, Odena A. Self-attention generative adversarial networks. In: International Conference on Machine Learning. 2019. pp. 7354-7363

[39] Vijay B, Alex K, Roberto C. Segnet: A deep convolutional encoder-decoder architecture for image segmentation. arXiv preprint arXiv:1511.00561 5; 2015

[40] Jinjin G, Hannan L, Wangmeng Z, Chao D. Blind super-resolution with iterative kernel correction. In: Proceedings of the IEEE Conference on Computer Vision and Pattern Recognition. 2019. pp. 1604-1613

[41] Sergey I, Christian S. Batch normalization: Accelerating deep network training by reducing internal covariate shift. In: International Conference on Machine Learning. 2015. pp. 448-456

[42] Takeru M, Toshiki K, Masanori K, Yuichi Y. Spectral normalization for generative adversarial networks. ICLR; 2018

[43] Diederik PK, Jimmy B. Adam: A method for stochastic optimization, 2014. cite arxiv:1412.6980. Comment: Published as a conference paper at the 3rd International Conference for Learning Representations. San Diego; 2015

[44] Adam P, Sam G, Francisco M, Adam L, James B, Gregory C, et al. Pytorch: An imperative style, high-performance deep learning library. In: Wallach H, Larochelle H, Beygelzimer A, dAlché-Buc F, Fox E, Garnett R, editors. Advances in Neural Information Processing Systems. Curran Associates, Inc.; 2019. pp. 8024-8035

[45] Adrian B, Jing Y, Georgios T. To learn image super-resolution, use a gan to learn how to do image degradation first. ECCV; 2018

[46] Brandon A, Bartosz L, Mahadev S. Openface: A general-purpose face recognition library with mobile applications. Technical report, CMU-CS-16-118, CMU School of Computer Science; 2016

Section 4

Multiview Imaging and 3D Reconstruction

Chapter 6

Spatiotemporal Fusion in Remote Sensing

Hessah Albanwan and Rongjun Qin

Abstract

Remote sensing images and techniques are powerful tools to investigate earth's surface. Data quality is the key to enhance remote sensing applications and obtaining clear and noise-free set of data is very difficult in most situations due to the varying acquisition (e.g., atmosphere and season), sensor and platform (e.g., satellite angles and sensor characteristics) conditions. With the increasing development of satellites, nowadays Terabytes of remote sensing images can be acquired every day. Therefore, information and data fusion can be particularly important in the remote sensing community. The fusion integrates data from various sources acquired asynchronously for information extraction, analysis, and quality improvement. In this chapter, we aim to discuss the theory of spatiotemporal fusion by investigating previous works, in addition to describing the basic concepts and some of its applications by summarizing our prior and ongoing works.

Keywords: spatiotemporal fusion, satellite images, depth images, pixel-level spatiotemporal fusion, feature-level spatiotemporal fusion, decision-level spatiotemporal fusion

1. Introduction

1.1 Background

Obtaining a high-quality satellite image with a complete representation of earth's surface is crucial to get clear interpretability of data, which can be used for monitoring and managing natural and urban resources. However, because of the internal and external influences of the imaging system and its surrounding environment, the quality of remote sensing data is often insufficient. The internal imaging system conditions include the spectral characteristics, resolution and other factors of the sensor, algorithms used to calibrate the images, etc. The surrounding environment refers to all external/environmental influences such as weather and season. These influences can cause errors and outliers within the images; for instance, shadow and cloud may cause obstructions in the scene and may occlude part of the information regarding an object. These errors must be resolved in order to produce high-quality remote sensing product (e.g., land-cover maps).

With the rapid and increasing development of satellite sensors and their capabilities, studies have shown that fusion of data from multisource, multitemporal images, or both is the key to recover the quality of a satellite image. Image fusion is known as the task of integrating two or more images into a single image [1–3]. The fusion of data essentially utilizes redundant information from multiple images to resolve or minimize uncertainties associated with the data, with goals such as to reject outliers, to replace and fill missing data points, and to enhance spatial and radiometric resolutions of the data. Fusion has been used in a wide range of remote sensing applications such as radiometric normalization, classification, change detection, etc. In general, there are two types of fusion algorithms: spatial-spectral [4–7] and spatiotemporal fusion [8–10]. Spatial-spectral fusion uses the local information in a single image to predict the pixels' true values based on spectrally similar neighboring pixels. It is used for various types of tasks and applications such as filling missing data (also known as image inpainting) and generating high-resolution images (e.g., pan-sharpening [11] and super-resolution [12]). It can include filtering approaches such as fusing information within a local window using methods such as interpolation [13, 14], maximum a posteriori (MAP), Bayesian model, Markov random fields (MRFs), and Neural Networks (NN) [4, 12, 15–18]. Although spatial-spectral fusion is efficient, it is not able to incorporate information from temporal images, which produce dramatic radiometric differences such as those introduced by meteorological, phenological, or ecological changes. For instance, radiometric distortions and impurities in an image due to metrological changes (e.g., heavy cloud cover, haze, or shadow) cannot be entirely detected and suppressed by spatial-spectral fusion since it only operates locally within a single image. To address this issue, researchers suggested spatiotemporal fusion, which encompasses spatial-spectral fusion and offers a filtering algorithm that is invariant to dynamic changes over time, in addition to being robust against noise and radiometric variations. Identifying spatiotemporal patterns is the core to spatiotemporal fusion, where the patterns are intended to define a correlation between shape, size, texture, and intensity of adjacent pixels across images taken at different times, of different types, and from different sources.

Spatiotemporal fusion has been an active area of study over the last few decades [9]. Many studies have shown that maximizing the amount of information through integrating the spatial, spectral, and temporal attributes can lead to accurate stable predictions and enhance the final output [8, 9, 19–21]. Spatiotemporal fusion can be applied within local and global fusion frameworks, where locally it can be performed using weighted functions and local windows around all pixels [22–24], and globally using optimization approaches [25, 26]. Additionally, spatiotemporal fusion can be performed on various data processing levels depending on the desired techniques and applications to be used [3]. It also can depend on the type of data used; for instance, per-pixel operations are well suited for images acquired from the same imaging system (i.e., same sensor) since they undergo similar calibration process and minimum spectral differences in terms of having the same number of bands and bandwidth ranges in the spectrum, whereas feature- or decision-level fusion is more flexible and able to handle heterogeneous data such as combing elevation data (e.g., LiDAR) with satellite images [27]. Fusion levels include:

Pixel-level image fusion: **This** is a direct low-level fusion approach. It involves pixel-to-pixel operation, where the physical information (e.g., intensity values, elevation, thermal values, etc.) associated with each pixel within two or more images is integrated into a single value [2]. It includes methods such as spatial and temporal adaptive reflectance fusion model (STARFM), Spatial and Temporal Reflectance Unmixing Model (STRUM), etc. [22–24].

Feature-level image fusion: It involves extracting and matching distinctive features from two or more overlapping images using methods such as dimensionality reduction like principal component analysis (PCA), linear discriminant analysis (LDA), SIFT, SURF, etc. [2, 28]. Fusion is then performed using the extracted features and the coefficients corresponding to them [2, 29]. Some other common methods that include spatiotemporal fusion on feature-level are sparse representation and deep learning algorithms [10, 30–38].

Decision-level image fusion is a high-level of fusion method that requires each image to be processed individually until an output (e.g., classification map). The outputs are then postprocessed using decision-level fusion techniques [2, 39]. This level of fusion can include the previous two levels of fusion (i.e., per-pixel operations or extracted features) within its operation [40, 41].

In this chapter, we will focus on the concept, methods, and applications of the spatiotemporal-based fusion at all levels of fusion. We will discuss all aspects of spatiotemporal fusion starting from its concepts, preprocessing steps, the approaches, and techniques involved. We will also discuss some examples that apply spatiotemporal fusion for remote sensing applications.

1.2 Contributions

This book chapter introduces the spatiotemporal analysis in fusion algorithms to improve the quality of remote sensing images. We will explore spatiotemporal fusion advantages and limitations, as well as, their applications and associated technicalities under three scenarios:

1. Pixel-level spatiotemporal fusion

2. Feature-level spatiotemporal fusion

3. Decision-level spatiotemporal fusion

1.3 Organization

The organization of this chapter is as follows: Section 2 describes remote sensing data and acquisition and generation processes and necessary preprocessing steps for all fusion levels. Section 3 talks about spatiotemporal fusion techniques under the three levels of fusion: pixel-level, feature-level, and decision-level, which can be applied to either multisource, multitemporal, or multisource multitemporal satellite images. Section 4 describes some applications applying spatiotemporal fusion, and finally Section 5 concludes the chapter.

2. Generic steps to spatiotemporal fusion

Spatiotemporal analysis allows investigation of data from various times and sources. The general workflow for any spatiotemporal fusion process is shown in **Figure 1**. The process description toward a fused image is demonstrated in **Figure 1(a)**, where it describes the process of input acquisition, preprocessing steps, and finally the fusion. Data in remote sensing are either acquired directly from a sensor (e.g., satellite images) or indirectly generated using algorithms (e.g., depth image from dense image matching algorithms [42]) (see **Figure 1(b)**). It also includes data from single or multiple sources (see **Figure 1(b)**); however, combing multisource and multitemporal images requires preprocessing steps to assure data consistency for analyses. The preprocessing steps can include radiometric and geometric correction and alignment (see **Figure 1(a)**). The main spatiotemporal fusion algorithm is then performed using one or more of the three levels of fusion as a base for their method. In this section, we will discuss the most common preprocessing steps in spatiotemporal fusion, as well as, the importance and previous techniques used in spatiotemporal fusion in the three levels of fusion to improve the quality of images and remote sensing applications.

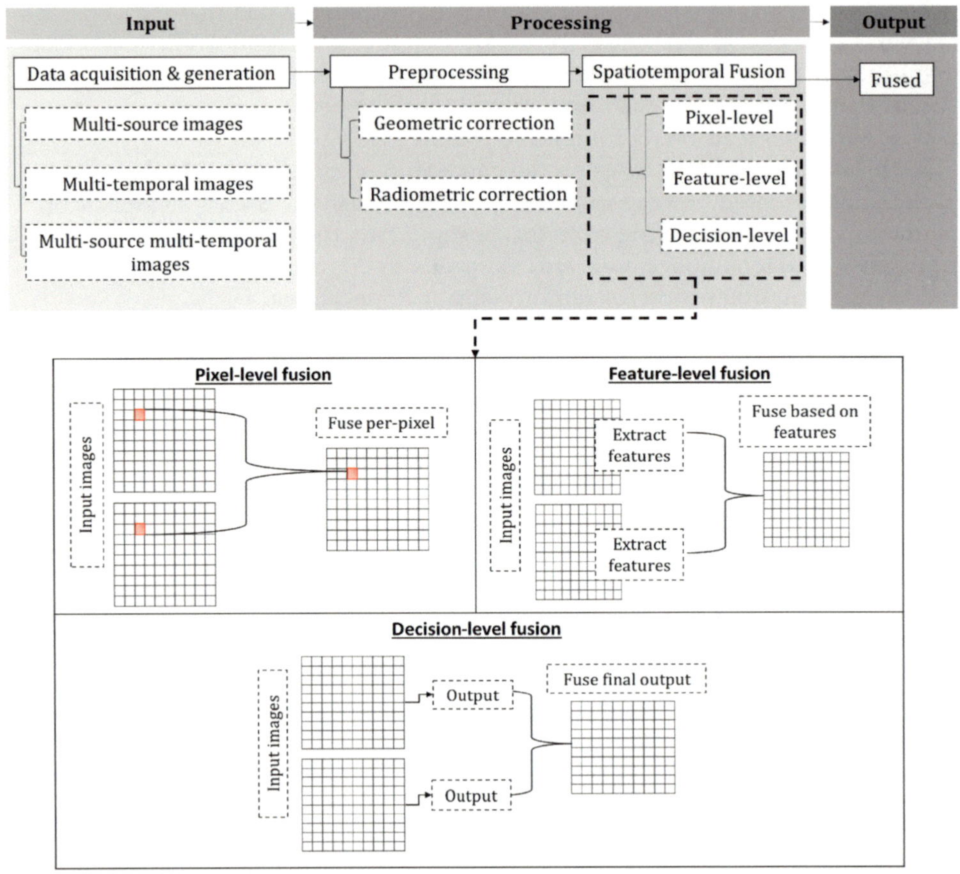

Figure 1.
The general workflow for spatiotemporal fusion. (a) The generic steps in spatiotemporal fusion, and (b) fusion based on type of data.

2.1 Data acquisition and generation

Today, there exists a tremendous number of satellite sensors with varying properties and configurations providing researchers with access to a large amount of satellite data. Remote sensing images can be acquired directly from sensors or indirectly using algorithms. It is also available with a wide range of properties and resolutions (i.e., spatial, spectral, and temporal resolutions), which are described in detail in **Table 1**.

2.1.1 Data acquisition

Generally, there exist two types of remote sensing sensor systems: active and passive sensors [43]. ***Active sensors*** record the signal that is emitted from the sensor itself and received back when it reflects off the surface of the earth. They include sensors like Light Detection and Ranging (LiDAR) and Radar. ***Passive sensors*** record the reflected signal off the ground after being emitted from a natural light source like the Sun. They include satellite sensors that produce satellite images such as Landsat, Satellite Pour l'Observation de la Terre (SPOT), MODIS, etc.

2.1.2 Data generation

Sometimes in remote sensing, the derived data can be also taken as measurements. Examples include depth images with elevation data derived through

Type of resolution	Spatial resolution	Spectral resolution	Temporal resolution
Definition	Describes the ground area covered by a single pixel in the satellite images. It is also known as the ground sampling distance (GSD) and can range from a few hundreds of meters to sub-meters. Satellite sensors like Moderate Resolution Imaging Spectroradiometer (MODIS) produce coarse-resolution images with 250, 500, and 1000 meters, while fine-resolution images are produced by satellites like very high-resolution (VHR) satellites at the sub-meter level [43].	Refers to the ability of satellite sensors to capture images with wide ranges of the spectrum. It includes hyperspectral (HS) images with thousands of bands or multispectral (MS) images with few numbers of bands (up to 10–15 bands) [43]. It may also include task-specific bands that are beneficial to study the environment and weather, like the thermal band as in Landsat 7 thematic mapper plus (ETM+) [43]. Spectral resolution also refers to the wavelength interval in the spectral signal domain; for instance, MODIS has 36 bands falling between 0.4 and 14.4 μm, whereas Landsat 7 (ETM+) has 7 bands ranging from 0.45 to 0.9 μm.	It is the ability of satellite sensors to capture an object or phenomena in certain periods of time, also known as the revisiting time of sensor at a certain location on the ground. Today, modern satellite systems allow monitoring earth's surface over short and regular periods of time; for instance, MODIS provides almost a daily coverage, while Landsat covers the entire earth surface every 16 days.

Table 1.
Satellite sensors' characteristics and resolutions.

photogrammetric techniques on satellite stereo or multi-stereo images [42], classification maps, change detection maps, etc. In this section, we will discuss two important examples of the commonly fused remote sensing data and their generation algorithms:

2.1.3 Depth maps (or digital surface model (DSM))

3D geometric elevation information can either be obtained directly using LiDAR or indirectly using dense image matching algorithms such as Multiview stereo (MVS) algorithms. However, because LiDAR data are expensive and often unavailable for historic data (before 1970s when LiDAR was developed), generating depth images using MVS algorithms is more convenient and efficient. MVS algorithms include several steps:

Images acquisition and selection to perform MVS algorithm requires having at least a pair or more of overlapping images captured from different viewing angles that assure selecting an adequate number of matching features. Specifically, this refers to the process of feature extraction and matching, where unique features are being detected and matched in pairs of images using feature detectors and descriptors methods such as Harris, SIFT, or SURF [44].

Dense image matching and depth map generation: Dense image matching refers to the process of producing dense correspondences between two or among multiple images, and with their pre-calculated geometrical relationship, depth/height information can be determined through ray triangulation [45]. The dense correspondences problem, with pre-calculated image geometry, turns to a 1-D problem in rectified image (also called epipolar image) [46], called disparity computation, which is basically the difference between the left and right views as shown below:

$$Disparity = \Delta x = x_l - x_r = \frac{\mathrm{f\,T}}{\mathrm{z}} \tag{1}$$

where x_l and x_r are distance of pixel in the left and right images accordingly, f is the focal length, T is the distance between the cameras, and z is the depth. The depth (z) is then estimated from Eq. [1] by taking the focal length times the distance between the cameras divided by the disparity as follows:

$$Depth = Z = \frac{ft}{|x_l - x_r|} \tag{2}$$

In addition, it is noted that assessing and selecting good pairs of images can improve the dense image matching and produce a more accurate and complete 3D depth map [47, 48].

2.1.4 Classification maps

Image classification can be divided into two categories: **1) Supervised classification** is a user-guided process, where classification depends on a prior knowledge about the data that are extracted from the predefined training samples by the user; some popular supervised classification methods include support vector machine (SVM), random forest (RF), decision trees DT, etc. [49–51]. 2) **Unsupervised classification** is a machine-guided process, where the algorithms classify the pixels in the image by grouping similar pixels to come up with specific patterns that define each class. These techniques include segmentation, clustering, nearest neighbor classification, etc. [49].

2.2 Preprocessing steps

2.2.1 Geometric correction

Image registration and alignment is an essential preprocessing step in any remote sensing application that processes two or more images. For accurate analyses of multisource multitemporal images, it is necessary that overlapping pixels in the images correspond to the same coordinates or points on the earth's surface. Registration can be performed manually by selecting control points (CPs) between a pair of images to determine the transformation parameters and wrap the images with respect to a reference image [52]. An alternative approach is an automated CP extraction that operates based on mutual information (MI) and similarity measures of the intensity values [52]. According to [53], there are a few common and sequential steps for image registration including the following steps:

Unique feature selection, extraction, and matching refers to the process where unique features are detected using feature extraction methods, then matched to their correspondences in a reference image. A feature can be a shape, texture, intensity of a pixel, edge, or an index such as vegetation and morphological index. According to [54, 55], features can be extracted based on the content of a pixel (e.g., intensity, depth value, or even texture) using methods such as SIFT, difference of Gaussian (DOG), Harris detection, and Histogram of oriented gradient (HOG) [53, 56–58] or based on patch of pixels [59–61] like using deep learning methods (e.g., convolutional neural networks (CNNs)), which can be used to extract complete objects to be used as features.

Transformation refers to the process of computing the transformation parameters (e.g., rotation, translation, scaling, etc.) necessary to convolve an image to a coordinate system that matches a reference image. The projection and transformation methods include similarity, affine, projective, etc. [53].

Resampling is the process where an image is converted into the same coordinate system as the reference image using the transformation parameters; it includes methods such as interpolation, bilinear, polynomial, etc. [53].

2.2.2 Radiometric correction

Radiometric correction is essential to remove spectral distortion and radiometric inconsistencies between the images. It can be performed either using absolute radiometric normalization (ARN) or relative radiometric normalization (RRN) [62–64]. ARN requires prior knowledge of physical information related to the scene (e.g., weather conditions) for normalization [63, 65–67], while, RRN radiometrically normalizes the images based on a reference image using methods such as dark object subtraction (DOS), histogram matching (HM), simple regression (SR), pseudo-invariant features (PIF), iteratively re-weighted MAD transformation, etc. [62, 64, 68].

3. Data analysis and spatiotemporal fusion

Pixels in remote sensing data are highly correlated over space and time due to earth's surface characteristics, repeated patterns (i.e., close pixels belong to the same object/class), and dynamics (i.e., season). The general algorithm for spatiotemporal fusion is demonstrated in **Figure 2**, where all levels of fusion follow the same ideology. The minimum image requirement for spatiotemporal fusion is a pair of images whether they are acquired from multiple sources or time, the input images are represented with t_1 to t_n in **Figure 2**. The red square can be either a single

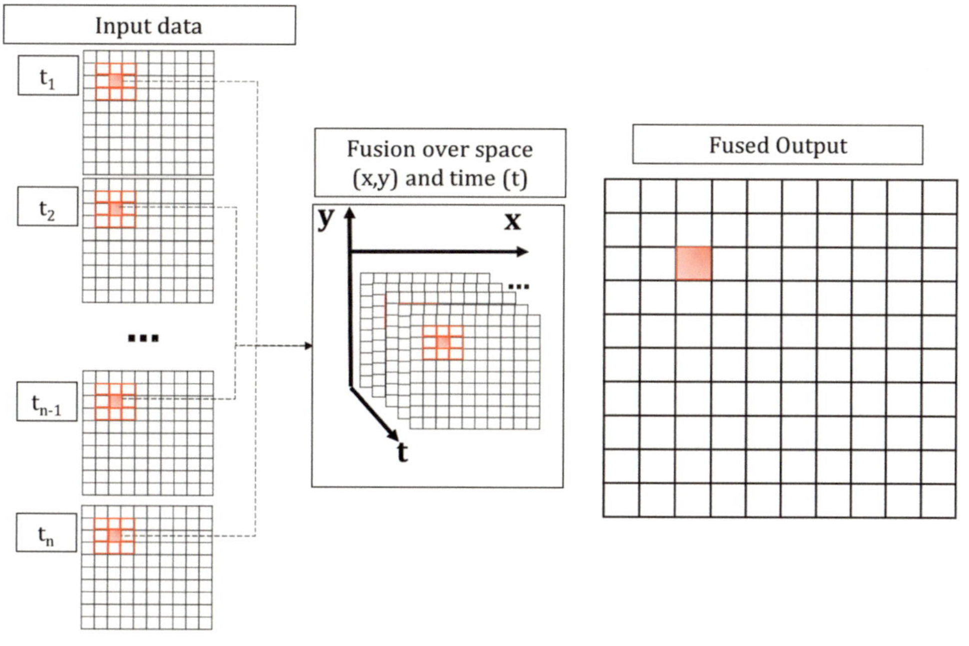

Figure 2.
The general concept of spatiotemporal fusion to process patch of pixels (the red square) spatially across different times (t).

raw pixel, an extracted feature vector, or processed pixel with valuable information (e.g., probability value indicating the class of a pixel). The fusion algorithm then finds the spatiotemporal patterns over space (i.e., the coordinates (x, y), and pixel content) and time (t) to predict accurate and precise values of the new pixels (see **Figure 2**). In this section, we will provide an overview of some previous works regarding spatiotemporal image fusion that emphasize on the importance of space-time correlation to enhance image quality and discuss this type of fusion in the context of three levels of fusion: pixel-level, feature-level, and decision-level.

3.1 Pixel-level spatiotemporal fusion

As mentioned in the introduction, pixel-based fusion is the most basic and direct approach to fuse multiple images by performing pixel-to-pixel operations; it has been used in a wide range of applications and is preferred because of its simplicity. Many studies performing pixel-level fusion algorithms realized the power of spatiotemporal analysis in fusion and used it in a wide range of applications such as monitoring, assessing, and managing natural sources (e.g., vegetation, cropland, forests, flood, etc.), as well as, urban areas [9]. Most of the pixel-level spatiotemporal fusion algorithms operate as a filtering or weighted-function method; they process a group of pixels in a window surrounding each pixel to compute the corresponding spatial, spectral, and temporal weights (see **Figure 3**). A very popular spatiotemporal fusion method that set the base for many other fusion methods is spatial and temporal adaptive reflectance fusion model (STARFM); it is intended to generate a high-resolution image with precise spectral reflectance by merging multisource fine- and coarse-resolution images [22]. Their method resamples the coarse-resolution MODIS image to have a matching resolution as the Landsat TM image, after that it computes the overall weight by calculating the spectral and temporal differences between the images. STARFM is highly effective in detecting phenological changes, but it fails to handle heterogeneous landscapes with rapid land-cover changes and around mixed pixels [22]. To address this issue, [20] have proposed Enhanced STARFM (ESTARFM); it applies a conversion coefficient to assess the temporal differences between fine- and coarse-resolution images. In [69], Hilker also addressed the problem of drastic land-cover change by proposing Spatial Temporal Adaptive Algorithm for mapping Reflectance Change (STAARCH), which applies Tasseled cap transformation [70] to detect the seasonal changes over

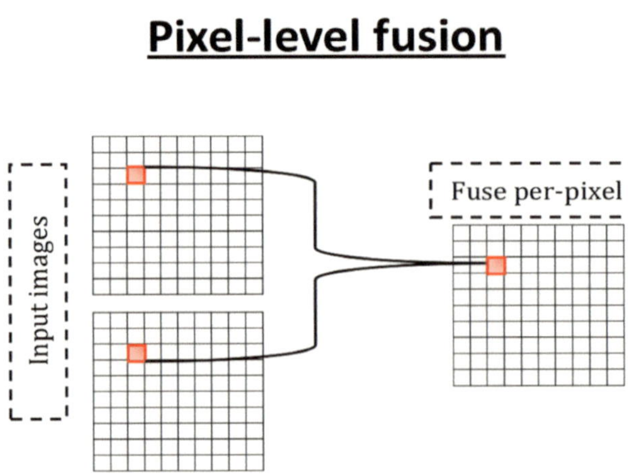

Figure 3.
Pixel-based fusion process diagram.

a landscape. For further improvement of these algorithms, studies have suggested using machine learning methods to identify similar pixels by their classes [71]. The authors also show an example on using machine learning unsupervised classification within the spatiotemporal fusion to enhance its performance. They used clustering on one of the images using the ISODATA method [72], where pixels are considered similar if the difference between the current and central pixel in the window is less than one standard deviation of the pixels in the cluster. Other methods use filtering algorithms to enhance the spatial and spectral aspects of images, in addition to embedding the temporal analysis to further enhance the quality and performance of an application. For instance, [73] proposed a method that combines the basic bilateral filter with STARFM to estimate land surface temperature (LST). In [19], they proposed a 3D spatiotemporal filtering as a preprocessing step for relative radiometric normalization (RRN) to enhance the consistency of temporal images. Their idea revolves around finding the spatial and spectral similarities using a bilateral filter, followed by assessing the temporal similarities for each pixel against the entire set of images. The temporal weight, which assesses the degree of similarity, is computed using an average Euclidean distance using the multitemporal data. In addition to the weighted-based functions, approaches such as unmixing-based and hybrid-based methods are also common in spatiotemporal fusion [74]. The unmixing-based methods predict the fine-resolution image reflectance by computing the mixed pixels from coarse-resolution image [75], while hybrid-based methods use a color mapping function that computes the transformation matrix from the coarse-resolution image and apply it on the finer resolution image [76].

3.2 Feature-level spatiotemporal fusion

Feature-level fusion is a more complex level of fusion, unlike pixel-based operations, it can efficiently handle heterogeneous data that vary in modality and source. According to [2], feature-based fusion can either be conducted directly using semantically equivalent features (e.g., edges) or through probability maps that transform images into semantically equivalent features. This characteristic allows fusion to be performed regardless of the type and source of information [27]. Fusion can then be performed using arithmetic (e.g., addition, division, etc.) and statistical (e.g., mean, median, maximum, etc.) operations; the general process of feature-based fusion is shown in **Figure 4**. The approach in [27] demonstrates a

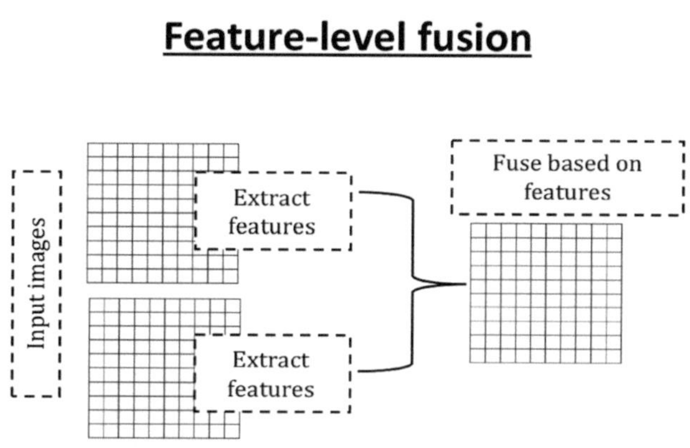

Figure 4.
Feature-based fusion diagram.

simple example on feature-level spatiotemporal fusion to investigate and monitor deforestation; in their method, they combined data from meduim-resolution synthetic aperture radar (SAR) and MS Landsat data, they extracted features related to vegetation and soil location (using scattering information and Normalized Difference Fraction Index (NDFI) respectively), finally, fusion was performed through decision tree classifier. Both [26, 62] point out to the most popular methods in feature-level fusion, which include Laplacian pyramid, gradient pyramid, morphological pyramid, high-pass filter, and wavelet transform methods [77–81]. A very famous fusion example in this category is inverse discrete wavelet (IDW) transform, which is a wavelet transform fusion approach; it uses temporal images with varying spatial resolutions to down-sample the coarse-resolution image. It basically extracts the wavelet coefficients from the fine-resolution image and uses them to down-sample the coarse-resolution image [82]. Sparse representation is another widely used learning-based method in feature-level fusion due to its good performance [8, 10, 30, 31]. All sparse representation algorithms share the same concept and core idea, where the general steps include: 1) dividing the input images into patches, 2) extracting distinctive features from the patches (e.g., high-frequency feature patches), 3) generating coefficients from the feature patches, 4) training jointly using dictionaries to find similar structures by extracting and matching feature patches, and finally, 5) fusion using the training information and extracted coefficients [8, 10, 30, 79, 83, 84].

Another state-of-the-art approach in feature- and decision-level fusion is deep learning or artificial neural networks (ANNs). They are currently a very active area of interest in many remote sensing fields (especially image classification) due to their outstanding performance that surpasses traditional methods [32–38, 76, 82–84]. They are also capable of dealing with multi-modality like images from varying sources and heterogeneous data, for instance, super-resolution and pan-sharpening images from different sensors, combining HS and MS images, combining images with SAR or LiDAR data, etc. [32–38]. In feature-level fusion, the ANN is either performed on the images for feature extraction or to learn from the data itself [38]. The extracted features from the temporal images or classification map are used as an input layer, which are then weighted and convoluted within several intermediate hidden layers to result in the final fused image [32–35, 37, 79]. For instance, [85] uses neural networks (CNN) to extract features from RGB image and a DSM elevation map, which are then fed into the SVM training model to generate an enhanced semantic labeling map. ANNs have also been widely used to solve problems related to change detection of bi-temporal images such as comparing multi-resolution images [86] or multisource images [87], which can be solved in a feature-learning representation fashion. For instance, the method in [87] directly compares stacked features extracted from a registered pair of images using deep belief networks (DBNs).

3.3 Decision-level spatiotemporal fusion

The decision-level fusion operates on a product level, where it requires images to be fully and independently processed until the meaningful output is obtained (e.g., classification or change detection maps) (see **Figure 5**). Decision-level fusion can adapt to different modularities like combing heterogeneous data such as satellite and depth images, which can be processed to common outputs (e.g., full/partial classification maps) for fusion [88]. Additionally, the techniques followed by this fusion type are often performed under the umbrella of Boolean or statistical operations using methods like likelihood estimation, voting (e.g., majority voting, Dempster-Shafer's estimation, fuzzy Logic, weighted sum, etc.) [88–90]. In [88],

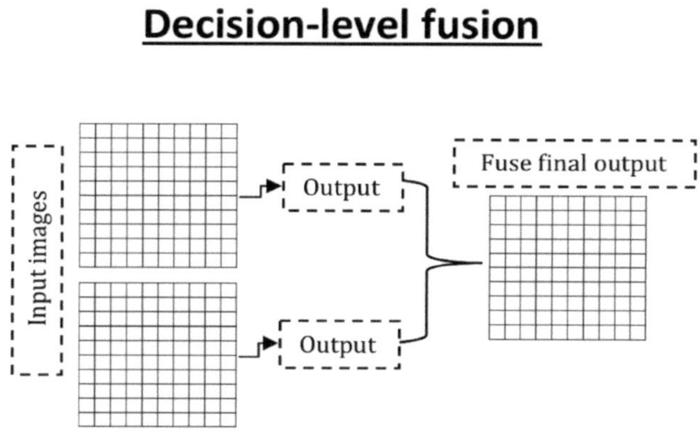

Figure 5.
Feature-based fusion diagram.

they provide an example on the mechanism of decision-level fusion; they developed a fusion approach to detect cracks and defects on ground surface, they first convert multitemporal images into spatial density maps using kernel density estimation (KDE), then, fused the pixels density values using a likelihood estimation method. In general, most of the decision-level fusion techniques rely on probabilistic methods, where they require generating an initial label map with each pixel upholding a probability value and indicating its belonging to a certain class, which can be generated using traditional classification methods like the supervised (e.g., random forest) or unsupervised (e.g., clustering or segmentation) classification (see Section 2.1.2.). Another advantage of the decision-level fusion is that it can be implemented while incorporating both levels of fusion, the pixel- and feature-level fusion. The method in [41] shows a spatiotemporal fusion algorithm that includes all levels of fusion, where they propose a post-classification refinement algorithm to enhance the classification maps. First, they generate probability maps for all temporal images using random forest classifier (as an initial classification map); then they use a recursive approach to iteratively process every pixel in the probability maps by fusing the multitemporal probability maps with the elevation from the DSMs using a 3D spatiotemporal filtering. Similarly, [40] have also proposed fusion of probability maps for building detection purposes, where they first generate the probability maps, then fuse them using a simple 3D bilateral filter.

Recently, more focus has been driven toward using spatiotemporal fusion to recover the quality of 3D depth images generated from MVS (e.g., DSM fusion). Median filtering is the oldest and most common fusion approach for depth images; it operates by computing the median depth of each pixel from a group of pixels at the same location in the temporal images [91]. The median filtering is robust to outliers and is efficient in filling missing depth values. However, the median filter only exploits the temporal domain; to further enhance its performance and the precision of the depth values, studies suggest spatiotemporal median filtering. In [92], the authors have proposed an adaptive median filtering that operates based on the class of the pixels; they use an adaptive window to isolate pixels belonging to the same class, then choose the median pixel based on the location (i.e., adaptive window) and temporal images. In [93], the authors also show that spatiotemporal median filtering can be improved by adopting an adaptive weighing-filtering function that involves assessing the uncertainty of each class in the spatial and temporal domains in the depth images using standard deviation. The uncertainty will then be used as the bandwidth parameter to filter each class individually. The authors in [47] also suggested a per-pixel fusing technique to select the depth value for each pixel by using a recursive K-median clustering approach that generates one to eight clusters until it reaches the desired precision.

Other complex yet efficient methods used in decision-level fusion are deep learning algorithms as mentioned previously in Section 2.3.2. [94]. They are either used as postprocessing refinement approaches or to learn end-to-end from a model [38]. For example, the method in [95] used a postprocessing enhancement step for semantic labeling, where they first generate probability maps using two different methods, RF and CNN using multimodal data (i.e., images and depth images), then they fused the probability maps using Conditional random fields (CRFs) as postprocessing approach. In [96], on the other hand, the authors used a model learning-based method, where they first semantically segment multisource data (i.e., image and depth image) using a SegNet network, then fuse their scores using a residual learning approach.

4. Examples on spatiotemporal fusion applications

4.1 Spatiotemporal fusion of 2D images

4.1.1 Background and objective

A 3D spatial-temporal filtering algorithm is proposed in [19] to achieve relative radiometric normalization (RRN) by fusing information from multitemporal images. RRN is an important preprocessing step in any remote sensing application that requires image comparison (e.g., change detection) or matching (e.g., image mosaic, 3D reconstruction, etc.). RRN is intended to enhance the radiometric consistency across set of images, in addition to reducing radiometric distortions that result due to sensor and acquisition conditions (as mentioned in Section 1.1.). Traditional RRN methods use a single reference image to radiometrically normalize the rest of the images. The quality of the normalized images highly depends on the reference image, which requires the reference image to be noise-free or to have minimum radiometric distortions. Thus, the objective of [19] is to generate high-quality radiometrically consistent images with minimum distortion by developing an algorithm that fuses the spatial, spectral, and temporal information across a set of images.

4.1.2 Theory

The core of the 3D spatiotemporal filter is based on the bilateral filter, which is used to preserve the spectral and spatial details. It is a weighting function that applies pixel-level fusion on images from multiple dates (see **Figure 4(a)**). The general form of this filter is as follows:

$$\bar{\mathrm{I}}_i = \int_{\Omega} w_{\mathrm{j},i} . \mathrm{I}_j . \mathrm{dj} \tag{3}$$

where the original and filtered images are indicated using I and $\bar{\mathrm{I}}$. The weight for every pixel at point j into the fused pixel i is indicated using $w_{\mathrm{j},i}$. The filtering is carried out on the entire space of the set of images Ω including all domains, that is, the spatial (i.e., pixels' coordinates (x, y)), the spectral (i.e., intensity value), and temporal (i.e., intensity of temporal images). The spatial and spectral weights are described by [97] and are indicated in Eqs. (4) and (5) respectively

$$w_{\text{spatial}} = \exp\left(\frac{|\, j_{\text{x}} - i_{\text{x}}|^2}{\sigma_{\vec{x}}} + \frac{\left|\, j_{\text{y}} - i_{\text{y}}\right|^2}{\sigma_{\vec{x}}}\right), j, i \in \Omega \tag{4}$$

$$w_{\text{spectral}} = \exp\left(-\frac{\left|I_j - I_i\right|^2}{\sigma_I}\right), j, i \in \Omega \tag{5}$$

where, I is the pixel value at x and y locations, and $\sigma_{\vec{x}}$ and σ_I are the spatial and spectral bandwidths respectively that set the degree of filtering based on the spatial and spectral similarities between the central pixel and nearby pixels. The novelty of this filter is in the design of the temporal weight, where it computes the resemblance between every image and the entire set of images using an average Euclidean distance as the follows

$$w_{\text{spectral}} = \exp\left(-\frac{|\, j_t - i_t|^2}{\sigma_T}\right), j, i \in \Omega \tag{6}$$

where $(\, j_t - i_t)$ are the difference between the current image being processed and all other images and σ_T is the degree of filtering along the temporal direction. Eq. (6) allows all images to contribute toward each other in enhancing the overall radiometric characteristics and consistency without requiring a reference image for the RRN process.

4.1.3 Experimental results and analysis

The 3D spatial-temporal filter was conducted on three experiments with varying resolutions and complexities. Experiments 1 and 2 were applied on urban and sub-urban areas respectively; each experiment had five medium-resolution images from Landsat 8 satellite (with 15- to 30- m spatial resolution). Experiment 3 was on a fine-resolution image from Planet satellite (with 3-m spatial resolution).

Figure 6(b) and **(c)** shows an example of the input and results of the filter using the data from experiment 1 (i.e., the urban area). The input images show a significant discrepancy in the radiometric appearance (see **Figure 6(b)**); however, the heterogeneity between multitemporal images is reduced after the filtering process (see **Figure 6(c)**). By comparing the original and filtered images in **Figure 6(c)**, we can notice that the land covers are more similar in the filtered images than in the original images. For instance, the water surface (shown in **Figure 6(c)** in blue bold dashed line) used to have a clear contrast in intensity in the original images, but after the filtering process, they become more spectrally alike in terms of intensity looks and ranges.

The experiments are also validated numerically using transfer learning classification (using SVM) to test the consistency between the normalized filtered images. The transfer learning classification uses a reference training data from one image and applies it to the rest of the images. The results in **Table 2** indicate that the filtered images have higher accuracy than the nonfiltered original images, where the average improvement in accuracy is ~6%, 19%, and 2% in all three experiments respectively. Reducing the uncertainty in the filtering process by not requiring a reference image for normalization was the key to this algorithm. The algorithm was formulated to take advantage of the temporal direction by treating all images in the

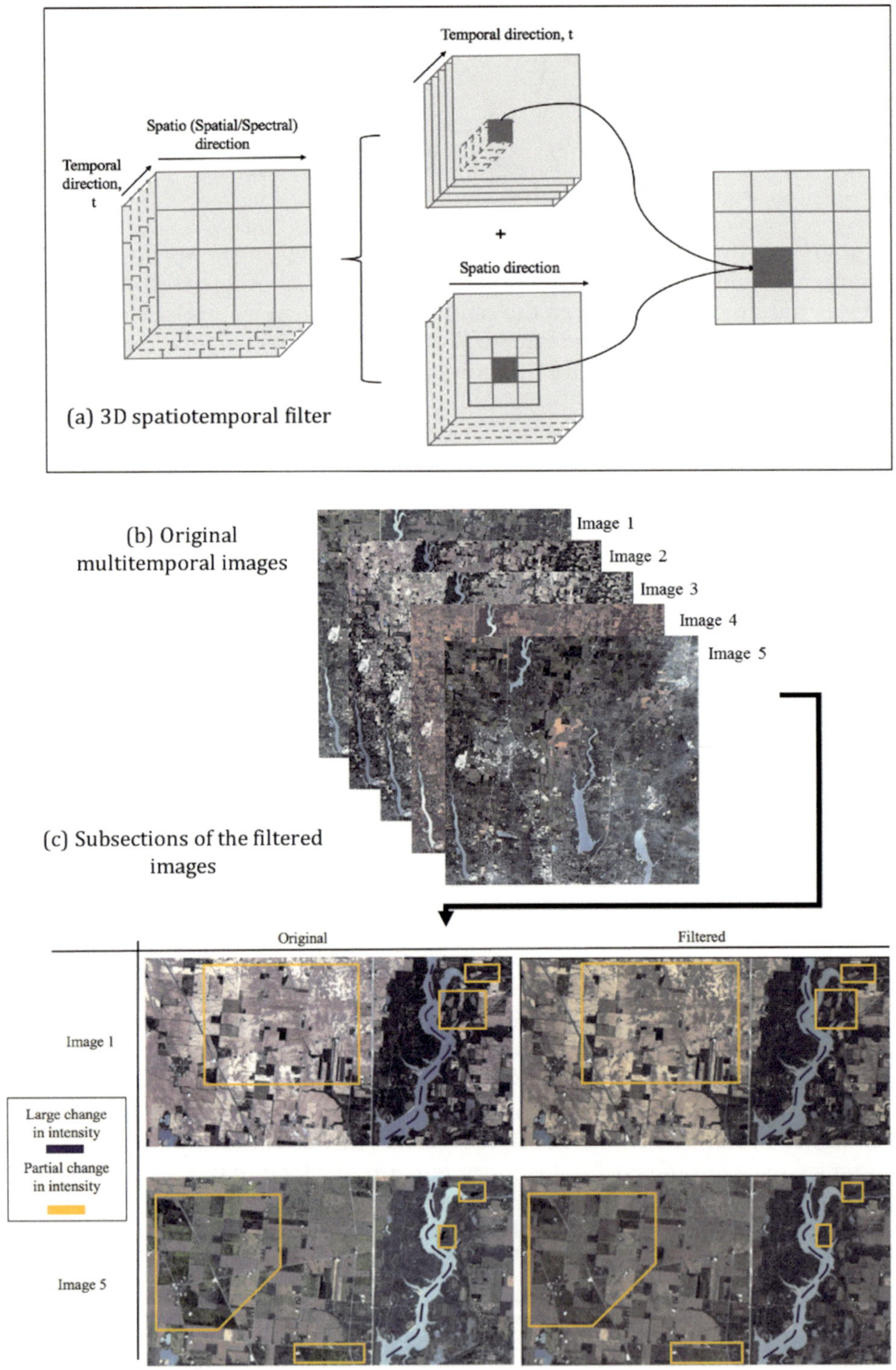

Figure 6.
Pixel-level fusion using 3D spatiotemporal bilateral filter to combine multitemporal images [19].

dataset as a reference. Therefore, it will have higher confidence to distinguish between actual objects and radiometric distortions (like clouds) in the scene when processing each pixel.

	Transfer learning classification				
Image	**1**	**2**	**3**	**4**	**5**
Exp. I Suburban					
Without filter	80.88	74.14	93.30	**93.59**	91.97
With filter	**91.99**	**91.96**	**93.95**	86.08	**94.30**
Exp. I - Urban					
Without filter	72.61	67.91	81.00	50.21	**93.75**
With filter	**89.29**	**90.60**	**91.35**	**77.82**	93.10
Exp. II					
Without filter	66.48	74.14	68.35	**67.17**	73.30
With filter	**66.75**	**76.20**	**72.06**	65.10	**78.54**

The bold numbers indicate an increase in the accuracy, and the numbers highlighted in gray indicate the reference image used for the training in the transfer learning classification.

Table 2.
The accuracy results for the 3D spatial-temporal filter [19].

4.2 Spatiotemporal fusion of multisource multitemporal images

4.2.1 Background and objective

Multitemporal and multisource satellite images often generate inconsistent classification maps. Noise and misclassifications are inevitable when classifying satellite images, and the precision and accuracy of classification maps vary based on the radiometric quality of the images. The radiometric quality is a function of the acquisition and sensor conditions as mentioned in the background in Section 1.1. The algorithm can also play a major role in the accuracy of the results; some classification algorithms are more efficient than others, while some can be sensitive to the spatial details in the images like complex dense areas and repeated patterns, which lead objects of different classes to have similar spectral reflectance. The acquisition time, type of algorithm, and distribution of objects in the scene are huge factors that can degrade the quality and generate inconsistent classification maps across different times. To address these issues, the authors in [41] proposed a 3D iterative spatiotemporal filtering to enhance the classification maps of multitemporal very high-resolution satellite images. Since the 3D geometric information is more stable and is invariant to spectral changes across temporal images, [41] proposed combining the 3D geometric information in the DSM with multitemporal classification maps to provide spectrally invariant algorithm.

4.2.2 Theory

The 3D iterative spatiotemporal filter is a fusion method that combines information from various types, sources, and times. The algorithm is a combination of feature and decision levels of fusion; it is described in detail in Algorithm 1. The first step is to generate initial probability maps for all images using random forest classification. The inference model is then built to recursively process every pixel in the probability maps using a normalized weighing function that computes the total weight $W_{3D}\left(x_j, y_j, t_n\right)$ based on the spatial ($W_{spatial}$), spectral ($W_{spectral}$), and temporal ($W_{temproral}$) similarities. The temporal weight is based on the elevation values in the DSMs. The probability value for every pixel is computed and updated using $W_{3D}\left(x_j, y_j, t_n\right)$ and the previous iteration until it satisfies the convergence condition, which requires the difference between the current and previous iterations to be under a certain limit.

Algorithm 1: Pseudo code of the proposed 3D iterative spatiotemporal filter [41]

Input: Initial probability maps P_c^0 (x_i, y_i, t_n), ortho photos I, and the band widths: σ_s and σ_r
Output: Final probability maps P_c^f (x_i, y_i, t_n)

For *every category/class c* ***do***

  While *not converge* ***do***

    For *every pixel (x,y) in the window w* ***do***

$$W_{spatial} \rightarrow \exp\left(\frac{\|x_i - x_j\|^2 + \|y_i - y_j\|^2}{2\sigma_s^2}\right)$$

$$W_{spectral} \rightarrow \exp\left(\frac{\|I(x_i, y_i) - I(x_j, y_j)\|^2}{2\sigma_r^2}\right)$$

Compute σ_h *for class c*

$$W_{nDSM} \rightarrow \exp\left(\frac{\|nDSM(x_i, y_i, t_m) - nDSM(x_j, y_j, t_n)\|^2}{2\sigma_h^2}\right)$$

$$W3D = W_{Spatial} * W_{Spectral} * W_{nDSM}$$

Update *the probability distribution map*

$$P_c^k(x_i, y_i, t_n) = \frac{1}{N * T} \sum \sum_{j \in N, n \in T} W_{3D}\left(x_j, y_j, t_n\right) * P_c^{k-1}\left(x_j, y_j, tn\right)$$

    End For

    Check *convergence*

$$\frac{P_c^k(x_i, y_i, t_n) - P_c^{k-1}(x_i, y_i, t_n)}{P_c^k(x_i, y_i, t_n)} * 100\% \rightarrow \begin{cases} \leq 5\% & Stop \\ > 5\% & Continue \end{cases}$$

  End While

End For

Compute *overall accuracy*

4.2.3 Experimental results and analysis

The proposed filter was applied to three datasets that include an open area, residential area, and school area. The input data include multisource and multitemporal very high-resolution images and DSMs; the probability maps were created for six types of classes: buildings, long-term or temporary lodges, trees, grass, ground, and roads (see **Figure 7(a)** for more details about the input data). **Figure 7 (b)** shows a sample of the filtering results. We can see that the initial classification of the building (circled with an ellipse) is mostly incorrectly classified to long-term lodge; however, it keeps improving as the filtering proceeds through the iterations.

The overall accuracy was reported, and it indicates that the overall enhancement in the accuracy is about ~2–6% (see **Table 3**). We can also notice that dense areas such as the residential area have the lowest accuracy range (around 85%), while the rest of the study areas had accuracy improvement in the 90% range. It indicates that the filtering algorithm is dependent on the degree of density and complexity in the

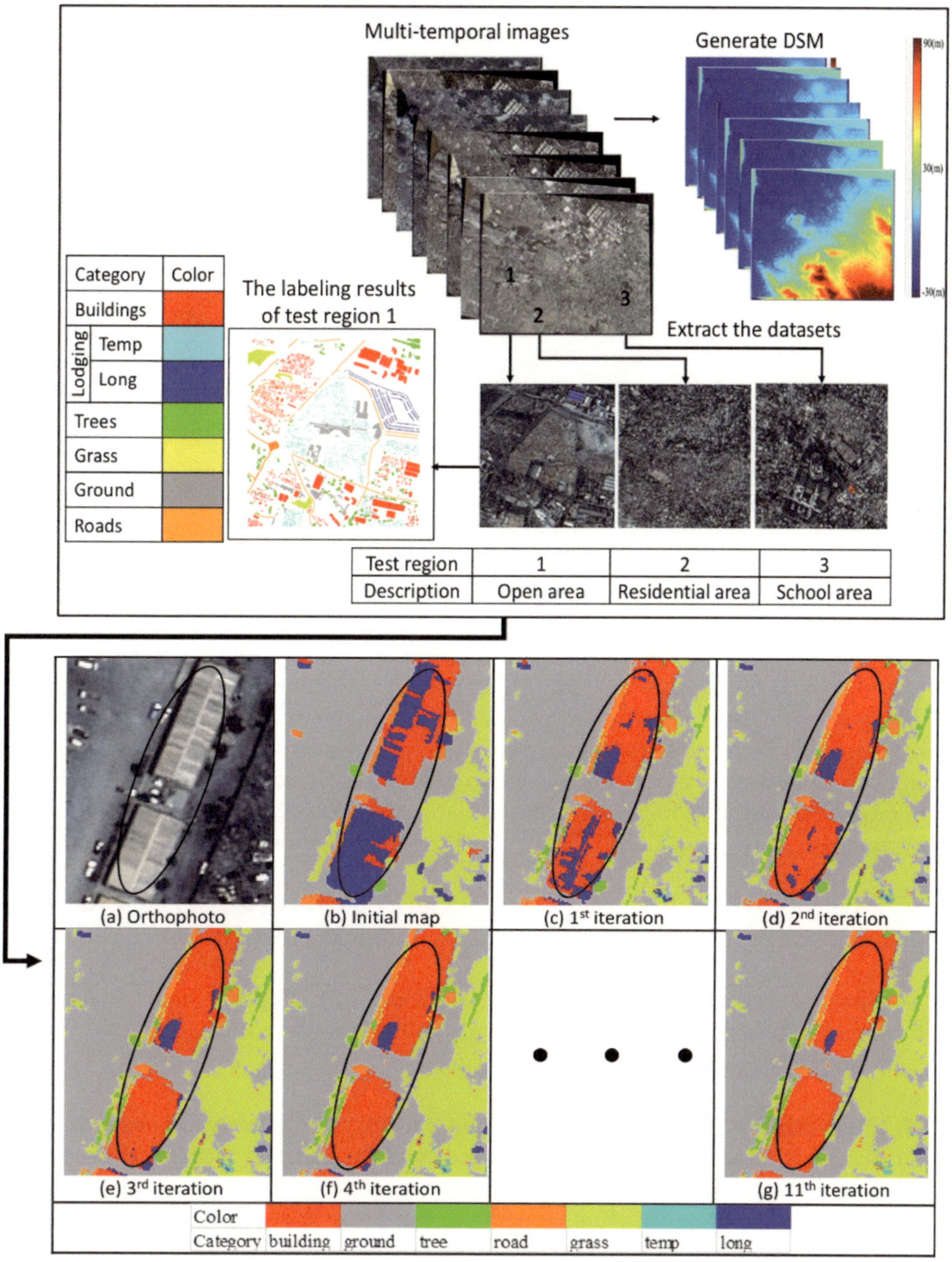

Figure 7.
3D iterative spatiotemporal filtering for classification enhancement [41].

scene, where objects are hard to distinguish in condensed areas due to mixed pixel and spectral similarity of different objects.

4.3 Spatiotemporal fusion of 3D depth maps

4.3.1 Background and objective

Obtaining high-quality depth images (also known as depth maps) is essential for remote sensing applications that process 3D geometric information like 3D

Date	Test region 1			Test region 2			Test region 3		
	Before (%)	**After (%)**	**Δ (%)**	**Before (%)**	**After (%)**	**Δ (%)**	**Before (%)**	**After (%)**	**Δ (%)**
2007	91.04%	95.21	+4.17	83.47	88.14	+4.67	91.12	95.85	+4.73
2010/1	93.21	96.45	+3.24	81.50	85.67	+4.17	93.06	96.82	+3.76
2010/6	91.93	96.26	+4.33	83.52	89.79	**+6.27**	88.82	94.87	**+6.05**
2010/12	89.08	95.57	**+6.49**	80.81	87.59	**+6.78**	88.58	94.86	**+6.28**
2012/3	92.19	95.92	+3.73	81.43	86.92	+5.49	91.44	97.08	+5.64
2013/9	90.40	96.56	**+6.16**	81.03	87.29	**+6.26**	94.99	97.54	+2.55
2014/7	95.11	97.27	+2.16	82.19	88.90	+6.17	90.39	96.58	+6.19
2015	92.74	96.35	+3.61	83.22	85.69	+2.47	94.61	97.19	+2.58
Average	92.09	96.20	4.24	82.15	87.50	5.29	91.63	96.35	4.72

Table 3.
The overall accuracy for classification results using the method in [41].

reconstruction. MVS algorithms are widely used approaches to obtain depth images (see Section 2.1.2.); however, depth maps generated using MVS often contain noise, outliers, and incomplete representation of depth like having missing data, holes, or fuzzy edges and boundaries. A common approach to recover the depth map is by fusing several depth maps through probabilistic or deterministic methods. However, most fusion techniques in image processing focus on the fusion of depth images from Kinect or video scenes, which cannot be directly applied on depth generated from satellite images due to the nature of images. The difference between depth generated from satellite sensors and Kinect or video cameras include:

1. Images captured indoor using Kinect or video cameras have less noise, since they are not exposed to external environmental influences like atmospheric effects.

2. Kinect or video cameras generate a large volume of images, which can improve dense matching, while the number of satellite images is limited due to the temporal resolution of the satellite sensor.

3. The depth from satellite images is highly sensitive to the constant changes in the environment and the spatial characteristics of the earth surface like the repeated patterns, complexity, sparsity, and density of objects in the scene, which can obstruct or create mismatching errors in the dense image matching process.

Most depth fusion algorithms for geospatial data focus on median filtering (see Section 4.3.), but it still needs some improvement in terms of robustness and adaptivity to the scene content. To address the aforementioned problems, [90] proposed an adaptive and semantic-guided spatiotemporal filtering algorithm to generate a single depth map with high precision. The adaptivity is implemented to address the issue of varied uncertainty for objects of different classes.

4.3.2 Theory

The adaptive and semantic-guided spatiotemporal filter is a pixel-based fusion method, where the depth of the fused pixel is inferred using multitemporal depths and a prior knowledge about the pixel class and uncertainty. A reference orthophoto is classified using a rule-based classification approach that uses normalized DSM (nDSM) with indices such as normalized difference vegetation index (NDVI). The uncertainty is then measured for all four classes (trees, grass, buildings, and ground and roads) using the standard deviation. The uncertainty is measured spatially using the classification map and also across the temporal images. The adaptive and semantic-guided spatiotemporal filter is intended to enhance the median filter, thus it uses height $h(i,j,t)_{med}$ as the base to the fused pixel, where the general form of the filter is expressed as

$$DSM_f(i,j) = \frac{1}{W_T} * \sum_{i=1}^{Width} \sum_{j=1}^{Height} W_r * W_s * W_h * h(i,j,t)_{med} \tag{7}$$

where DSM_f is the fused pixel; i, j are the pixel's coordinates; h_{med} is the median height value from the temporal DSMs; and the spectral, spatial, and temporal height weights are expressed as W_r, W_s, and W_h respectively. The W_r and W_s are described in Eqs. (4) and (5) that measure the spectral and spatial components from the orthophoto. The W_h is a measure of similarity for the height data across temporal images, and it can be computed using the following formula:

$$W_h(i,j) = exp^{\frac{-||hmed - h(i,j,t)||^2}{2\,\sigma_h^2}} \tag{8}$$

where $\sigma_h$is the adaptive height bandwidth, which varies based on the class of pixel as follows:

$$\sigma_h = \begin{cases} \sigma_{Building} \rightarrow if\ pixel\ (i,j)\ is\ building \\ \sigma_{Ground/road} \rightarrow if\ pixel\ (i,j)\ is\ ground/road \\ \sigma_{tree} \rightarrow if\ pixel\ (i,j)\ is\ tree \\ \sigma_{grass} \rightarrow if\ pixel\ (i,j)\ is\ grass \\ \sigma_{water} \rightarrow if\ pixel\ (i,j)\ is\ water \end{cases} \tag{9}$$

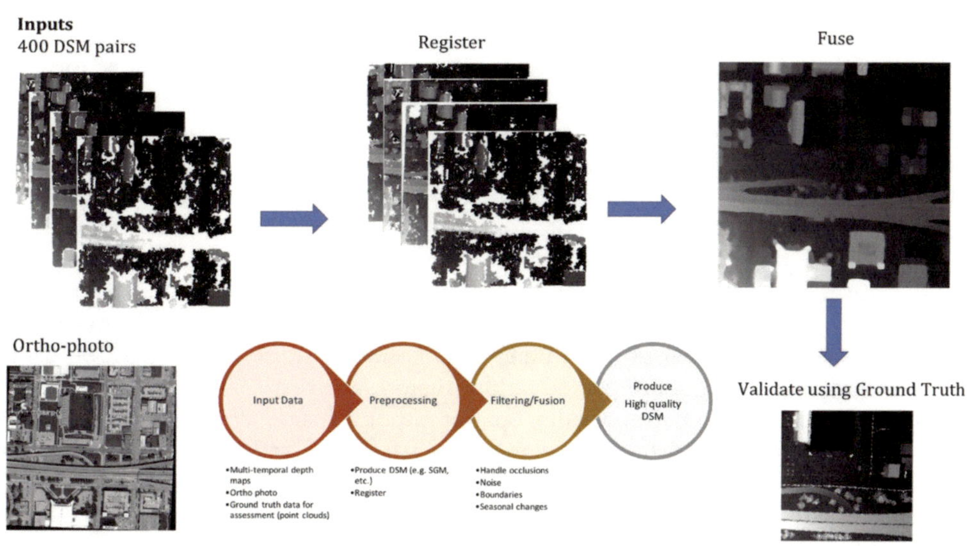

Figure 8.
Process description of adaptive and semantic-guided spatiotemporal filtering [93].

4.3.3 Experimental results and analysis

The method in [90] was experimented on three datasets with varying complexities. The satellite images are taken from the World-View III sensor, and depth is generated using MVS algorithm on every image pair using RSP (RPC Stereo Processor) software developed by [95] and semi-global matching (SGM) algorithm [42]. **Figure 8** describes the procedures followed by the fusion algorithm, in addition to the visual results where it shows that noise and missing elevation points were recovered in the fused image. The validation of three experiments shows that this fusion technique can achieve up to 2% increase in the overall accuracy of the depth map.

5. Conclusions

Spatiotemporal fusion is one of the powerful techniques to enhance the quality of remote sensing data, hence, the performance of its applications. Recently, it has been drawing great attention in many fields, due to its capability to analyze and relate the space-interaction on ground, which can lead to promising results in terms of stability, precision, and accuracy. The redundant temporal information is useful to develop a time-invariant fusion algorithm that leads to the same inference from the multitemporal geospatial data regardless of the noise and changes that occur occasionally due to natural (e.g., metrology, ecology, and phenology) or instrumental (e.g., sensor conditions) causes. Therefore, incorporating spatiotemporal analysis in any of the three levels of fusion can boost their performance, where it can be flexible to handle data from multiple sources, types, and times. Despite the effectiveness of spatiotemporal fusion, there are still some issues that may affect the precision and accuracy of the final output. These considerations must be taken into account while designing the spatiotemporal fusion algorithm. For example, spatiotemporal analysis for per-pixel operations is highly sensitive to mixed pixels especially for coarse-resolution images where one pixel may contain the spectral information of more than one object. The accuracy of the spatiotemporal fusion can also be sensitive to the complexity of the scene, where in densely congested areas such as cities the accuracy may be less than open areas or sub-urban areas (as mentioned in the examples in Section 4.). This is due to the increase in the heterogeneity of the images in these dense areas. This issue can be solved using adaptive spatiotemporal fusion algorithms, which is a not widely investigated area of study in current practices. Feature and decision levels of fusion can partially solve this problem by learning from patches of features or classified images, but their accuracy will also be under the influence of the feature extraction algorithm or the algorithm to derive the initial output. For instance, mismatching features can result in fusing unrelated features or data points, thus produce inaccurate coefficients for the feature-level fusion model. Another observation is the lack of studies that relates the number of temporal images and the fusion output accuracy, which is useful to decide the optimal number of input images for fusion. Additionally, it is rarely seen that the integrated images are picked before fusion, where assessing and choosing good images can lead to better results. Spatiotemporal fusion algorithms are either local or global approaches, the local algorithms are simple and forward like pixel-level fusion or local filtering like the methods in [19, 22], while global methods tend to perform extensive operations for optimization purposes like in [25]. In future works, we aim to explore how these explicitly modeled spatiotemporal fusion algorithms can be enhanced by the power of more complex and inherent models such as deep learning-based models to drive more important remote sensing applications.

Acknowledgments

The authors would like to express their gratitude to Planet Co. for providing them with the data; to sustainable institute at the Ohio state university, Office of Naval Research (Award No. N000141712928) for partial support of the research; and to the Johns Hopkins University Applied Physics Laboratory and IARPA and the IEEE GRSS Image Analysis and Data Fusion Technical Committee for making the benchmark satellite images available.

Author details

Hessah Albanwan[1] and Rongjun Qin[1,2]*

1 Department of Civil, Environmental and Geodetic Engineering, The Ohio State University, Columbus, Ohio, USA

2 Department of Electrical and Computer Engineering, The Ohio State University, USA

*Address all correspondence to: qin.324@osu.edu

References

[1] Li SZ, Jain AK. Encyclopedia of Biometrics. 1st ed. Boston, MA: Springer US; 2015. DOI: 10.1007/978-1-4899-7488-4 [Accessed: 31 March 2020]

[2] Mitchell HB. Image Fusion. Berlin, Heidelberg: Springer Berlin Heidelberg. Epub ahead of print; 2010. DOI: 10.1007/978-3-642-11216-4

[3] Pohl C, Genderen JLV. Review article multisensor image fusion in remote sensing: Concepts, methods and applications. International Journal of Remote Sensing. 1998;**19**:823-854

[4] Dian R, Li S, Fang L, et al. Multispectral and hyperspectral image fusion with spatial-spectral sparse representation. Information Fusion. 2019;**49**:262-270

[5] Fauvel M, Tarabalka Y, Benediktsson JA, et al. Advances in spectral-spatial classification of Hyperspectral images. Proceedings of the IEEE. 2013;**101**:652-675

[6] Wang L, Zhang J, Liu P, et al. Spectral-spatial multi-feature-based deep learning for hyperspectral remote sensing image classification. Soft Computing. 2017;**21**:213-221

[7] Kang X, Li S, Benediktsson JA. Spectral-spatial Hyperspectral image classification with edge-preserving filtering. IEEE Transactions on Geoscience and Remote Sensing. 2014; **52**:2666-2677

[8] Chen B, Huang B, Xu B. A hierarchical spatiotemporal adaptive fusion model using one image pair. The International Journal of Digital Earth. 2017;**10**:639-655

[9] Chen B, Huang B, Bing X. Comparison of spatiotemporal fusion models: A review. Remote Sensing. 2015;7:1798-1835

[10] Song H, Huang B. Spatiotemporal satellite image fusion through one-pair image learning. IEEE Transactions on Geoscience and Remote Sensing. 2013; **51**:1883-1896

[11] Ehlers M, Klonus S, Johan Åstrand P, et al. Multi-sensor image fusion for pansharpening in remote sensing. International Journal of Image and Data Fusion. 2010;**1**:25-45

[12] Shen H, Ng MK, Li P, et al. Super-resolution reconstruction algorithm to MODIS remote sensing images. The Computer Journal. 2008;**52**:90-100

[13] Nguyen H, Cressie N, Braverman A. Spatial statistical data fusion for remote sensing applications. Journal of the American Statistical Association. 2012; **107**:1004-1018

[14] Bertalmio M, Sapiro G, Caselles V, et al. Image inpainting. In: Proceedings of the 27th annual conference on Computer graphics and interactive techniques - SIGGRAPH '00. ACM Press; 2000. pp. 417-424

[15] Kasetkasem T, Arora M, Varshney P. Super-resolution land cover mapping using a Markov random field based approach. Remote Sensing of Environment. 2005;**96**:302-314

[16] Pathak D, Krahenbuhl P, Donahue J, et al. Context Encoders: Feature Learning by Inpainting. In: 2016 IEEE Conference on Computer Vision and Pattern Recognition (CVPR). NV, USA: Las Vegas; 2016, pp. 2536-2544

[17] Eismann MT, Hardie RC. Application of the stochastic mixing model to hyperspectral resolution enhancement. IEEE Transactions on Geoscience and Remote Sensing. 2004;**42**:1924-1933

[18] Wei Q, Dobigeon N, Tourneret J-Y. Bayesian fusion of hyperspectral and

multispectral images. In: IEEE International Conference on Acoustics, Speech and Signal Processing (ICASSP). Florence, Italy: IEEE; 2014. pp. 3176-3180

[19] Albanwan H, Qin R. A novel spectrum enhancement technique for multi-temporal, multi-spectral data using spatial-temporal filtering. ISPRS Journal of Photogrammetry and Remote Sensing. 2018;**142**:51-63

[20] Zhu X, Chen J, Gao F, et al. An enhanced spatial and temporal adaptive reflectance fusion model for complex heterogeneous regions. Remote Sensing of Environment. 2010;**114**:2610-2623

[21] Gómez C, White JC, Wulder MA. Optical remotely sensed time series data for land cover classification: A review. ISPRS Journal of Photogrammetry and Remote Sensing. 2016;**116**:55-72

[22] Gao F, Masek J, Schwaller M, et al. On the blending of the Landsat and MODIS surface reflectance: Predicting daily Landsat surface reflectance. IEEE Transactions on Geoscience and Remote Sensing. 2006;**44**:2207-2218

[23] Gevaert CM, García-Haro FJ. A comparison of STARFM and an unmixing-based algorithm for Landsat and MODIS data fusion. Remote Sensing of Environment. 2015;**156**:34-44

[24] Jia K, Liang S, Zhang N, et al. Land cover classification of finer resolution remote sensing data integrating temporal features from time series coarser resolution data. ISPRS Journal of Photogrammetry and Remote Sensing. 2014;**93**:49-55

[25] Tang Q, Bo Y, Zhu Y. Spatiotemporal fusion of multiple-satellite aerosol optical depth (AOD) products using Bayesian maximum entropy method: merging satellite AOD products using BME. Journal of Geophysical Research-Atmospheres. 2016;**121**:4034-4048

[26] Melgani F, Serpico SB. A markov random field approach to spatio-temporal contextual image classification. IEEE Transactions on Geoscience and Remote Sensing. 2003; **41**:2478-2487

[27] Reiche J, Souzax CM, Hoekman DH, et al. Feature level fusion of multi-temporal ALOS PALSAR and Landsat data for mapping and monitoring of tropical deforestation and Forest degradation. The IEEE Journal of Selected Topics in Applied Earth Observations and Remote Sensing. 2013; **6**:2159-2173

[28] Ross A. Fusion, feature-level. In: Li SZ, Jain AK, editors. Encyclopedia of Biometrics. Boston, MA: Springer US; 2015. pp. 751-757

[29] Sasikala M, Kumaravel N. A comparative analysis of feature based image fusion methods. Information Technology Journal. 2007;**6**:1224-1230

[30] Huang B, Song H. Spatiotemporal reflectance fusion via sparse representation. IEEE Transactions on Geoscience and Remote Sensing. 2012; **50**:3707-3716

[31] Wu B, Huang B, Zhang L. An error-bound-regularized sparse coding for spatiotemporal reflectance fusion. IEEE Transactions on Geoscience and Remote Sensing. 2015;**53**:6791-6803

[32] Palsson F, Sveinsson JR, Ulfarsson MO. Multispectral and Hyperspectral image fusion using a 3-D-convolutional neural network. IEEE Geoscience and Remote Sensing Letters. 2017;**14**:639-643

[33] Masi G, Cozzolino D, Verdoliva L, et al. Pansharpening by convolutional neural networks. Remote Sensing. 2016; **8**:594

[34] Shao Z, Cai J. Remote sensing image fusion with deep convolutional neural network. The IEEE Journal of Selected Topics in Applied Earth Observations and Remote Sensing. 2018;**11**:1656-1669

[35] Song H, Liu Q, Wang G, et al. Spatiotemporal satellite image fusion using deep convolutional neural networks. The IEEE Journal of Selected Topics in Applied Earth Observations and Remote Sensing. 2018;**11**:821-829

[36] Tuia D, Flamary R, Courty N. Multiclass feature learning for hyperspectral image classification: Sparse and hierarchical solutions. ISPRS Journal of Photogrammetry and Remote Sensing. 2015;**105**:272-285

[37] Zhong J, Yang B, Huang G, et al. Remote sensing image fusion with convolutional neural network. Sensing and Imaging. 2016;**17**:10

[38] Zhu XX, Tuia D, Mou L, et al. Deep learning in remote sensing: A comprehensive review and list of resources. IEEE Geoscience and Remote Sensing Magazine. 2017;**5**:8-36

[39] Osadciw L, Veeramachaneni K. Fusion, decision-level. In: Li SZ, Jain AK, editors. Encyclopedia of Biometrics. Boston, MA: Springer US; 2015. pp. 747-751

[40] Qin R, Tian J, Reinartz P. Spatiotemporal inferences for use in building detection using series of very-high-resolution space-borne stereo images. International Journal of Remote Sensing. 2016;**37**:3455-3476

[41] Albanwan H, Qin R, Lu X, et al. 3D iterative spatiotemporal filtering for classification of multitemporal satellite data sets. Photogrammetric Engineering and Remote Sensing. 2020;**86**:23-31

[42] Hirschmuller H. Accurate and efficient stereo processing by semi-global matching and mutual information. In: IEEE Computer Society Conference on Computer Vision and Pattern Recognition (CVPR'05). San Diego, CA, USA: IEEE; 2005. pp. 807-814

[43] Jensen JR. Remote Sensing of the Environment: An Earth Resource Perspective. 2nd ed. Pearson Prentice Hall: Upper Saddle River, NJ; 2007

[44] Mikolajczyk K, Schmid C. A performance evaluation of local descriptors. IEEE Transactions on Pattern Analysis and Machine Intelligence. 2005;**27**:1615-1630

[45] Mikhail EM, Bethel JS, McGlone JC. Introduction to Modern Photogrammetry. New York: Chichester: Wiley; 2001

[46] Habib AF, Morgan MF, Jeong S, et al. Epipolar geometry of line cameras moving with constant velocity and attitude. ETRI Journal. 2005;**27**:172-180

[47] Facciolo G, De Franchis C, Meinhardt-Llopis E. Automatic 3D reconstruction from multi-date satellite images. In: IEEE Conference on Computer Vision and Pattern Recognition Workshops (CVPRW). Honolulu, HI: IEEE; 2017. pp. 1542-1551

[48] Qin R. A critical analysis of satellite stereo pairs for digital surface model generation and a matching quality prediction model. ISPRS Journal of Photogrammetry and Remote Sensing. 2019;**154**:139-150

[49] Congalton RG. A review of assessing the accuracy of classifications of remotely sensed data. Remote Sensing of Environment. 1991;**37**:35-46

[50] Foody GM, Mathur A. A relative evaluation of multiclass image classification by support vector machines. IEEE Transactions on Geoscience and Remote Sensing. 2004; **42**:1335-1343

[51] Xiong Y, Zhang Z, Chen F. Comparison of artificial neural network and support vector machine methods for urban land use/cover classifications from remote sensing images a case study of Guangzhou, South China. In: 2010 International Conference on Computer Application and System Modeling (ICCASM 2010). 2010. pp. V13-52-V13-56

[52] Brown LG. A survey of image registration techniques. ACM Computing Surveys. 1992;**24**:325-376

[53] Goshtasby A. 2-D and 3-D Image Registration for Medical, Remote Sensing, and Industrial Applications. Hoboken, NJ: J. Wiley & Sons; 2005

[54] Yu Y, Liu F. Dense connectivity based two-stream deep feature fusion framework for aerial scene classification. Remote Sensing. 2018;**10**: 1158

[55] Boureau Y-L, Bach F, LeCun Y, et al. Learning mid-level features for recognition. In: IEEE Computer Society Conference on Computer Vision and Pattern Recognition. San Francisco, CA, USA: IEEE; 2010. pp. 2559-2566

[56] Dalal N, Triggs B. Histograms of oriented gradients for human detection. In: IEEE Computer Society Conference on Computer Vision and Pattern Recognition (CVPR'05). San Diego, CA, USA: IEEE; 2005. pp. 886-893

[57] Harris C, Stephens M. A combined corner and edge detector. In: Procedings of the Alvey Vision Conference 1988. Manchester: Alvey Vision Club; 1988. pp. 23.1-23.6

[58] Lowe DG. Distinctive image features from scale-invariant Keypoints. International Journal of Computer Vision. 2004;**60**:91-110

[59] Lazebnik S, Schmid C, Ponce J. Beyond bags of features: Spatial pyramid matching for recognizing natural scene categories. In: IEEE Computer Society Conference on Computer Vision and Pattern Recognition - Volume 2 (CVPR'06). New York, NY, USA: IEEE; 2006. pp. 2169-2178

[60] Ranzato M Aurelio, Boureau Y-Lan, Cun YL. Sparse feature learning for deep belief networks. In: Platt JC, Koller D, Singer Y, et al, editors. Advances in Neural Information Processing Systems 20. Curran Associates, Inc.; 2008. pp. 1185-1192

[61] Yang Y, Newsam S. Bag-of-visual-words and spatial extensions for land-use classification. In: Proceedings of the 18th SIGSPATIAL International Conference on Advances in Geographic Information Systems - GIS '10. San Jose, California: ACM Press; 2010. p. 270

[62] Yuan D, Elvidge CD. Comparison of relative radiometric normalization techniques. ISPRS Journal of Photogrammetry and Remote Sensing. 1996;**51**:117-126

[63] Young NE, Anderson RS, Chignell SM, et al. A survival guide to Landsat preprocessing. Ecology. 2017; **98**:920-932

[64] Elvidge CD, Yuan D, Weerackoon RD, et al. Relative radiometric normalization of Landsat multispectral scanner (MSS) data using a automatic scattergram-controlled regression. Photogrammetric Engineering and Remote Sensing. 1995;**61**:1255-1260

[65] Moran MS, Jackson RD, Slater PN, et al. Evaluation of simplified procedures for retrieval of land surface reflectance factors from satellite sensor output. Remote Sensing of Environment. 1992;**41**:169-184

[66] VERMOTE E, KAUFMAN YJ. Absolute calibration of AVHRR visible and near-infrared channels using ocean

and cloud views. International Journal of Remote Sensing. 1995;**16**:2317-2340

[67] Slater PN, Biggar SF, Holm RG, et al. Reflectance- and radiance-based methods for the in-flight absolute calibration of multispectral sensors. Remote Sensing of Environment. 1987;**22**:11-37

[68] Paolini L, Grings F, Sobrino JA, et al. Radiometric correction effects in Landsat multi-date/multi-sensor change detection studies. International Journal of Remote Sensing. 2006;**27**:685-704

[69] Hilker T, Wulder MA, Coops NC, et al. A new data fusion model for high spatial- and temporal-resolution mapping of forest disturbance based on Landsat and MODIS. Remote Sensing of Environment. 2009;**113**:1613-1627

[70] Crist EP, Cicone RC. A physically-based transformation of thematic mapper data—the TM Tasseled cap. IEEE Transactions on Geoscience and Remote Sensing. 1984;**GE-22**:256-263

[71] Knauer K, Gessner U, Fensholt R, et al. An ESTARFM fusion framework for the generation of large-scale time series in cloud-prone and heterogeneous landscapes. Remote Sensing. 2016;**8**:425

[72] Ball GH, Hall DJ. Isodata, a Novel Method of Data Analysis and Pattern Classification. Menlo Park, Calif: Stanford Research Institute; 1965

[73] Huang B, Wang J, Song H, et al. Generating high spatiotemporal resolution land surface temperature for urban Heat Island monitoring. IEEE Geoscience and Remote Sensing Letters. 2013;**10**:1011-1015

[74] Kwan C, Zhu X, Gao F, et al. Assessment of spatiotemporal fusion algorithms for planet and worldview images. Sensors. 2018;**18**:1051

[75] Ma J, Zhang W, Marinoni A, et al. An improved spatial and temporal reflectance Unmixing model to synthesize time series of Landsat-like images. Remote Sensing. 2018;**10**:1388

[76] Kwan C, Budavari B, Gao F, et al. A hybrid color mapping approach to fusing MODIS and Landsat images for forward prediction. Remote Sensing. 2018;**10**:520

[77] Chen S, Wang W, Liang H. Evaluating the effectiveness of fusing remote sensing images with significantly different spatial resolutions for thematic map production. Physics and Chemistry of the Earth, Parts A/B/C. 2019;**110**:71-80

[78] Chavez PSJ, Sides SC, Anderson JA. Comparison of three different methods to merge multiresolution and multispectral data: LANDSAT TM and SPOT panchromatic. AAPG Bulletin (American Association of Petroleum Geologists) (USA). 1990;**74**(6):265-303. Available from: https://www.osti.gov/biblio/6165108 [Accessed: 23 April 2020]

[79] Zhang Q, Liu Y, Blum RS, et al. Sparse representation based multi-sensor image fusion for multi-focus and multi-modality images: A review. Information Fusion. 2018;**40**:57-75

[80] Zhang Q, Ma Z, Wang L. Multimodality image fusion by using both phase and magnitude information. Pattern Recognition Letters. 2013;**34**: 185-193

[81] Liu Y, Jin J, Wang Q, et al. Region level based multi-focus image fusion using quaternion wavelet and normalized cut. Signal Processing. 2014;**97**:9-30

[82] Mallat SG. A theory for multiresolution signal decomposition: The wavelet representation. IEEE Transactions on Pattern Analysis and Machine Intelligence. 1989;**11**:674-693

[83] Li S, Yin H, Fang L. Remote sensing image fusion via sparse representations

over learned dictionaries. IEEE Transactions on Geoscience and Remote Sensing. 2013;**51**:4779-4789

[84] Wei Q, Bioucas-Dias J, Dobigeon N, et al. Hyperspectral and multispectral image fusion based on a sparse representation. IEEE Transactions on Geoscience and Remote Sensing. 2015; **53**:3658-3668

[85] Lagrange A, Le Saux B, Beaupere A, et al. Benchmarking classification of earth-observation data: From learning explicit features to convolutional networks. In: IEEE International Geoscience and Remote Sensing Symposium (IGARSS). Milan, Italy: IEEE; 2015. pp. 4173-4176

[86] Zhang P, Gong M, Su L, et al. Change detection based on deep feature representation and mapping transformation for multi-spatial-resolution remote sensing images. ISPRS Journal of Photogrammetry and Remote Sensing. 2016;**116**:24-41

[87] Gong M, Zhan T, Zhang P, et al. Superpixel-based difference representation learning for change detection in multispectral remote sensing images. IEEE Transactions on Geoscience and Remote Sensing. 2017; **55**:2658-2673

[88] Heideklang R, Shokouhi P. Decision-level fusion of spatially scattered multi-modal data for nondestructive inspection of surface defects. Sensors. 2016;**16**:105

[89] Du P, Liu S, Xia J, et al. Information fusion techniques for change detection from multi-temporal remote sensing images. Information Fusion. 2013;**14**: 19-27

[90] Nunez J, Otazu X, Fors O, et al. Multiresolution-based image fusion with additive wavelet decomposition. IEEE Transactions on Geoscience and Remote Sensing. 1999;**37**:1204-1211

[91] Kuschk G. Large Scale Urban Reconstruction from Remote Sensing Imager. 2013. Available form: https://www.semanticscholar.org/paper/LARGE-SCALE-URBAN-RECONSTRUCTION-FROM-REMOTE-Kuschk/91cd21f39b27088e6a9ba8443558281074356f16 [Accessed: 27 April 2020]

[92] Qin R, Fang W. A hierarchical building detection method for very high resolution remotely sensed images combined with DSM using graph cut optimization. Photogrammetric Engineering and Remote Sensing. 2014; **80**:873-883

[93] Albanwan H, Qin R. Enhancement of depth map by fusion using adaptive and semantic-guided spatiotemporal filtering. In: Annals. Photogramm. Remote Sens. Spatial Inf. Sci. 2020. ISPRS Congress (2020/2021). Nice, Fr: ISPRS; 2020

[94] Jing L, Wang T, Zhao M, et al. An adaptive multi-sensor data fusion method based on deep convolutional neural networks for fault diagnosis of planetary gearbox. Sensors. 2017;**17**:414. DOI: 10.3390/s17020414

[95] Paisitkriangkrai S, Sherrah J, Janney P, et al. Semantic Labeling of aerial and satellite imagery. IEEE Journal of Selected Topics in Applied Earth Observations and Remote Sensing. 2016;**9**:2868-2881

[96] Audebert N, Le Saux B, Lefèvre S. Semantic segmentation of earth observation data using multimodal and multi-scale deep networks. In: Lai S-H, Lepetit V, Nishino K, et al, editors. Computer Vision – ACCV 2016. Cham: Springer International Publishing; 2016. pp. 180–196

[97] Tomasi C, Manduchi R. Bilateral filtering for gray and color images. In: Sixth International Conference on Computer Vision (IEEE Cat. No.98CH36271). 1998. pp. 839-846

Chapter 7

3D Reconstruction through Fusion of Cross-View Images

Rongjun Qin, Shuang Song, Xiao Ling and Mostafa Elhashash

Abstract

3D recovery from multi-stereo and stereo images, as an important application of the image-based perspective geometry, serves many applications in computer vision, remote sensing, and Geomatics. In this chapter, the authors utilize the imaging geometry and present approaches that perform 3D reconstruction from cross-view images that are drastically different in their viewpoints. We introduce our project work that takes ground-view images and satellite images for full 3D recovery, which includes necessary methods in satellite and ground-based point cloud generation from images, 3D data co-registration, fusion, and mesh generation. We demonstrate our proposed framework on a dataset consisting of twelve satellite images and 150 k video frames acquired through a vehicle-mounted Go-pro camera and demonstrate the reconstruction results. We have also compared our results with results generated from an intuitive processing pipeline that involves typical geo-registration and meshing methods.

Keywords: cross-view 3D fusion, photogrammetry, remote sensing, mesh reconstruction, 3D modeling

1. Introduction

3D data generation often requires expensive data collection such as aerial photogrammetric or LiDAR flight [1, 2]. Depending on the required accuracy, resolution and other specs of the final products, the efforts in data collection and processing can exponentially grow. Alternative and low-cost data sources are of particular interest for wide-area 3D modeling [3]. Satellite sensors running 24/7 offer overview images covering large regions with single scans, which comparatively come with lower cost than aerial flights and do not require physical access to the area of interest [4]. On the other hand, there exist many ground-view images coming either from crowdsourcing platforms or collected using relatively low-cost equipment (e.g., video frames from low-cost cameras) that provides high-resolution information of objects. Both the overview and the ground-view data are complementary to each other and their view differences being approximately 90° forms cross-view dataset, a fusion of which may yield a low-cost solution for city-scale 3D modeling. This chapter describes our ongoing work (an earlier work is described in [5]) in an attempt to address this challenging task by proposing an integrated framework to fuse the 3D results of satellite overview and ground-view video frames to generate 3D textured mesh models presenting both top and side view features.

IntechOpen

The available commercial satellite images often have 0.3–0.5 m GSD (ground sampling distance) and ground-view images can easily reach a GSD of a few millimeters. With significantly different resolution, the resulting 3D geometry may be associated with different uncertainties, which adds additional challenges for the fusion task of these two types of data, which include:

1. The quality of 3D output separately generated from satellite images and ground-view images are scene-specific and may differ in terms of completeness and accuracy. Algorithms and basic principles for addressing image-based 3D modeling are relative standard, thus the image quality and their respective characteristics play a major role in the reconstruction results, such as the photo-consistency/temporal differences/illumination among images, their geometric setup, completeness in terms of coverage, intersection angles, etc.

2. Due to the large view differences, the overview and ground-view dataset may share very limited region in common, and additionally the 3D output from the ground-view dataset may come with no geo-referencing information and may contain non-rigid topographic distortions (e.g., trajectories drift or distortions due to inaccurate interior/exterior orientation estimation), which further add challenges in 3D geo-registration of the dataset.

3. The combined 3D point clouds are from two sources with different resolution, uncertainty, and radiometric properties of textures, which present difficulties in both the geometric reconstruction of meshes and the texture mappings. Thus, obtaining visually consistent textured meshes the preserve information to the maximal extent is extremely challenging.

We introduce in our proposed method major contributions to address the above-mentioned challenges to form a complete fusion pipeline. These contributions are: (1) we introduce a monocular video-frame-based 3D reconstruction pipeline to achieve the minimal geometric distortion by leveraging the speed and accuracy in a photogrammetric reconstruction pipeline called MetricSFM. (2) We introduce a cross-view geo-registration and fusion algorithm that takes point clouds generated from satellite multi-view stereo (MVS) images and from ground-view videos, to co-register the ground-view point clouds to the overview point clouds; (3) we extend a view-based meshing approach to accommodate point clouds with images coming from different cameras. The rest of this chapter is organized as follows: Section 2 introduces related works and the overview of the proposed pipeline; Section 3 introduces our methodologies of the components of the pipeline in details, Section 4 describes the experiment dataset and the results of the 3D reconstruction; and Section 5 concludes this chapter by discussing potential works moving forward.

2. Related works and an overview of the proposed pipeline

The uses of multi-source 3D data have been attempted for different purposes, such as for localization, geo-registration, image synthesis, cartographical model generation [6–9], and planetary applications using different types of sensors [10–14]. For example, [8] utilized a combination of UAV (Unmanned Aerial Vehicles) images and mobile LiDAR (Light Detection and Ranging) for 3D model generation, where the geo-registrations are performed using manually measured ground control points (GCP) from the LiDAR data, followed by a Bundle

Adjustment [15] of the UAV images. All were performed following a surveying-grade processes, thus minimal topographical distortions needed to be addressed in critical or non-optimally collected data (e.g., monocular video collection with a single trajectory).

Correlating the satellite overview and ground view images is extremely challenging because the areas in common can sometimes be barely the ground or even less (due to vegetations and moving objects). There are two types of approaches to address relevant tasks, such as (1) cross-view images localization [9, 16, 17] and (2) cross-view image synthesis [6, 7]. Since the traditional feature-based matching methods fail in cross-view data, the major technical approaches for cross-view data instead are to learn deep representations between cross-view data, with various strategies for learning scene-level descriptors used to match cross-view data, combing learned semantics and geometric transformation. A few early works also explored the use of manually crafted features for such a task [16, 18]. Most of the existing methods exploring 3D data co-registration require a certain common regions, and the transformation is often assumed to be simple models such as similarity or rigid transformations [19, 20]. Thus, exploring methods for registering wide-area, cross-view dataset potentially with complex geometric distortions are particularly of interest and can offer tangible solutions for low-cost 3D data generation.

Meshing point clouds seems to be a standard practice with many applicable algorithms available [21]. However, for image-based point clouds, meshing requires the use of the visibility information between the view and each point [22, 23] which sometimes are not easily available for multi-source data as first of all, they may share different camera model, and second of all, standard software packages generating point clouds from images do not offer such visibility information. As a result, a standard practice of using multi-source image-based point clouds only takes point-cloud-based meshing methods [21], which are designed for very dense point clouds and do not necessarily work well for point clouds with the level of uncertainty and complexity as the image-based point clouds.

Despite these challenges, we consider the problem of turning the MVS satellite images and ground-view Go-pro data to be approachable, if scenario-specific information and intermediate results of the stereo reconstruction pipeline are available. To achieve, we have the following three considerations:

1. Monocular ground-view video frames taking alongside the street do not offer an optimal camera network, thus it is possible that the results of the 3D reconstruction contain geometric distortion, for example, trajectory drifts, or topographic distortion due to the incorrectly estimated interior/exterior orientations [24], which will further add challenges to the geo-registration, we therefore consider to optimize our photogrammetric reconstruction workflow by considering self-calibration for each incremental reconstruction to minimize the potential trajectory drift.

2. We observed that in an urban environment, the boundary of objects from the satellite point clouds, for example, buildings, might coincide well with the boundary produced by projecting the façade point clouds to the ground; therefore it can be seen as a view-invariant feature for co-registering the satellite point clouds and ground-view point clouds.

3. Meshing methods will unlikely to work well on the combined point clouds (from satellite and ground-view point clouds) without the use of visibility information. Although theoretically possible, re-implementing a meshing

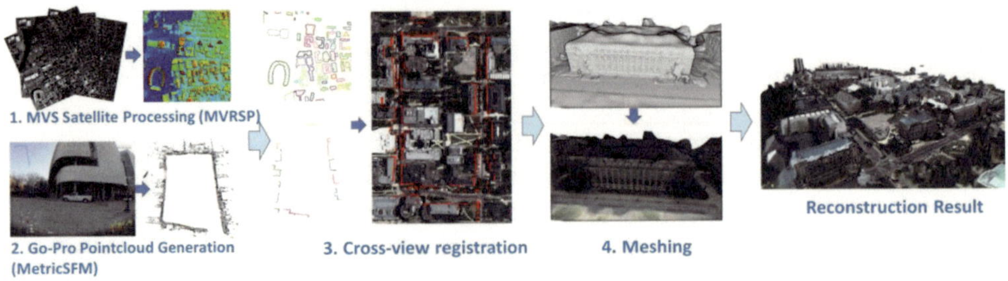

Figure 1.
The general workflow of our processing pipeline.

algorithm considering different camera models can be painstakingly trivial. We consider the satellite point clouds to be associated with an orthophoto under a parallel projection, thus the visibility can be easily computed and incorporated into an image-based meshing [23] and texture mapping pipeline [25].

To sum, our proposed data generation pipeline considers three major components. As shown in **Figure 1**, which includes separate 3D data generation (for MVS satellite images and ground-level video frames), geo-registration, and meshing.

The MVRSP (based on [4, 26, 27]) and MetricSFM are, respectively, our developed system for processing the satellite data and ground-level video frames. A cross-view registration method is performed for overview and ground-view point cloud registration, which utilize the boundary information derived from both types of point clouds. Finally, the co-registered point clouds are processed by a modified meshing and texture mapping algorithm that innovatively consider both perspective and parallelly projected image (satellite orthophoto) in an integrated optimization framework.

3. Methodology

3.1 Multi-view (MVS) satellite image processing

The MVS satellite processing follows methods in [4, 26], which takes a pair-wise reconstruction followed by a DSM (Digital Surface Model) fusion as shown in **Figure 2**. Given a set of images, we will first apply an analysis algorithm presented

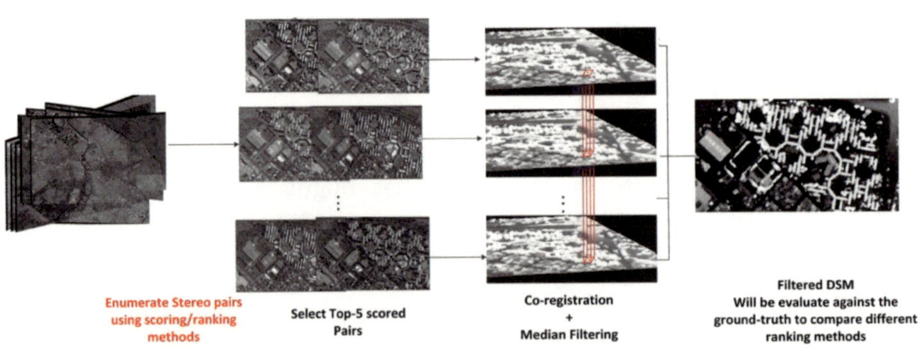

Figure 2.
A workflow of the multi-view satellite image processing [28].

Figure 3.
3D reconstruction of the central area in London (ca. 50 km^2). Left: overview of part of the area; right: top, enlarged RGB (red, green, blue) color image, bottom, pseudo color image (near infrared, red, green).

in [28] to rank the matchability of the satellite stereo pairs (enumerated from the existing images), and then we take the top five stereo pairs to perform relative orientation and stereo dense matching using a software called RPC stereo processor [4, 27]. The core matching algorithm uses a hierarchical semi-global matching [29] with modifications to accommodate large-format images [30]. The use of multiple stereo pairs enables sufficient redundancies for high-quality 3D reconstruction, and the images consist of both Worldview I/II images (data will be introduced in Section 4). The produced individual DSMs resulting from different stereo pairs are co-registered with a shift-based registration which search for translation parameters in reference to one of the pairs (which is used to be the first pair in the pair ranking), and the co-registered DSMs are fused following an adaptive depth-fusion method [26] that utilizes the color information of the orthophoto, which were shown to achieve better accuracy than a simple median depth filtering. The readers may refer to specific details of the reconstruction in [4, 26, 28].

A typical digital surface model generated using our pipeline is shown in **Figure 3**, which indicates a 3D reconstruction result of the central area of the city of London. Worldview-III images with a 0.3-m resolution are used, thus the resulting surface models are with the same resolution.

3.2 3D reconstruction from ground-view monocular image sequences

Monocular 3D reconstruction refers to the process of recovering shape of objects using images taken from a single video camera. As compared to typical stereo/multi-stereo images captured from well-distributed angles, such video sequences present sub-optimal camera network in which the pose estimation is often inaccurate for metrically correct 3D reconstruction. Oftentimes, the structure from motion and SLAM (simultaneous localization and mapping) approaches are used to compute the camera poses and generate 3D semi-dense or dense point clouds. These methods although provide visually pleasant trajectories and point clouds, they may often be metrically incorrect and present drifting problems. In this section, we introduce a monocular 3D reconstruction system that leverages the speed of a typical SLAM system and rigorous photogrammetric optimization. We first present typical components for 3D reconstruction and then briefly introduce the processing workflow of the system.

3.2.1 A 3D reconstruction pipeline

Figure 4 presents a typical image-based 3D reconstruction pipeline. Raw images or undistorted images (through pre-calibrated parameters) are taken as the input and follow a series steps named feature extraction and matching, relative orientation, bundle adjustment and dense image matching, and output intrinsic and extrinsic orientation parameters and dense point clouds. Among these steps, the GPS (global positioning system) or IMU (inertial measurement unit) can be optionally taken as observations to bring global datum. Below we briefly introduce these components and their specifics in a ground-view image sequence scenario:

Camera intrinsic and extrinsic parameters: the camera intrinsic parameters refer to the internal geometry of the camera and often considered as focal length, principal points, and lens distortions. The extrinsic parameters refer to the poses (position and facing) of each image, normally represented by six parameters: three for a point in Euclidean coordinate (camera perspective center) and three rotation angles (sometimes are represented directly as rotation matrix).

Pair selection: pair selection tells the system what are the images that are likely to observe the same object, such that a connected graph can be built [31, 32] to formulate observations to recover 3D geometry. In the ground-view scenario, this can be simply formulated using the timestamp of the frames.

Feature extraction and matching: features represent areas or points of interest in images and denote special pieces of information. In 3D reconstruction, points are the most popular feature representations due to their simplicity and flexibility. Point features can be understood as corners or spots that are distinctive and easily identifiable across different images with various levels of perspective differences and typical features are SIFT (Scale-Invariant Feature Transform) [33], SURF (Speeded up robust features) [34], ORB (Oriented FAST and Rotated BRIEF) [35], etc. Once these points are extracted, feature matching aims to associate identical points across different images, which essentially represents corresponding rays from different images. Typically done with an exhaustive search, feature matching in a ground-view video frame scenario can be speed up by considering the fact of horizontal moving thus to reduce the search space [36].

Incremental relative orientation/pose estimation: the incremental relative orientation refers to the process starting with a two-view relative orientation, followed by sequentially orienting the rest of the images given the feature point correspondences. Often the estimation process needs to address blunders in the observations and the state-of-the-art procedure takes RANSAC (random sampling consensus) [37] for robust and automated relative pose estimation. RANSAC used a random sampling strategy that starts with randomly sampled feature matches (observations) instead of all the observations for relative orientation (model estimation), runs the same process for multiple times, and selects the model (estimated orientation parameters) accounting for most of the observations with reasonable residual. This has dramatically improved the automation in relative orientation and subsequently the incremental procedure, as it theoretically only requires the error

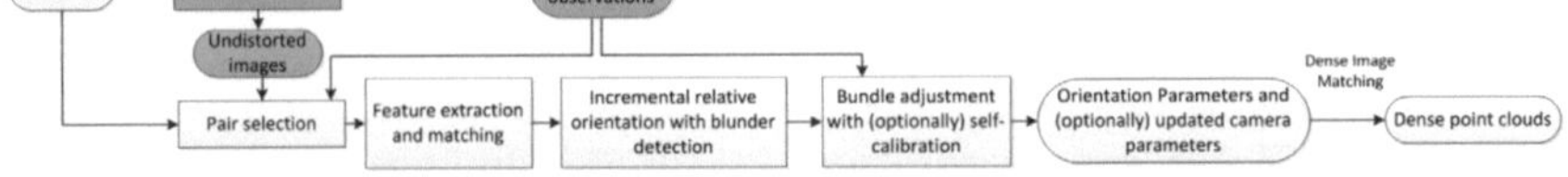

Figure 4.
A typical 3D reconstruction pipeline, dark-gray blocks indicate optional steps.

rate of the matches be larger than 50%, while apparently the state-of-the-art feature extractors and matchers do much better with images in most of the applications.

Bundle adjustment: is a refinement process for the intrinsic and extrinsic camera parameters simultaneously with the 3D coordinated of the scene points since the measurements are prone to errors [38]. It involves a global minimization scheme using robust nonlinear least-squares algorithm such as Levenberg-Marquardt [39]. This often comes with a procedure called self-calibration [40] that simultaneously estimates the lens distortions of the camera. In a ground-view video frame scenario, because the bundle adjustment is particularly time consuming, it may sometimes be simplified to only perform local bundle adjustment instead of considering all available images.

3.2.2 3D reconstruction using ground-view image sequences

Ground-view image sequences formulate a specific scenario in which a typical 3D reconstruction pipeline can be customized to accommodate the need for speed and accuracy. Our general workflow is presented in **Figure 5**. It is similar to a SLAM pipeline [36] with the differences that the local and full bundle adjustment considers the estimation of camera lens distortion parameters. Typically, the system starts with an initialization module that aims at estimating the camera pose for the two images used in the initialization by utilizing the matched features between them, this is in line with the first half of incremental relative orientation as mentioned above. Moreover, this module generates initial 3D points of the scene by triangulating the matched feature points from the two images. After generating the initial reconstruction, the tracking module (in dashed box) starts to localize every image by finding its pose, which is similar to the second half of the relative orientation which sequentially add image frames to the system. In this module, the temporal relation between the images is used by assuming a constant velocity motion model so that we can get an initial estimate of the current image pose. Thus, using the estimated pose, we can directly project the 3D points into the current image and perform window-based search for the potential feature matches with the projected points. Consequently, we can save computations by searching correspondences only inside this window instead of searching in the whole image. Then, using these correspondences, the current camera pose can be estimated. It should be noted that the concept of keyframes are used to identify important frames in which the poses will be optimized through bundle adjustment, because frames that are estimated through a constant velocity are considered to close enough to interpolate. For images that fail the constant velocity motion model, the tracking module performs full feature matches to find feature in previous frames that have an associated map point using a spatial resection (i.e., a Perspective-n-Point (PnP) algorithm) [41] by taking existing 3D points and 2D correspondences to compute their pose, and such images are then taken as the new keyframes, in the meantime features with no 3D correspondences will be triangulated as candidates of 3D map points.

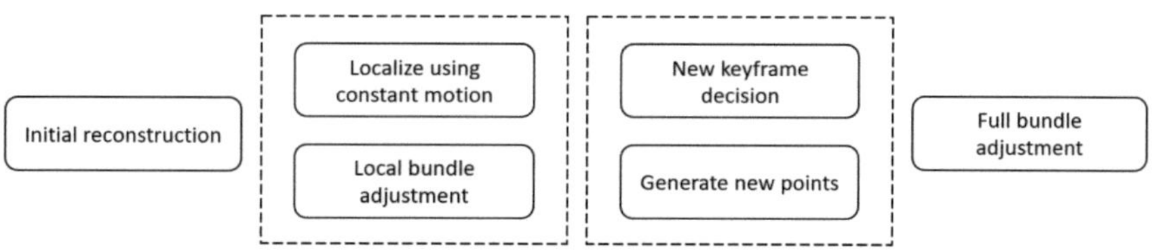

Figure 5.
A 3D reconstruction pipeline using ground-view video frames.

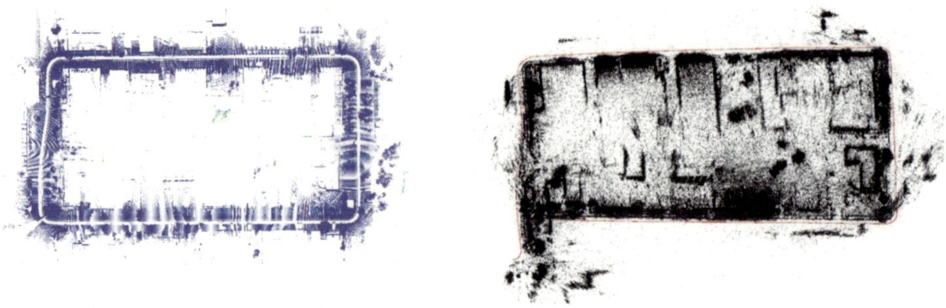

Figure 6.
The 3D reconstruction result, left: ground truth trajectory from mobile LiDAR, right: our result without loop closure (7500 frames).

Once the tracking module accumulates frames to a pre-defined number, a full bundle adjustment is used interchangeably with local bundle adjustment to refine the estimated measurements. These aforementioned processes are implemented in an in-house software package called MetricSFM. A sample from the 3D reconstruction results is shown in **Figure 6**.

3.3 Cross-view 3D point co-registration and fusion

Non-rigid distortion of the ground-view data (e.g., trajectory drift) and very limited overlapping region among cross-view data make them difficult to be registered without significant manual effort. Based on the assumption that the object boundaries (e.g., buildings) from the over-view data should coincide with footprints of façade points from ground-view, we tackle these problems by proposing a fully automated geo-registration method for cross-view data, which utilizes semantically segmented object boundaries as view-invariant features under a global optimization framework. Taking the over-view point clouds generated from satellite stereo/multi-stereo images and the ground-view point clouds from monocular video frames as the input, the proposed method takes a "two-step" strategy to solve the non-rigid cross-view registration problem using object boundaries, which is further optimized through a constrained bundle adjustment to keep 2D-3D consistencies.

3.3.1 Building boundary extraction from ground-view and over-view point clouds

The building extraction on the over-view point cloud is achieved by converting the point cloud into a digital surface model (DSM), on which the well-developed morphological top-hat [42, 43] can be used to extract a binary mask for all the high objects like tree and building. For satellite orthophoto containing multi-spectral information, the NDVI (Normalized Difference Vegetation Index) [44] can be extracted to further remove the trees from the binary masks. The ground-view building detection is based on the observation that the building façade points are usually vertical to the horizontal ground plane. We therefore determine the vertical direction by calculating the normal vector for all the points and then selecting the direction with the largest number of normal vectors pointing to the vertical directions. Once the vertical direction is obtained, all the ground-view points are projected onto the horizontal plane, which is followed by a classical region growing method [45] to extract point cloud segments. Finally, those segments with the number of points greater than a threshold are kept as the extracted ground-view buildings. The results of building boundary extraction from both over-view and ground-view data can be seen in **Figure 7**.

3.3.2 Individual building segment matching

In order to efficiently search for accurate registration parameters locally to address potential topographical errors of the point clouds (e.g., drifted trajectory resulting metrically incorrect point clouds), we developed a simple 2D point cloud registration algorithm that performs sampled exhaustive search. Given the over-view point set P_d of size n_d as the reference point cloud, and the ground-view point set P_s of size n_s as the matching point cloud, with the scale difference s between two point sets. Firstly, the distance map (as **Figure 8(b)** shows) for P_d is calculated using distance transformation [46, 47], in which the distance of each pixel (colored in gray-level, darkest referring to the closest distance) to the region of interest (in our scenario this refers to the boundary from the overview data). P_s is centralized by subtracting the central point for each point from P_s. Assuming a fixed scale determined by sparse known observations such as GPS positions, we perform an exhaustive-search through the rotation and translation space to find the optimal parameters. The final rotation parameter and translation parameter were found as ones that minimize the co-registration error in the distance map, and an example result is shown in **Figure 8(c)**.

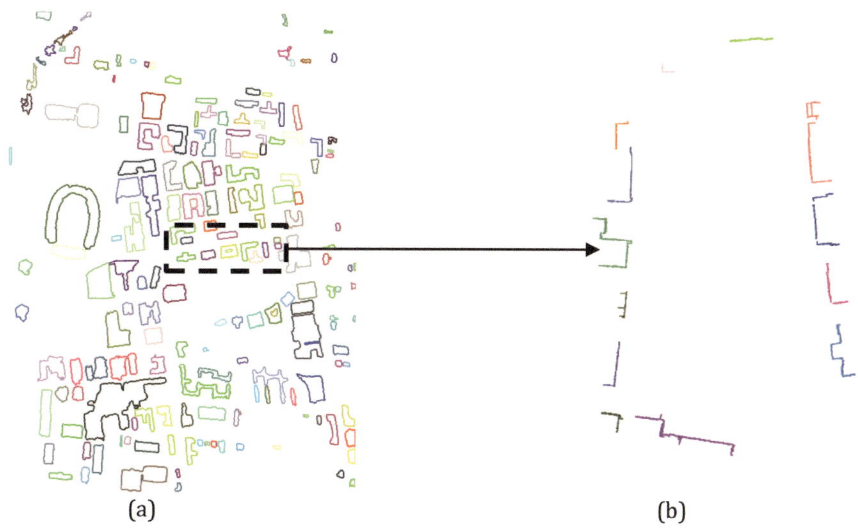

Figure 7.
Illustration of building boundary extraction results from (a) over-view and (b) ground-view data.

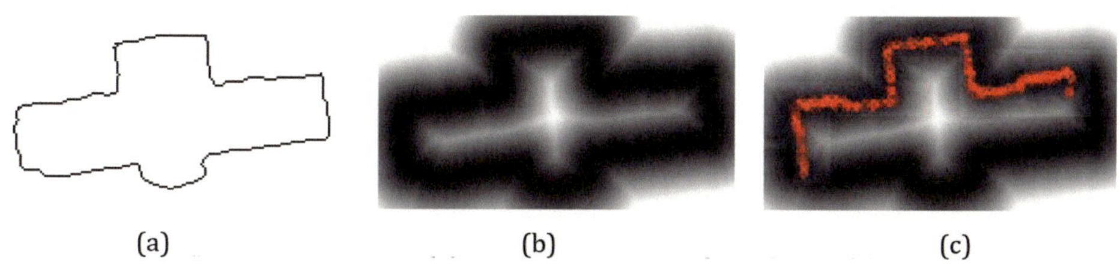

Figure 8.
Exhaustive search-based local matching algorithm. Given the over-view building boundary points P_d as destination in (a), the distance map in (b) is calculated where the intensity of pixel denotes the closest distance to P_d, then the global solution in (c) is obtained by our proposed method. Red points represent the ground-view point P_s.

3.3.3 Global optimization for consistent building segment matching using graph-cut

In the previous building segment matching step, a list of transformations $\mathcal{T} = \{T_i, i = 1, 2, \ldots\}$ is generated, which constitutes the final hypotheses for each building segments. We consider that the transformation hypothesis for neighboring building segments to be similar, therefore, we consider formulating this constrain in an energy minimization problem (Eq. (1)):

$$\mathrm{E}(\mathcal{T}) = \sum_{\mathrm{B}} \mathrm{D}(\mathrm{B}, T) + \sum_{\mathrm{B}_i, \mathrm{B}_j} \mathrm{V}_{\mathrm{B}_i, \mathrm{B}_j}\left(T_{\mathrm{B}_i}, T_{\mathrm{B}_j}\right), \tag{1}$$

where $\mathrm{D}(\mathrm{B}, T)$ is the data term for teach building segment B with a transformation T in $\mathcal{T}$, and $\mathrm{V}_{\mathrm{B}_i, \mathrm{B}_j}\left(T_{\mathrm{B}_i}, T_{\mathrm{B}_j}\right)$ is the smooth term that penalizes differences of two transformations T_{B_i} and T_{B_j} of the building segments B_i and B_j.

3.3.3.1 Data term

Given a building B and a transformation T, we first collect its k-adjacent buildings (including B), measured using distance between barycentric coordinates. These segments after transformation are used to verify how close they are to the over-view building segments. To robustify the evaluation, we consider counting the number of points that are close enough to the overview building segments, as follows (Eq. (2)):

$$\mathrm{D}(\mathrm{B}, T) = \sum_{\mathrm{p} \in \mathrm{B}} \mathrm{c}(\mathrm{p}, \mathrm{p}') = \begin{cases} 0, \text{if } \mathrm{d}(\mathrm{p}, \mathrm{p}') < \mathrm{d}_{th} \\ 1, \text{otherwise} \end{cases} \tag{2}$$

where $\mathrm{c}(\mathrm{p}, \mathrm{p}')$ is the cost of a point p that belongs to the building B, which equals to 0 if the distance $\mathrm{d}(\mathrm{p}, \mathrm{p}')$ between p and its closest point p' in the over-view building boundaries is smaller than d_{th}, and equals to 1 otherwise. This formulation can effectively keep the value range of the data term limited. For example, the value of $\mathrm{d}(\mathrm{p}, \mathrm{p}')$ can be very large if an incorrect transformation converts the point p far away from p'; however, $\mathrm{c}(\mathrm{p}, \mathrm{p}')$ can eliminate the influence of this mistake to generate more reasonable cost value.

3.3.3.2 Smooth term

The smooth term $\mathrm{V}_{\mathrm{B}_i, \mathrm{B}_j}\left(T_{\mathrm{B}_i}, T_{\mathrm{B}_j}\right)$ penalizes the transformation associate with two neighboring buildings being too different, shown in Eq. (3):

$$\mathrm{V}_{\mathrm{B}_i, \mathrm{B}_j}\left(T_{\mathrm{B}_i}, T_{\mathrm{B}_j}\right) = \begin{cases} p1, \text{if} \left\|\theta_{\mathrm{B}_i} - \theta_{\mathrm{B}_j}\right\| < \theta_{th} \text{ and } \left\|t_{\mathrm{B}_i} - t_{\mathrm{B}_j}\right\| < t_{th} \\ p2, \text{otherwise} \end{cases} \tag{3}$$

where θ is the rotation angle in 2D and t is translation, and we assign a small penalty $p1$ to neighboring segments with transformation different smaller than a given threshold, otherwise we assign a larger penalty. The weights and thresholds can be determined based on the noise level of data. The solution Eq. (1) can be achieved efficiently through graph-cut algorithm [48].

3.3.4 Bundle adjustment for pose refinement

The co-registration is further performed in the vertical direction using the overlapping ground points, and this is followed by a bundle adjustment of all image poses such that they are consistent with the registered ground-view point clouds. This is achieved by weighting the unknown poses to be close to the poses after the transformation. An additional bundle adjustment benefits the poses to be strictly following the epipolar constraints thus offers consistent 2D-3D relationship for further processing such as texture mapping.

Both the overview and ground-view point clouds are then combined, and their overlapping point clouds were fused as follows: for areas where both satellite point clouds and ground-view point clouds exist, we take the ground-view point clouds as it with a resolution presents higher accuracy and certainty. An example of co-registered cross-view point clouds is shown in **Figure 9**.

3.4 Meshing and texture mapping of cross-view fused point clouds

3.4.1 Mesh reconstruction of cross-view fused point cloud

As mentioned in Section I (Introduction), a point cloud-based meshing method [21] is unlikely to yield visually consistent meshes (an example is shown in **Figure 14**). Therefore, our solution considers the use of image information for mesh reconstruction. The base method [23] takes the constructed Delaunay tetrahedra of the point clouds as the input to extract the surface. These tetrahedra can be viewed as a connected graph, in which the tetrahedra are the nodes and shared/common faces are edges. **Figure 10** shows the procedure: black triangles denote cameras, dash arrows denote visual rays, each point in 3D space can be determined by at least two rays, which connect the object points and camera centers, here we call it ray visibility. Based on ray visibility, tetrahedra intersected with rays are evaluated by their probability to be in a free space (outer space), and tetrahedra behind the ray endpoint are evaluated by their probability belonging to the full space (inner space). Such a graph labeling can be casted to a s-t minimal cut problem and solved with maxflow algorithms [49]. The final surfaces are the common faces of the tetrahedra labeled as free and full spaces (**Figure 10**).

Our pipeline extends from this base algorithm by incorporating point clouds generated from the satellite images. The following steps give streamline from source points to surface mesh model.

Delaunay 3D triangulation: 3D triangulation or tetrahedralization is extended from 2D triangulation, which partitions a polyhedron into non-overlapping basic 3D elements, where the vertices of tetrahedra take the vertices of the original

Figure 9.
Co-registered cross-view point clouds are fused (left: before; right: after) by only keeping the high resolution results. Non-textured points are over-view satellite point clouds.

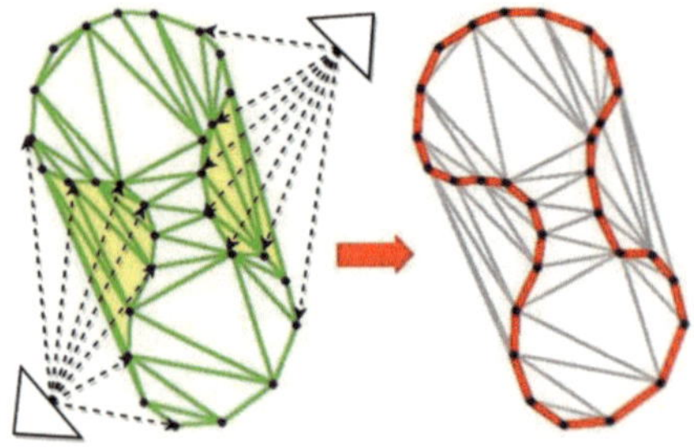

Figure 10.
Left: Green network is Delaunay triangulation, yellow region (free space) is tetrahedra which intersected with rays (dash arrows), and white region is tetrahedra labeled as full space. Right: red lines are surfaces between full and free space, which are common faces shared by those tetrahedra (artwork from [50] with minor edit).

polyhedron. Delaunay tetrahedron reconstruction [51] divides the convex hull of points into compact simplices, where neither extremely long edge nor extremely sharp angle is included. Many well-known commercial packages and open source projects have implemented the algorithm that creates Delaunay tetrahedron from point set, here we use CGAL [52] an open source computational geometric algorithm library to construct tetrahedra.

Visibility: each ray will propagate its confidence to intersected nodes (tetrahedra) and edges (triangle faces) of the tetrahedra graph. The algorithm was implemented by an open-sourced project OpenMVS [53]. Dense points and their associated images with poses are the most common source of visibility in our framework, often under a perspective geometry. However, the geometric model of satellite camera sensors is different (e.g., rational polynomial coefficients) [4]. By considering that the point clouds can be associated with the orthophoto through a parallel projection, we proposed a two-step method: (1) project satellite point on to grid, only the highest point is recorded in each cell. (2) Create vertical visual rays from those points.

Assigning weights for the graph: our method follows a so-called soft visibility weighting model that was used by the base algorithm. The readers may refer to the original paper [23] for more detail.

Solving min-cut problem: once weighting procedure for the edges is done, we use IBFS (incremental breadth first search) [54] maximum flow algorithm to solve minimum *s-t* cut problem. And finally, the common faces between source and sink tetrahedra are extracted to build up optimum surface model.

3.4.2 Texture mapping of cross-view fused point cloud

Our texture mapping framework is based on Waechter's work [25] which has been well practiced and widely used by rather popular open source projects, for example, OpenMVS [53]. Texturing a 3D model from multiple registered images is typically performed in a two steps approach: (1) select view(s) should be used to texture each face yielding a preliminary texture and (2) optimize the texture to avoid seams between adjacent texture patches.

Best view selection: the base method [25] determines face visibility (distinct from ray visibility) for all combinations of views and faces by first performing back face and view frustum culling, then renders faces onto images, using depth buffer to determine the nearest faces. Lempitsky et al. [51, 52, 55] compute a labeling that assign a view to be used as texture for each mesh face using a pairwise Markov random field energy formulation. We consider the ground-view images are perspective, and the satellite orthophotos are in parallel projection. Our texture mapping considers the orthophoto as one of the images with only few simple modifications: we balanced data term of ortho images to compensate resolution gap and make ortho images as the default sources for texturing.

Seamless texture fusion: in Waechter et al.'s method [25], they proposed a global and local color adjustment method to blur the seams, which extended Lempitsky and Ivanov's [55] color adjustment approach. The original approach only accounts for color difference on vertices to measure color difference along the seam line, called global adjustment. The extended method added a local adjustment with Poisson editing [56] affect border strip of image patches. In our case, since the resolution of orthophoto is way lower than the ground-view images, prior to applying the fusion of image patches, we up-sampled orthophoto to the same resolution as that of the ground-view images. After color balancing and Poisson editing, color differences can be well-adjusted and seams are successfully been blurred.

4. Data description

We take the Ohio State University (OSU) Columbus Campus as our test site, of which we have collected 12 overlapping satellite images consisting of WorldView-I and WorldView-II images (information shown in **Table 1**). These images selectively form 31 pairs used for the reconstruction based on the method of [28], and many of these images are not from the same year thus creating challenges for the reconstruction. **Table 2** provides an overview of the first 10 pairs used from the acquired images: not all of these pairs form in-track stereo, while the large redundancy does provide the advantage in producing more accurate surface model. **Figure 11** shows the generated digital surface model. The achieved RMSE (root-mean-squared-error) is 1.26 m evaluated through LiDAR point clouds, and the RMSE reached 0.60 m by excluding changed buildings, rivers, and trees.

We have also collected approximately 300 GB of Go-pro videos covering a trajectory equivalent to 33 km, and the reconstruction for the ground-view images take 150 k frames (with a resolution of 1500 $\times$ 2000 pixels per frame) out of these videos. **Figure 12** shows the reconstructed point clouds of approximately two thirds

	Acquisition time	Sensor	Off nadir (degree)	Sun elevation angle (degree)	Resolution (meter)	Cloud cover percentage (%)
1	2009-04-01	WorldView-01	1.80	52.40	0.50	0.00
2	2010-04-15	WorldView-01	15.40	58.20	0.52	0.00
3	2010-09-25	WorldView-02	13.00	48.30	0.49	0.04
4	2010-09-25	WorldView-02	19.20	48.30	0.52	0.01
5	2011-10-08	WorldView-02	4.30	43.80	0.47	0.00
6	2012-01-09	WorldView-01	20.00	26.10	0.55	0.00
7	2012-01-09	WorldView-01	32.70	26.20	0.67	0.00
8	2013-08-06	WorldView-02	15.80	64.20	0.50	0.00
9	2013-12-28	WorldView-01	22.90	24.50	0.57	0.00
10	2014-06-06	WorldView-02	23.50	70.80	0.54	0.00
11	2015-04-17	WorldView-02	25.60	56.80	0.56	0.00
12	2019-01-05	WorldView-02	19.90	26.60	0.52	0.00

Table 1.
Twelve overlapping satellite images used for satellite-based 3D reconstruction.

Pair	Intersection angle (degree)	Sun difference angle (degree)	Time difference (days)	Left image ID	Right image ID
1	6.20	0.00	0	3	4
2	12.70	0.10	0	6	7
3	13.60	5.80	379	1	2
4	2.90	1.60	719	6	9
5	9.80	1.70	719	7	9
6	8.70	4.50	378	3	5
7	14.90	4.50	378	4	5
8	7.70	6.60	304	8	10
9	2.10	14.00	315	10	11
10	5.70	30.20	1359	11	12

Table 2.
Examples of metadata of pairs used for satellite-based 3D reconstruction. These data come in level 1. The image ID refers to those in ***Table 1****.*

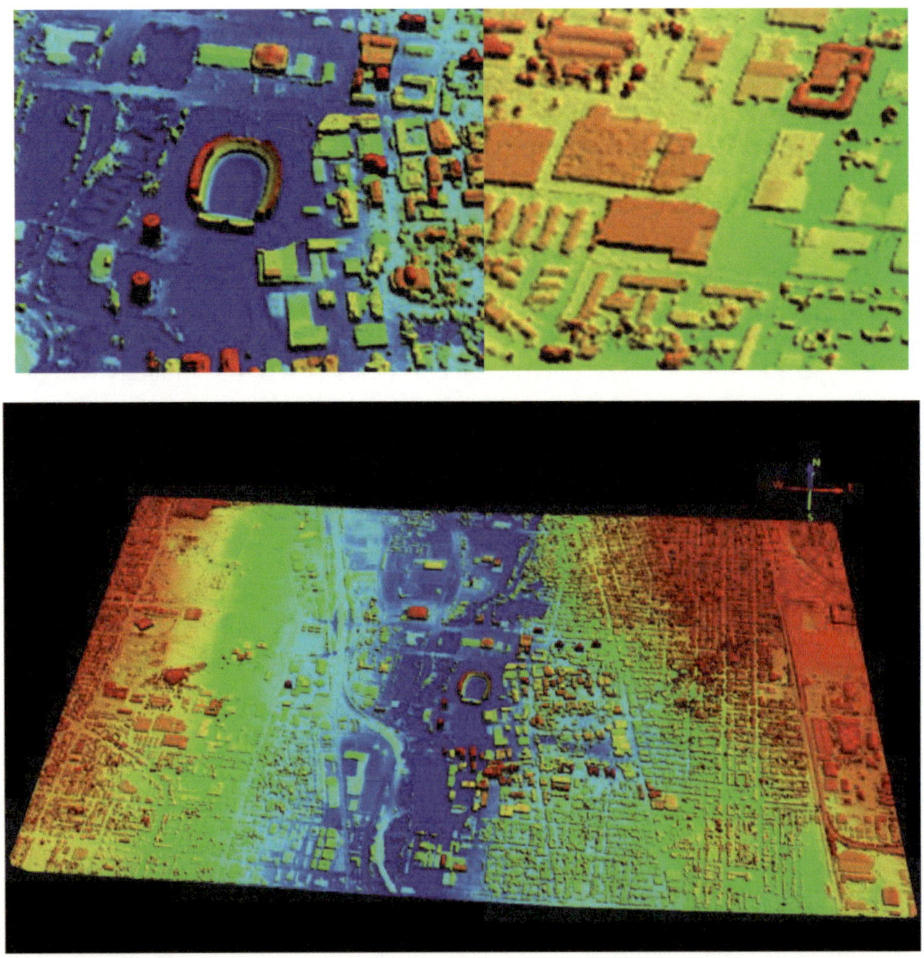

Figure 11.
The generated digital surface models of the OSU campus using our satellite data processing pipeline. The top-row shows enlarged views.

Figure 12.
Dense reconstruction using our processing pipeline for two thirds of the campus region, totaling 7 billion color points.

of the region. The pose estimation time takes approximately 20 hours and dense matching takes 4 h in a normal i-7 desktop computer.

5. Experiment results

We demonstrate that the resulting geometry shows completeness in terms of the rooftop and façade information (for places where ground-view images are available). **Figure 13** provides an overview of the registered point clouds and a comparison showing the mis-registration using a typical point cloud based algorithm [20].

With the registered point clouds, we can generate the meshes using our proposed meshing pipeline introduced in Section 3.4. **Figure 14** shows the reconstructed meshes (shaded and textured) using our pipeline, and we have also included the results from a pure point cloud-based meshing method, which visually demonstrates much worse results. In **Figure 15**, we have also included the reconstruction results of a relatively larger region using our reconstructed pipeline.

5.1 Accuracy evaluation

We have compared the resulting combined model with the ground truth Airborne LiDAR data as shown in **Figure 16**, in which we include two sample areas (top and bottom row of **Figure 16**). Since the airborne LiDAR does not cover the façade information, we evaluate the accuracy of the results using resampled DSM to the same grid. It is expected that the combined model with the incorporated street-view point clouds should have better accuracy given the more accurate point clouds of the (partial) ground and building boundaries. From **Figure 16**, we can observe that the satellite DSM (left column), due to the lower resolution, shows blurred object boundaries, as compared to the combined model (middle column). **Figure 17** plots the error distributions, and it evidences our observations in **Figure 16**: the object boundaries in the satellite DSM show larger errors than the combined model, and it can be also seen in some regions of the ground that the combined model presents less error due to the captured fine ground structures (marked in red circle of **Figures 16** and **17**, bottom row). **Table 3** calculates the RMSE (root mean squared error) of these two areas, and it shows that the combined model improves at 0.20 m in accuracy for

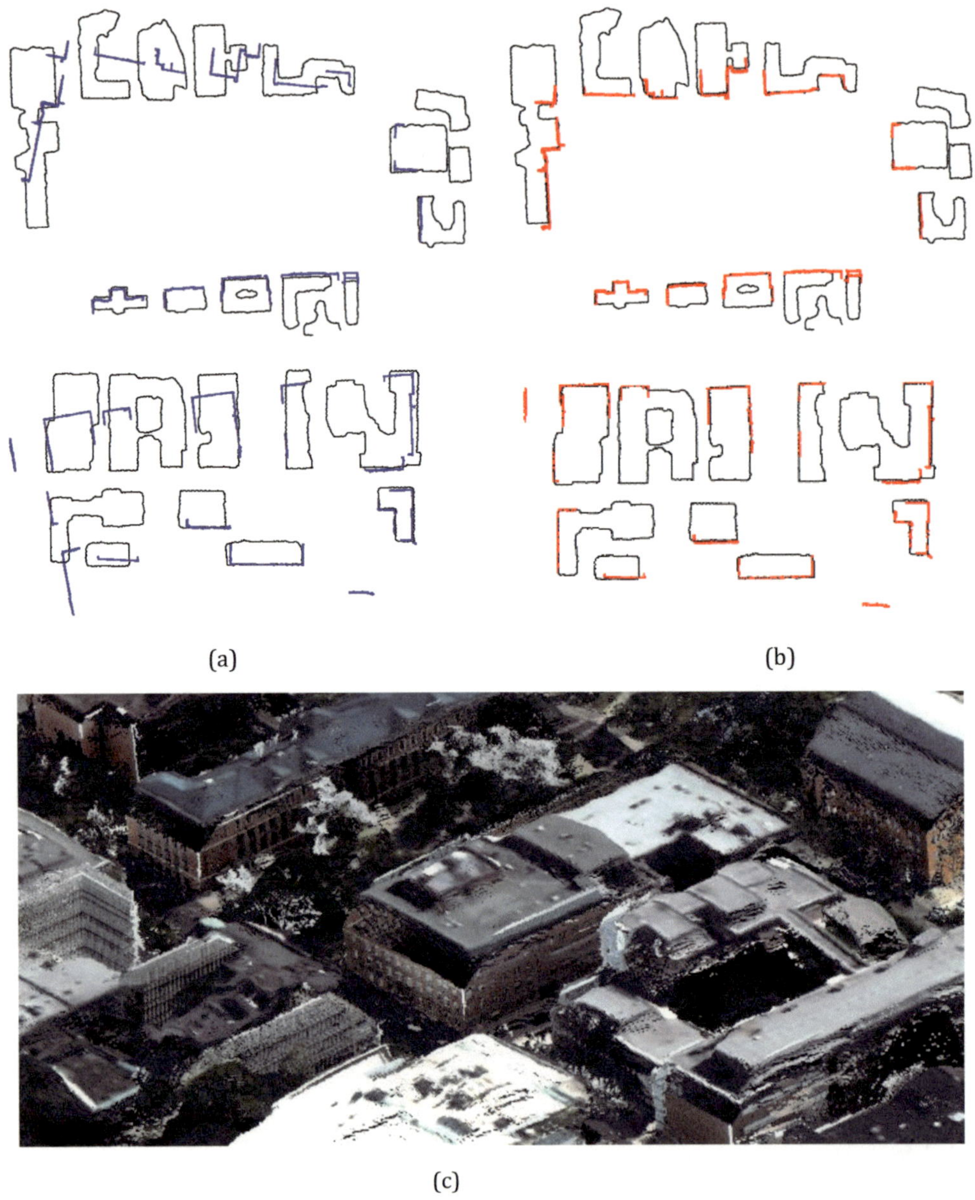

Figure 13.
Registration result of ICP (a) and our method (b) on the distorted ground-view trajectory. (c) Part of the registered ground-view point clouds generated on 150 k Go-Pro images.

area 1 and 1 m for area 2. This shows significant improvement in terms of data accuracy, and we should note that this evaluate is only on the DSM and it is expected that if the façade data evaluation is considered (if ground truth of the façade geometry is available), the accuracy improvement can be significantly more.

6. Conclusion

In this chapter, we propose a framework for fusing results from cross-view images for 3D mesh reconstruction. We present our processing framework (**Figure 1**) that

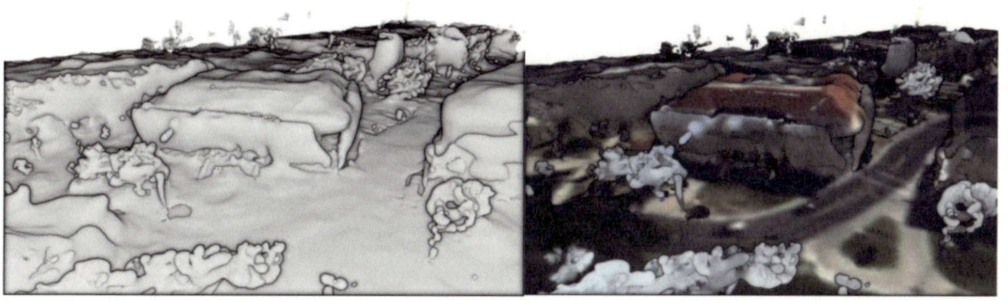

(a)

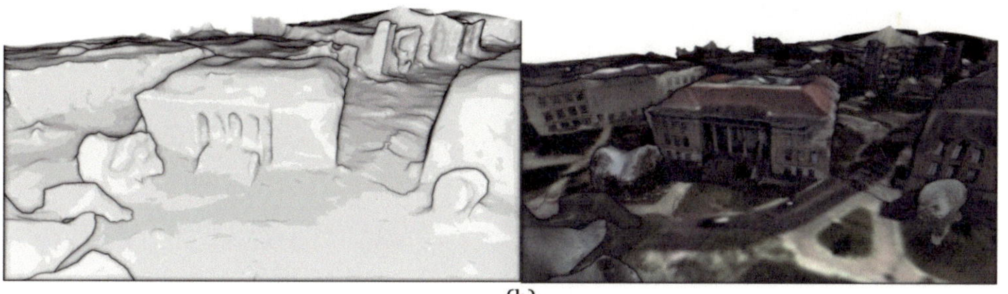

(b)

Figure 14.
Left: shaded mesh model. Right: textured mesh model. (a) Reconstructed mesh using Poisson reconstruction. (b) Reconstructed mesh using our reconstruction method.

Figure 15.
A screenshot of the generated textured mesh of the OSU campus area using our proposed pipeline, which includes information from the top-view and details on the facades.

consists of three major components: (1) 3D reconstruction separately from the top-view satellite images and ground-level images; (2) cross-view geo-registration between the satellite point clouds and ground-view point clouds; 3) meshing reconstruction based on the combined satellite and ground point clouds. In each of these components, we present our developed systems and on-going research efforts in addressing the potential challenges (introduced in Section 1.1) and the in-progress results. We demonstrate that our proposed pipeline can achieve visually more consistent textured meshes, in comparison to a standard and intuitive processing method. The proposed framework and the attempts for integrating satellite and ground-view images and

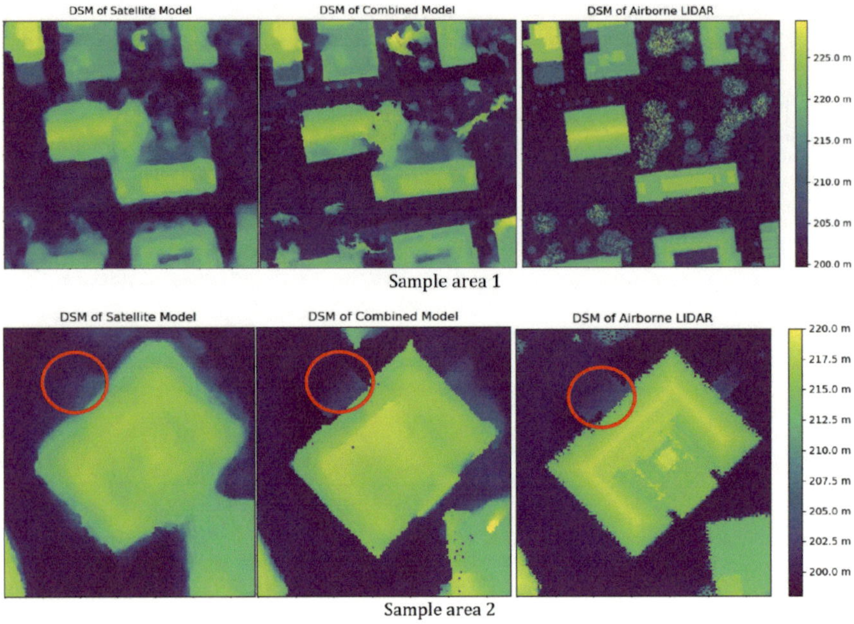

Figure 16.
DSM from satellite stereo (left column)/combined model (middle column)/airborne LIDAR (right column). Top and bottom row indicates two difference samples (sample area 1 and sample area 2). The red-circled region shows that a ground structure is well compared in the combined model, as compared to the satellite DSM.

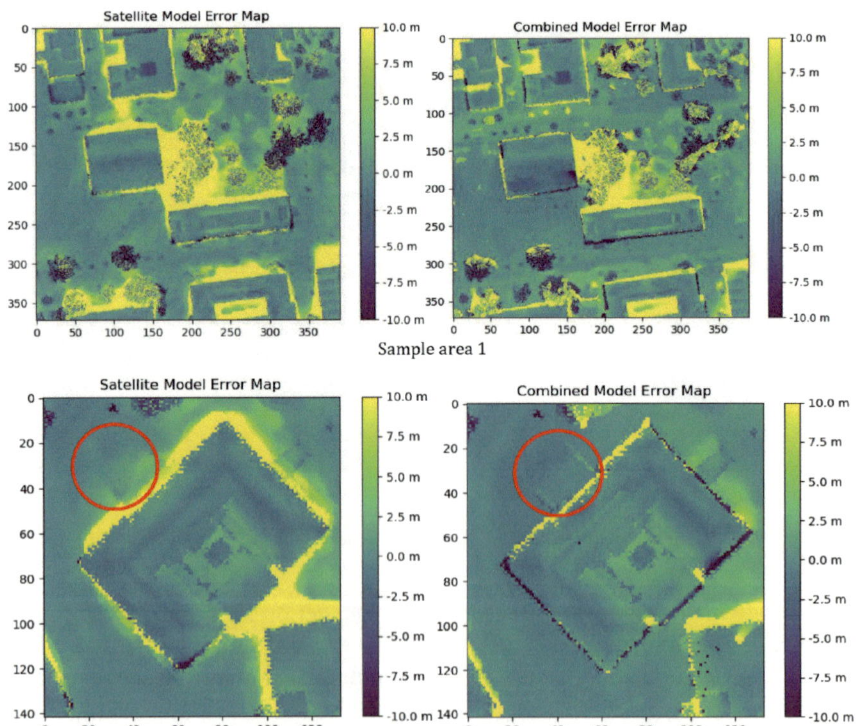

Figure 17.
Error maps of satellite model (left column) and combined model (right column) evaluated against the LiDAR DSM. Top and bottom row indicates two difference samples (sample area 1 and sample area 2). The red circled region shows smaller errors in the combined model due to that the ground structure is well captured.

	RMSE (m) – Area 1	RMSE (m) – Area 2
Satellite model	4.315	3.505
Combined model	4.138	2.532

Table 3.
Error evaluation.

converting them to textured models can be of particular interest for data collection in areas where standard datasets such as aerial/UAV (unmanned aerial vehicle) photogrammetric/LiDAR flights. We have demonstrated that DSM generated from the combined model using our workflow can be 1-m more accurate than the satellite DSM and is expected to be much more accurate if the evaluation on the façade is considered (as the satellite DSM does not have façade information at all). Our future works include further optimizing individual modules of our processing pipeline and part of these modules will be made available once they are optimized for practical uses.

Acknowledgements

This work is supported by the Office of Naval Research (Award No. N000141712928). The satellite datasets are provided by Digital-Globe. The authors appreciate the helpful support of Mr. Xiaohu Lu and Dr. Xu Huang in their prior work.

Author details

Rongjun Qin[1,2]*, Shuang Song[1], Xiao Ling[1] and Mostafa Elhashash[2]

1 Department of Civil, Environmental and Geodetic Engineering, The Ohio State University, Columbus, Ohio, USA

2 Department of Electrical and Computer Engineering, The Ohio State University, USA

*Address all correspondence to: qin.324@osu.edu

References

[1] Haala N, Cavegn S. High density aerial image matching: State-of-the-art and future prospects. In: International Archives of the Photogrammetry, Remote Sensing & Spatial Information Sciences. Vol. 41. Netherlands: Copernicus Publications; 2016

[2] Schwarz B. LIDAR: Mapping the world in 3D. Nature Photonics. 2010;**4**:429

[3] Bosch M, Kurtz Z, Hagstrom S, Brown M. A multiple view stereo benchmark for satellite imagery. In: Presented at the Proceedings of the IEEE Applied Imagery Pattern Recognition (AIPR) Workshop, October 2016. 2016

[4] Qin R. RPC stereo processor (RSP) –a software package for digital surface model and orthophoto generation from satellite stereo imagery. In: ISPRS Annals of Photogrammetry, Remote Sensing and Spatial Information Sciences. Vol. III. Netherlands: Copernicus Publications; 2016. pp. 77-82

[5] Qin R, Song S, Huang X. 3D data generation using low-cost cross-view images. In: Presented at the the International Archives of Photogrammetry and Remote Sensing. ISPRS Congress 2020 (Delayed to 2021 Due to Coronavirus), Nice, France. 2020

[6] Regmi K, Borji A. Cross-view image synthesis using conditional gans. In: Proceedings of the IEEE Conference on Computer Vision and Pattern Recognition. 2018. pp. 3501-3510

[7] Lu X, Li Z, Cui Z, Oswald MR, Pollefeys M, Qin R. Geometry-aware satellite-to-ground image synthesis for urban areas. In: Presented at the IEEE Conference on Computer Vision and Pattern Recognition (CVPR). 2020

[8] Gruen A, Huang X, Qin R, Du T, Fang W, Boavida J, et al. Joint processing of Uav imagery and terrestrial Mobile mapping system data for very high Resolution City Modeling. In: ISPRS-International Archives of the Photogrammetry, Remote Sensing and Spatial Information Sciences. Vol. 1. Netherlands: Copernicus Publications; 2013. pp. 175-182

[9] Lin T-Y, Cui Y, Belongie S, Hays J. Learning deep representations for ground-to-aerial geolocalization. In: Proceedings of the IEEE Conference on Computer Vision and Pattern Recognition. 2015. pp. 5007-5015

[10] Kwan C, Chou B, Ayhan B. Enhancing stereo image formation and depth map estimation for Mastcam images. In: 2018 9th IEEE Annual Ubiquitous Computing, Electronics & Mobile Communication Conference (UEMCON). 2018. pp. 566-572

[11] Qin R, Kwan C, Ayhan B. Generation of stereo images for Mastcam imagers. In: Algorithms, Technologies, and Applications for Multispectral and Hyperspectral Imagery XXVI. Bellingham, Washington, USA: SPIE; 2020. p. 1139207

[12] Ayhan B, Kwan C. Mastcam image resolution enhancement with application to disparity map generation for stereo images with different resolutions. Sensors. 2019;**19**:3526

[13] Boyle R. NASA Uses Microsoft's HoloLens and ProtoSpace to Build its Next Mars Rover in Augmented Reality. Seattle, Washington, USA: GeekWire; 2018. Available from: https://www.geekwire.com/2016/nasa-uses-microsoft-hololens-build-mars-rover-augmented-reality/

[14] Kwan C, Chou B, Ayhan B. Stereo image and depth map generation for images with different views and resolutions. In: 2018 9th IEEE Annual

Ubiquitous Computing, Electronics & Mobile Communication Conference (UEMCON). 2018. pp. 573-579

[15] Triggs B, McLauchlan PF, Hartley RI, Fitzgibbon AW. Bundle adjustment—A modern synthesis. In: Vision Algorithms: Theory and Practice. Springer; 2000. pp. 298-372

[16] Lin T-Y, Belongie S, Hays J. Cross-view image geolocalization. In: Proceedings of the IEEE Conference on Computer Vision and Pattern Recognition. 2013. pp. 891-898

[17] Tian Y, Chen C, Shah M. Cross-view image matching for geo-localization in urban environments. In: Proceedings of the IEEE Conference on Computer Vision and Pattern Recognition. 2017. pp. 3608-3616

[18] Castaldo F, Zamir A, Angst R, Palmieri F, Savarese S. Semantic cross-view matching. In: Proceedings of the IEEE International Conference on Computer Vision Workshops. 2015. pp. 9-17

[19] Gruen A, Akca D. Least squares 3D surface and curve matching. ISPRS Journal of Photogrammetry and Remote Sensing. 2005;**59**:151-174

[20] Rusinkiewicz S, Levoy M. "efficient variants of the ICP algorithm," in 3-D digital imaging and Modeling. In: Proceedings. Third International Conference on, 2001. 2001. pp. 145-152

[21] Kazhdan M, Bolitho M, Hoppe H. Poisson surface reconstruction. In: Proceedings of the Fourth Eurographics Symposium on Geometry Processing. 2006

[22] Tran S, Davis L. 3D surface reconstruction using graph cuts with surface constraints. In: European Conference on Computer Vision. 2006. pp. 219-231

[23] Labatut P, Pons JP, Keriven R. Robust and efficient surface reconstruction from range data. In: Computer Graphics Forum. Hoboken, New Jersey, US: Wiley; 2009. pp. 2275-2290

[24] Kerl C, Sturm J, Cremers D. Dense visual SLAM for RGB-D cameras. In: 2013 IEEE/RSJ International Conference on Intelligent Robots and Systems. New York, US: IEEE; 2013. pp. 2100-2106

[25] Waechter M, Moehrle N, Goesele M. Let there be color! Large-scale texturing of 3D reconstructions. In: European Conference on Computer Vision. 2014. pp. 836-850

[26] Qin R. Automated 3D recovery from very high resolution multi-view satellite images. In: ASPRS (IGTF) Annual Conference, March 12–16, Baltimore, Maryland, USA. 2017. p. 10

[27] Qin R. RPC stereo processor (RSP) – a software package for digital surface model and orthophoto generation from satellite stereo imagery. In: ISPRS Annals of Photogrammetry, Remote Sensing and Spatial Information Sciences, Vol. (to Appear in ISPRS Congress July 2016). 2016

[28] Qin R. A critical analysis of satellite stereo pairs for digital surface model generation and a matching quality prediction model. ISPRS Journal of Photogrammetry and Remote Sensing. 2019;**154**:139-150

[29] Hirschmüller H. Stereo processing by semiglobal matching and mutual information. IEEE Transactions on Pattern Analysis and Machine Intelligence. 2008;**30**:328-341

[30] Qin R. Change detection on LOD 2 building models with very high resolution spaceborne stereo imagery. ISPRS Journal of Photogrammetry and Remote Sensing. 2014;**96**:179-192

[31] N. Snavely, "Bundler: Structure from Motion (SFM) for Unordered Image Collections," Available online: phototour. cs. washington. edu/bundler/ (accessed on 12 July 2013), 2010

[32] Snavely N, Seitz SM, Szeliski R. Skeletal graphs for efficient structure from motion. In: 2008 IEEE Conference on Computer Vision and Pattern Recognition. 2008. pp. 1-8

[33] Lowe DG. Distinctive image features from scale-invariant keypoints. International Journal of Computer Vision. 2004;**60**:91-110

[34] Bay H, Tuytelaars T, Van Gool L. Surf: Speeded up robust features. In: Computer Vision–ECCV 2006. New York, US: Springer; 2006. pp. 404-417

[35] Rublee E, Rabaud V, Konolige K, Bradski G. ORB: An efficient alternative to SIFT or SURF. In: 2011 International Conference on Computer Vision. 2011. pp. 2564-2571

[36] Mur-Artal R, Tardós JD. Orb-slam2: An open-source slam system for monocular, stereo, and rgb-d cameras. IEEE Transactions on Robotics. 2017;**33**: 1255-1262

[37] Fischler MA, Bolles RC. Random sample consensus: A paradigm for model fitting with applications to image analysis and automated cartography. Communications of the ACM. 1981;**24**: 381-395

[38] Förstner W, Wrobel BP. Photogrammetric Computer Vision. 1st ed. New York, US: Springer International Publishing; 2016

[39] Nocedal J, Wright S. Numerical Optimization. New York, US: Springer Science & Business Media; 2006

[40] Gruen A, Beyer HA. System calibration through self-calibration. In: Gruen TSHA, editor. Calibration and Orientation of Cameras in Computer Vision. Vol. 34. New York, US: Springer; 2001. -163, 193

[41] Lepetit V, Moreno-Noguer F, Fua P. Epnp: An accurate o (n) solution to the pnp problem. International Journal of Computer Vision. 2009;**81**:155

[42] Qin R, Fang W. A hierarchical building detection method for very high resolution remotely sensed images combined with DSM using graph cut optimization. Photogrammetry Engineering and Remote Sensing. 2014; **80**:37-48

[43] Vincent L. Morphological grayscale reconstruction in image analysis: Applications and efficient algorithms. IEEE Transactions on Image Processing. 1993;**2**:176-201

[44] Carlson TN, Ripley DA. On the relation between NDVI, fractional vegetation cover, and leaf area index. Remote Sensing of Environment. 1997; **62**:241-252

[45] Tremeau A, Borel N. A region growing and merging algorithm to color segmentation. Pattern Recognition. 1997;**30**:1191-1203

[46] Fabbri R, Costa LDF, Torelli JC, Bruno OM. 2D Euclidean distance transform algorithms: A comparative survey. ACM Computing Surveys (CSUR). 2008;**40**:1-44

[47] Meijster A, Roerdink JB, Hesselink WH. A general algorithm for computing distance transforms in linear time. In: Mathematical Morphology and its Applications to Image and Signal Processing. New York, US: Springer; 2002. pp. 331-340

[48] Boykov Y, Veksler O, Zabih R. Fast approximate energy minimization via graph cuts. IEEE Transactions on Pattern Analysis and Machine Intelligence. 2001;**23**:1222-1239

[49] Orlin JB. Max flows in O (nm) time, or better. In: Proceedings of the Forty-Fifth Annual ACM Symposium on Theory of Computing. 2013. pp. 765-774

[50] S. Clark. (2020. The Surface Grower Algorithm. Available from: http://www.cs.carleton.edu/cs_comps/0405/shape/surface_grower.html

[51] Van Kreveld M, Schwarzkopf O, de Berg M, Overmars M. Computational Geometry Algorithms and Applications. New York, US: Springer; 2000

[52] Fabri A, Pion S. CGAL: The computational geometry algorithms library. In: Proceedings of the 17th ACM SIGSPATIAL International Conference on Advances in Geographic Information Systems. 2009. pp. 538-539

[53] D. Cernea, OpenMVS: Open Multiple View Stereovision, 2015. Available from: https://openmvg.readthedocs.io/en/latest/software/MVS/OpenMVS/

[54] Goldberg AV, Hed S, Kaplan H, Tarjan RE, Werneck RF. Maximum flows by incremental breadth-first search. In: European Symposium on Algorithms. 2011. pp. 457-468

[55] Lempitsky V, Boykov Y, Ivanov D. Oriented visibility for multiview reconstruction. In: European Conference on Computer Vision. 2006. pp. 226-238

[56] Pérez P, Gangnet M, Blake A. Poisson image editing. In: ACM Transactions on Graphics (TOG). Vol. 22. New York, US: ACM Publications; 2003. pp. 313-318

Section 5

Digital Terrain Model and Digital Surface Model Generation

Chapter 8

Practical Digital Terrain Model Extraction Using Image Inpainting Techniques

Chiman Kwan, David Gribben, Bulent Ayhan and Jude Larkin

Abstract

In some applications such as construction planning and land surveying, an accurate digital terrain model (DTM) is essential. However, in urban and sub-urban areas, the terrain may be covered by trees and man-made structures. Although digital surface model (DSM) obtained by radar or LiDAR can provide a general idea of the terrain, the presence of trees, buildings, etc. conceals the actual terrain elevation. Normally, the process of extracting DTM involves a land cover classification followed by a trimming step that removes the elevation due to trees and buildings. In this chapter, we assume the land cover types have been classified and we focus on the use of image inpainting algorithms for DTM generation. That is, for buildings and trees, we remove those pixels from the DSM and then apply inpainting techniques to reconstruct the terrain pixels in those areas. A dataset with DSM and hyperspectral data near the U. Houston area was used in our study. The DTM from United States Geological Survey (USGS) was used as the ground truth. Objective evaluation results indicate that some inpainting methods perform better than others.

Keywords: digital terrain model (DTM), digital surface model (DSM), image inpainting, vegetation extraction, land classification

1. Introduction

There are several ways to obtain DTM. The oldest method is to do this manually by measuring the terrain elevations of some selected points of a given area. The process is time-consuming, tedious, and prone to human errors. In recent years, people have started to use LiDAR to generate DTM. The obtained DTM is in general satisfactory even though the point density may not be very dense as compared to optical stereo imaging approach [1]. Radar has been used as well. It is well known that LiDAR and radar equipment are expensive. Due to availability of low-cost drones, stereo imaging has been gaining popularity. Near infrared (NIR) together with color imagers have been used in recent years to generate DSM. However, due to the presence of vegetation and buildings, some additional processing steps are needed in order to obtain DTM from DSM.

In recent years, hyperspectral images [2–4] are gaining popularity in various applications, including anomaly detection [5–7], target classification [8, 9], search and rescue operations [10], and many others. Due to the availability of hundreds of contiguous spectral bands, accuracies of anomaly detection and target classification have been improved quite significantly. Hyperspectral images can also be used for accurate land cover classification [11–16]. Many methods have been developed in the past [17–19] for target detection in hyperspectral images. It will be ideal that hyperspectral images are available for land cover classification so that more accurate DTM can be obtained. However, equipment cost, requirement on data storage, and computational burden are limiting the widespread usage of hyperspectral imagers.

In contrast, low-cost color and NIR images are relatively inexpensive, have low computational cost, and low data storage. If one is given only color (RGB) and near infrared (NIR) images, however, it will be difficult to obtain accurate land cover classification for the following reasons. First, the accuracy of using only RGB and NIR bands for land cover classification is low as compared to that of using hyperspectral images. This point will be clear later in Section 3. Improving land cover classification using only color and NIR images will be a good contribution to the community. In recent years, there are some new developments along this direction. In particular, people have developed methods to synthesize spectral bands from color and NIR images. One technique is known as Extended Morphological Attribute Profile (EMAP) [20]. Several notable applications have appeared in the literature [16, 17]. Second, even after the pixels related to trees and man-made structures are identified and removed from the DSM, we still need to face an important practical issue. How can one recover the missing terrain pixels in the DSM to build a DTM? Conventional approaches use simple interpolation such as bilinear or bicubic interpolations [1]. However, the accuracy of DTM may be compromised. In recent years, there have been new developments in interpolation methods, termed as image inpainting methods. Those recent methods can be categorized into several groups. The first group is similar to bicubic interpolation methods. Some representative methods include bicubic, Laplacian [21], and inpaint-nans [22]. The second group uses nonlocal sparse representation for inpainting. Well-known methods include Local Matrix Completion Sparse (LMCS) [23], field of expert (FOE) [24], and Transformic [25]. The last group is the deep learning-based methods. One representative method is known as generative inpainting (GenIn) [26].

In this chapter, we propose a low-cost and accurate approach to DTM generation. Suppose we are given a DSM and only the color and NIR images. Our approach consists of four steps. First, we perform land cover classification using only color and NIR images. Various methods can be applied in this step. The key innovation is to apply synthetic spectral bands to enhance the land cover performance. It was demonstrated that the land cover performance using synthetic bands can yield performance very close to that of the hyperspectral image. Second, since there may be more than 10 types of land covers, we observed that it is more accurate to consolidate some of the land cover types into only five groups. Third, the trees and man-made structures are then removed from the DSM. Fourth, various conventional and deep learning inpainting methods are applied to generate the DTM. Comparisons show that GenIn has consistent performance in DTM construction.

This chapter is organized as follows. In Section 2, we will briefly review the methods and data. Section 3 will discuss the land cover classification results and how we consolidate 15 land cover types into only five groups. Section 4 focuses on the various DTM reconstruction results. Finally, some concluding remarks will be given in Section 5.

2. Methods and data

2.1 Land cover classification methods

In this research, we have used the following nine methods for land cover classification. We will not go into the details of each method. Instead, we briefly list the names and provide some references for their sources.

We categorize the methods into three groups. In the first group are simple and efficient methods, including Matched Subspace Detection (MSD) [18], Adaptive Subspace Detection (ASD) [18], and Reed-Xiaoli Detection (RXD) [19]. These methods have been used in hyperspectral image processing in the past. In the second group are kernel versions of the first group and they are: Kernel MSD (KMSD) [18], Kernel ASD (KASD) [18], and Kernel RXD (KRXD) [19]. The kernel-based algorithms are computationally expensive and may not be suitable for real-time applications. The third group contains Sparse Representation (SR) [27] algorithm, Joint Sparse Representation (JSR) [27] algorithm, and Support Vector Machine (SVM) [28, 29] algorithm. In the past, we have used the above three methods in group 3 for soil detection using multispectral images [27].

2.2 Inpainting methods

We have applied seven methods in this project. They are briefly summarized below:

Bicubic: in a recent paper by researchers at Cyprus, a bicubic interpolation method was used in [1].

Inpaint_nans: we denote this as "inpaint" in our later experiments. This method was developed by D'Errico [22]. This is a very simple method that only uses the neighboring pixels to estimate the missing pixels, which will be referred as NaNs (not a number).

FOE: the Field of Experts method (FOE) was developed by Roth [24]. This method uses pre-trained models that are used to filter out noise and obstructions in images.

Laplacian: this method [21] fills in each missing pixel using the Laplacian interpolation formula by finding the mean of the surrounding known values.

Local Matrix Completion Sparse (LMCS) [23]: in LMCS, which was developed by us, a search is performed for each missing pixel to find a pixel with the most similar neighbors. After the search, the missing pixel is replaced with the found pixel. This method performs very well with images containing repeating patterns.

Transformic: the Transformic method was developed by Mansfield [25]. It is similar to the LMCS in that it searches the whole image for a patch that is similar to the neighbors of the missing pixel.

Generative Inpainting (GenIn) [26]: a new inpainting method, Generative Inpainting (GenIn), which is a deep learning-based method [26], was considered in our research. It was developed at the University of Illinois and aims to outperform typical deep learning methods that use convolutional neural network (CNN) models. GenIn builds on CNN and Generative Adversarial Networks (GANs) in an effort to encourage cohesion between created and existing pixels.

2.3 EMAP

In this section, we briefly introduce EMAP, which has been shown to yield good classification performance when one only has a few spectral bands available. Given an input grayscale image f and a sequence of threshold levels $\{Th_1,,Th_2,,...Th_n\}$, the attribute profile (AP) of f is obtained by applying a sequence of thinning and thickening attribute transformations to every pixel in f as follows:

$$AP(f)=\{\phi_1(f),\ \phi_2(f),\ ...\phi_n(f), f,\ \gamma_1(f),\ \gamma_2(f),\ ...\gamma_n(f)\} \quad (1)$$

where ϕ_i and $\gamma_i\ (i=1,,2,,...n)$ are the thickening and thinning operators at threshold Th_i, respectively. The EMAP of f is then acquired by stacking two or more APs using any feature reduction technique on multispectral/hyperspectral images, such as purely geometric attributes (e.g., area, length of the perimeter, image moments, shape factors), or textural attributes (e.g., range, standard deviation, entropy).

$$EMAP(f)=\{AP_1(f),\ AP_2(f)...AP_m(f)\} \quad (2)$$

More technical details about EMAP can be found in [20, 30–32]. In this work, the "area (a)" and "length of the diagonal of the bounding box (d)" attributes of EMAP [17] were used. The lambda parameters for the area attribute of EMAP, which is a sequence of thresholds used by the morphological attribute filters, were set to 10 and 15, respectively. The lambda parameters for the length attribute of EMAP were set to 50, 100, and 500. With this parameter setting, EMAP creates 11 synthetic bands for a given single band image. One of the bands comes from the original image.

2.4 IEEE dataset

From the IEEE GRSS Data Fusion package [11], we obtained the ground truth classification maps, the hyperspectral image of the University of Houston area, and the LiDAR data of the same area. The instrument used to collect the dataset is simply a hyperspectral and LiDAR sensor. The hyperspectral image contains 144 bands ranging in wavelength from 380 to 1050 nm with spatial resolution of 0.25 m. The LiDAR sensor has the same spatial resolution of 0.25 m.

As shown in **Table 1**, there are a number of datasets used for analysis. The first group is the RGB (band # 60, 30, 22 in the hyperspectral data) and the NIR band (band #103). It should be noted that the above selection of bands is not the same as band selection in the literature [33]. In band selection, the objective is to select the most informative bands out of the available hyperspectral bands. In our case, we are restricted to only having a few bands. We call this group Dataset-4 (DS-4). The second group is the four band group put through EMAP augmentation to produce 44 bands as each band produces 10 other bands in addition to the original band

Dataset label	Bands present in the corresponding dataset
Dataset-4 (DS-4)	RGB and the NIR bands (respectively bands # 60, # 30, # 22, and # 103 in the hyperspectral data)
Dataset-44 (DS-44)	RGB and the NIR bands. Forty bands obtained by EMAP augmentation applied to RGB and the NIR bands
Dataset-144 (DS-144)	Hyperspectral dataset

Table 1.
Dataset labels and the corresponding bands.

[denoted as Dataset-44 (DS-44)]. The third group is the full hyperspectral image of 144 bands [denoted as Dataset-144 (DS-144)].

3. Consolidation of the number of land cover classes

Before studying the performance of inpainting techniques on the IEEE GRSS Data Fusion dataset, in order to create a consensus about the best classification method, the number of classes was reduced from 15 to 5. As shown in **Table 1**, the first three grass classes (Healthy, Stressed, and Synthetic) were consolidated into simply grass; tree, soil, and water maintained their individual classifications; and then all other classes were grouped into one class as man-made structures. This was done simply because some of the man-made classes—road, highway, railway, and both parking lots—were consistently misclassified and often as the other classes in this group. The same is true for the grass classes. By consolidating the classes, the classification method selection process was made easier. The averages listed in **Table 2** are a summation of all non-kernel methods averages. This is shown to illustrate how low performing some types are even among the high-performing methods.

Table 3, extracted from a recent work [34], corresponds to the accuracy for the full 15 class models while **Table 4** is for consolidated 5 classes. Comparing the two tables, it can be seen that the new class combination results in much improved results in all cases. Each method has an overall improvement of at least 13% and most methods saw an improvement of over 20%. It is clear from **Table 4** that JSR clearly stands out as the best performing method. JSR goes from being the best performing method in one band case to every band case as well as overall average when using the new class arrangement. Yet, every band case of JSR returns over 90% accuracy, when previously the smaller number band cases returned results near 50%.

New class #	Class type	Class #	Avg. accuracy (5)
1	Healthy grass	1	72.93
	Stressed grass	2	56.67
	Synthetic grass	3	91.90
2	Tree	4	70.98
3	Soil	5	82.99
4	Water	6	61.29
5	Residential	7	54.82
	Commercial	8	48.16
	Road	9	39.23
	Highway	10	43.00
	Railway	11	45.20
	Parking lot 1	12	36.94
	Parking lot 2	13	36.69
	Tennis court	14	64.03
	Running track	15	94.22

Table 2.
Combining classes down from 15 classes to 5 classes and the average accuracy of each class.

OA	DS-4 (%)	DS-44 (%)	DS-144 (%)	Avg. (%)
ASD	22.59	22.75	21.11	22.15
MSD	0.11	48.65	55.56	34.77
RXD	28.93	46.09	42.69	39.24
KASD	6.16	79.70	53.57	46.48
KMSD	26.32	69.26	53.61	49.73
KRXD	5.72	64.14	71.79	47.22
SR	39.99	64.45	57.46	53.97
JSR	59.83	80.77	72.57	71.06
SVM	70.43	82.64	78.68	77.25

Table 3.
Overall accuracies using 15 classifications of the 9 classification methods and each band combination.

OA	DS-4 (%)	DS-44 (%)	DS-144 (%)	Avg. (%)
ASD	47.17	69.89	65.75	60.94
MSD	63.31	71.32	81.94	72.19
RXD	57.50	68.98	62.29	62.92
KASD	42.67	94.50	82.64	73.27
KMSD	63.53	91.87	75.18	76.86
KRXD	45.62	86.35	88.40	73.46
SR	55.11	90.61	85.50	77.07
JSR	**93.15**	**94.55**	**93.84**	**93.85**
SVM	91.59	92.25	87.72	90.52

Bold numbers indicate the best performing method of each column.

Table 4.
Overall accuracies using five classes for the nine classification methods and each band combination.

It should be noted that the results related to the 44-band (DS-44) case are observed to perform better than the 4-band (DS-4) and 144-band (DS-144) cases. It may be easier to understand why DS-44 is better than DS-4. A simple explanation is that the DS-44 data contain some synthetic spectral information, which enriches the spectral content. The explanation for why DS-144 case is worse than DS-44 case is because there are a lot of redundancies in the various bands in the DS-144 data. The data redundancies appear to cause some conflicts in the classifiers. Other researchers have observed similar behaviors [11] before and sometimes they call this the curse of dimension.

4. DTM extraction by removing man-made structures and trees

4.1 Ground truth DTM

The ground truth being used is the 1/9 arc second-resolution Digital Elevation map produced by USGS. Additional maps used for comparison in this investigation are the Cloth Simulation Filter (CSF) method [35] and the 1 arc second-resolution USGS DE map. However, CSF and USGS can only be used for general comparison as their inputs are not dependent on the different numbers of bands. CSF simply uses the LiDAR image while USGS is an already completed product. The three DTMs are shown in **Figure 1**. It can be seen that the USGS 1/9 arc second map is more accurate.

4.2 Individual inpainting results

The different methods used to compare digital terrain models (DTMs) through inpainting were "inpaint_nans," "LMCS," "Laplacian," "Transformic," and "CSF." However, CSF must be considered separate from others as it is not dependent on the same image bands that the other inpainting techniques are dependent on. In this study, the best resolution (1/9 arc second) USGS satellite radar imagery was used as the ground truth.

With a consistently well-performing method available for the composition of DTMs, which is JSR, we now look at the performance of inpainting methods judging against a general ground truth of the USGS Digital Elevation maps. Our goal is to remove Class 2 (trees) and Class 5 (manmade structures) from the DSM. The missing pixels will be interpolated by using inpainting techniques. The names of the methods tested against this ground truth were: inpaint_nans, LMCS, Laplace, Transformic, and FOE. There is also the added variation of downsizing the image four times versus maintaining the full-size image to demonstrate affected accuracy because the downsized results save considerable time.

After JSR classifier is applied to the EMAP images (DS-44) and the man-made objects areas are identified by JSR, these identified man-made and trees areas are removed from the LiDAR image (DSM). Inpainting techniques are then applied to those missing pixel areas in the LiDAR image. The filled-in LiDAR image with inpainting methods corresponds to the estimated DTM. **Figure 2** contains the DTMs, generated from the four times downsized DS-44 EMAP images for each method (excluding CSF). The purpose of downsizing by four times was because of computational issues. It took many hours to finish the inpainting for some of the methods. The images from **Figure 2** can be compared to the ground truth and fully produced products of CSF and the lower resolution USGS. The LMCS results have issues near the boundary of the image because LMCS cannot handle missing pixels near the image boundary.

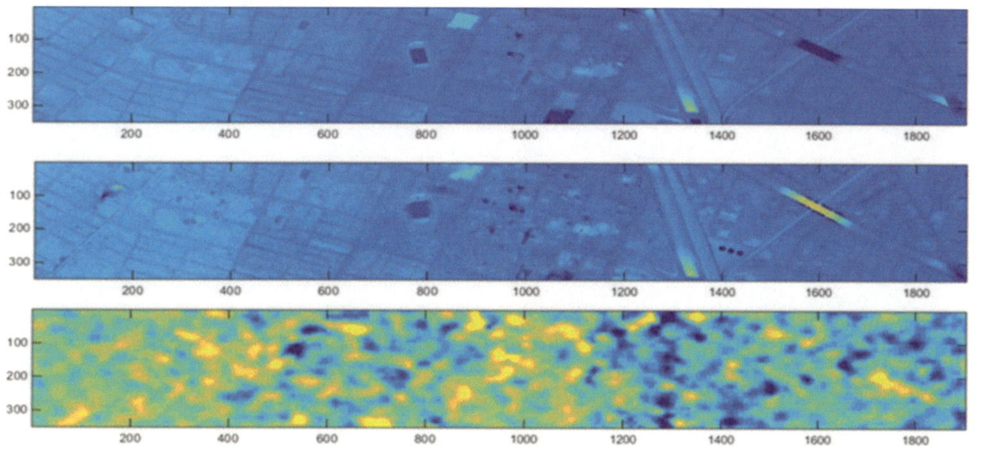

Figure 1.
USGS 1/9 arc second resolution (top), CSF (middle), and USGS 1 arc second-resolution (bottom) DTMs.

Figure 1 displays the full-size ground truth maps. **Figure 3** contains the estimated DTMs using full-size DS-44 EMAP images. The inpainting maps in **Figure 2** and **Figure 3** can also be compared against **Figure 1**.

Clearly the lower resolution USGS image is not a great product to use for the digital terrain map. However, it is useful to show a low-resolution picture of what the Houston area could look like without classification and inpainting.

To find an objective statistical proof of accuracy of the different inpainting methods, there are five different metrics that can be used. By taking the difference between the DTM of a given inpainting method and the ground truth map (USGS)—then calculating mean, standard deviation, root mean squared, and the min and max of each instance—we can find a general standard of accuracy for each method. The visual observation from LMCS shows that performance is poor on the edges of each map, as is expected given that it does not calculate any inpainting on the edges. The same can also be said to a lesser extent of inpaint_nans. To help alleviate that inaccuracy, a cropped comparison of downsized and full-size versions is conducted for all methods, which gets rid of these problematic areas on the edges.

The performance metrics for the DS-44 case can be seen in **Table 5**. In the DS-44 case, we observe that two techniques, Laplacian and Transformic, performed better than the rest. While Transformic's mean value is the smallest, the other four metrics have better values in Laplacian. For comparison purposes, the performance metrics for the CSF method and USGS lower resolution elevation map are also included in **Table 6**. Overall, CSF performs pretty well for the mean; however, because of the non-removed bridge, all other metrics are relatively poor performing. The 1 arc second resolution USGS image performs poorly in all accuracy categories. It can be

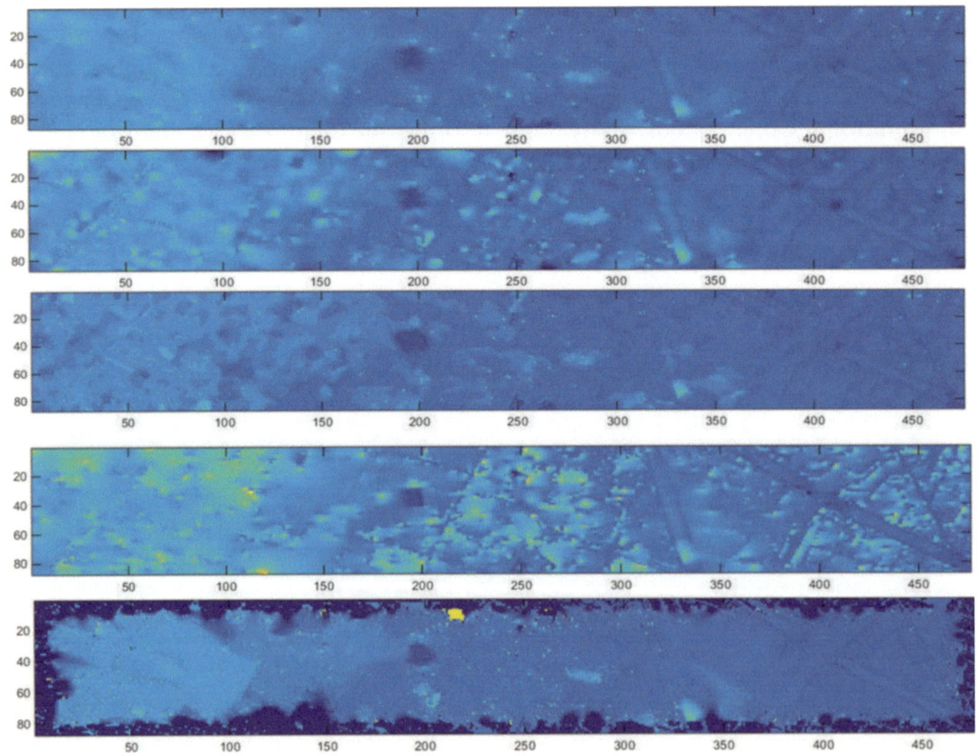

Figure 2.
DTMs generated from the four times downsized DS-44 EMAP images: first row: Laplace; second row: inpaint_ nans; third row: Transformic; fourth row: FOE; and fifth row: LMCS.

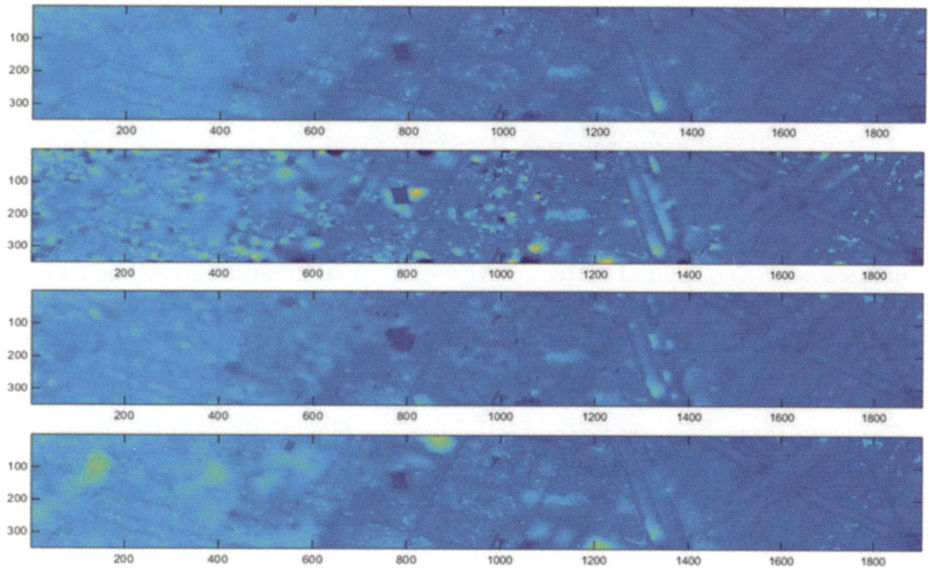

Figure 3.
DTMs generated from the full-size DS-44 EMAP images. We could not generate LMCS, which took many days and we stopped the program. First row: Laplace; second row: inpaint_nans; third row: Transformic; fourth row: FOE.

	Inpaint_nans	LMCS	Laplacian	Transformic	FOE
Mean	0.39	0.24	0.34	**0.08**	0.38
Sigma	0.74	0.82	**0.58**	0.67	0.64
RMS	0.84	0.85	**0.67**	**0.67**	0.74
Min	**−3.43**	−11.87	**−3.43**	−3.55	**−3.43**
Max	6.38	18.45	**6.30**	6.56	6.60

Bold numbers indicate the best performing method of each row.

Table 5.
Mean, standard deviation (sigma), root mean square (RMS), min, and max accuracy results using five inpainting methods for the DS-44 case.

also noticed from **Table 6** that these values for CSF and USGS are worse than the best performing individual cases that are shown in **Table 5**.

4.3 Fusion of different inpainting results

In an effort to improve the inpainting performance metrics, three different fusion methods are utilized. The pixel level fusion methods were used in [36]. For the first fusion method, alpha trimmed mean filter (ATMF), the worst and best performing methods for a given accuracy measurement are removed and then the three in-between results are averaged before re-taking the accuracy measurements to see how the results were improved. The second fusion method, weighted method, weighs each method based on a specific accuracy measurement and averages those results. The final fusion method, F3, simply averages the three best performing methods for each accuracy measurement.

In order to perform these operations, it was necessary to rank each of the methods based on the three main accuracy measurements: mean, standard deviation

(STD, also denoted in other tables as sigma), and root mean squared (RMS). This was done for exclusively DS-44 results. It includes both the full-sized results and the four times down-sampled results. **Table 7** shows the performance rankings for various combinations of band number with respect to three performance metrics: mean, sigma, and root mean squared (RMS). From the results in **Table 7**, it is clear that overall the downsized results return much more accurate values than the full-sized values in most cases.

Table 8 shows the performance metrics for the DS-44 case when three different fusion methods were applied to the best five individual inpainting methods' results where the ranking was conducted with respect to three performance metrics separately (mean, STD, and RMS). F3 produces the lowest mean value and relatively lower sigma and RMS values in comparison to others.

Table 9 shows the performance metrics for the special case (which we name as combo) when three different fusion methods are applied to the best five individual inpainting methods' results from both 44-bands inpainting results where the ranking is conducted with respect to three performance metrics separately (mean, STD, and RMS). In this case, F3 method produces lower mean, sigma, and RMS values with respect to ranking according to the mean performance metric.

Table 10 shows a summary of the best performing individual cases (no fusion) and the best performing cases with fusion for DS-44 case with fusion. From **Table 10**, it can be noticed that the F3 (with respect to ranking according to lowest mean) improves the RMS value slightly when compared with the RMS values of the best performing individual inpainting method results (Laplacian and Transformic in DS-44). However, when all performance metrics are considered as a whole, we cannot clearly state F3 performs the best in all performance accuracy metrics but improves a few of the parameters.

	CSF	USGS 1 arc second
Mean	0.37	4.70
Sigma	1.02	3.10
RMS	1.08	5.63
Min	−5.81	−7.83
Max	15.98	19.04

Table 6.
Accuracy values for CSF and USGS lower resolution map.

Mean			STD			RMS		
Rank	Method	Value	Rank	Method	Value	Rank	Method	Value
1	4 × T	0.08	1	4 × LP	0.58	1	4 × LP	0.67
2	4 × LMCS	0.24	2	4 × FOE	0.64	2	4 × T	0.67
3	4 × LP	0.34	3	Full T	0.65	3	4 × FOE	0.74
4	4 × FOE	0.38	4	4 × nans	0.74	4	4 × nans	0.84
5	4 × nans	0.39	5	4 × LMCS	0.82	5	4 × LMCS	0.85

Transformic is T and Laplacian is LP.

Table 7.
Ranking results for various combinations of band number and accuracy measurement for DS-44 case.

ATMF				Weighted				F3			
DS-44	**Mean**	**STD**	**RMS**	**DS-44**	**Mean**	**STD**	**RMS**	**DS-44**	**Mean**	**STD**	**RMS**
Mean	0.58	0.64	0.56	Mean	0.29	0.51	0.44	Mean	0.22	0.62	0.53
Sigma	0.68	0.67	0.67	Sigma	0.60	0.60	0.60	Sigma	0.61	0.67	0.67
RMS	0.89	0.93	0.87	RMS	0.67	0.79	0.75	RMS	0.64	0.91	0.86
Min	−5.85	−3.47	−3.50	Min	−4.46	−4.36	−4.46	Min	−5.93	−3.50	−3.54
Max	6.77	6.75	6.68	Max	6.37	6.42	6.36	Max	6.40	6.61	6.61

From left to right, ATMF, weighted, and fusion 3; methods for combining generated DTM maps for DS-44 case.

Table 8.
Performance metrics based on fusion algorithms.

ATMF				Weighted				F3			
Combo	Mean	STD	RMS	Combo	Mean	STD	RMS	Combo	Mean	STD	RMS
Mean	0.61	0.35	0.25	Mean	0.29	0.56	0.73	Mean	0.22	0.66	0.56
Sigma	0.70	0.61	0.63	Sigma	0.60	0.62	0.70	Sigma	0.61	0.68	0.68
RMS	0.93	0.70	0.68	RMS	0.67	0.84	1.01	RMS	0.64	0.95	0.88
Min	−5.83	−3.39	−3.45	Min	−4.46	−3.42	−4.12	Min	−5.93	−3.38	−3.43
Max	7.55	6.62	6.48	Max	6.37	6.85	7.03	Max	6.40	7.55	7.44

From left to right, ATMF, weighted, and fusion 3; methods for combining generated DTM maps for both band instances.

Table 9.
Accuracy values.

4.4 Comparison with deep learning inpainting

Using the pre-trained model provided by the GenIn package [26] for an image the size of about 350 by 1900 pixels (that covers the University of Houston campus and surrounding area), the computation time observed is roughly 2 minutes.

The accuracy of the GenIn model as compared to the other inpainting techniques is competitive and, cases, if not overall, is a more accurate result. In **Table 11**, statistics from GenIn together with the statistics from other inpainting techniques for the IEEE dataset are provided. In regards to mean, root mean square (RMS), and the maximum difference (max), GenIn outperforms all other techniques. For the sigma metric, it is the second-best performing method. The minimum difference accuracy measure is the only underperforming value coming in as the fourth best performing statistic. However, it is still the second-best value available, closely trailing the other three techniques.

It is also helpful to visualize GenIn's digital terrain map estimation as compared to the ground truth. In **Figure 4**, an image of the U. Houston area can be observed after GenIn is applied on that area's LiDAR data. **Figure 5** corresponds to the USGS 1/9 arc second Digital Elevation map that is used as the ground truth for the area.

The GenIn-generated results are found to be a very close reproduction of the ground truth. In some instances, it is observed that it provides more realistic results than the ground truth. As an example, in the horizontal right and vertical center

	No fusion		With fusion
Metric	**Best DS-44 (Laplacian)**	**Best DS-44 (Transformic)**	**Best DS-44 (F3-mean)**
Mean	0.34	**0.08**	0.22
Sigma	**0.58**	0.67	0.61
RMS	0.67	0.67	**0.64**
Min	**−3.43**	−3.55	−5.93
Max	**6.30**	6.56	6.40

Bold numbers indicate the best performing method of each row.

Table 10.
Summary of the best performing individual and fusion cases.

4 × crop	Inpaint-nans	LMCS	Laplacian	Transformic	FOE	GenIn
Mean	0.39	0.24	0.34	0.08	0.38	**0.23**
Sigma	0.74	0.82	0.58	0.67	0.64	0.59
RMS	0.84	0.85	0.67	0.67	0.74	**0.63**
Min	−3.43	−11.87	−3.43	−3.55	−3.43	−3.50
Max	6.38	18.45	6.30	6.56	6.60	**6.29**

Bold numbers indicate the best performing method of each row.

Table 11.
Comparison of GenIn statistics with respect to other inpainting methods' performances for IEEE dataset.

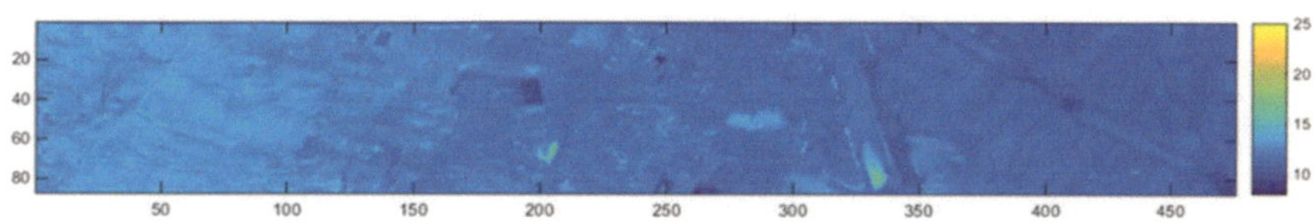

Figure 4.
GenIn digital terrain map for the U. Houston (UH) area. Scale is from 8 to 25 m.

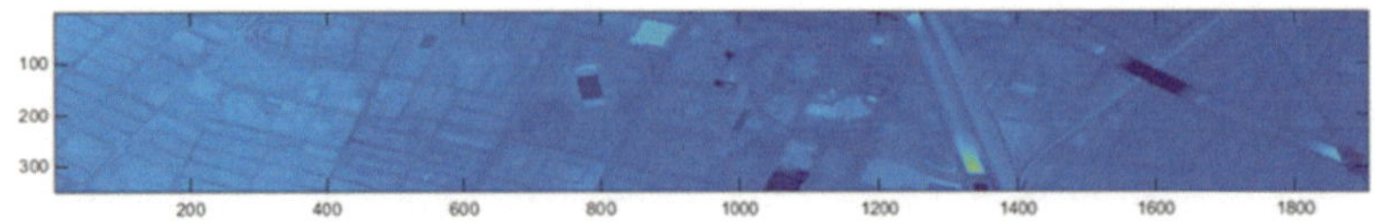

Figure 5.
USGS 1/9 arc second digital elevation map for the UH area. Scale is from 8 to 25 m.

of the plot in **Figure 5**, there is a deep dark spot that is observed, which is to be denoted as a low spot. However, this is caused because of a highway bridge that runs over a railway and could be considered a miscalculated section of the Digital Elevation map. The GenIn-generated map produces no such deep dark spot and instead smoothly removes the bridge and because it does this, it then slightly suffers in the resultant accuracy statistics.

5. Conclusions

In this research, we investigated the feasibility of using only color and NIR images for accurate DTM extraction. We assume the DSM is also available. Our approach involves several steps. The first step is to use color and NIR images for land cover classification. After some extensive experiments, it was observed that using only four bands cannot achieve accurate land cover classification. A morphological filtering approach was applied to generate synthetic spectral bands. Using nine land cover classification algorithms, it was observed that the use of synthetic bands significantly improved the land cover classification accuracy for the well-known IEEE dataset. The second step is to consolidate the many land cover types into only five groups. This was observed to further improve the accuracy. The third step is to apply nine inpainting algorithms to recover DTM from DSM. It was observed that the deep learning algorithm yielded more consistent performance.

Here, we also briefly mention a few future research directions. One direction is to focus on DSM generation using color images. The second direction is to obtain ortho-rectified images for the color and NIR images. A third direction is to build a software prototype that integrates DSM generation tool, ortho-rectification tool, land cover classification tool, and DTM reconstruction tool.

Acknowledgements

This research was supported by DOE under contract # DE-SC0019936.

Author details

Chiman Kwan*, David Gribben, Bulent Ayhan and Jude Larkin
Applied Research LLC, Rockville, MD, USA

*Address all correspondence to: chiman.kwan@signalpro.net

References

[1] Skarlatos D, Marinos V. Vegetation removal from UAV derived DSMS using combination of RGB and NIR imagery. ISPRS Annals of Photogrammetry, Remote Sensing and Spatial Information Sciences. 2018;**IV-2**:255-262

[2] Lee CM, Cable ML, Hook SJ, Green RO, Ustin SL, Mandl DJ, et al. An introduction to the NASA hyperspectral infrared imager (HyspIRI) mission and preparatory activities. Remote Sensing of Environment. 2015;**167**:6-19

[3] Zhou J, Kwan C, Budavari B. Hyperspectral image super-resolution: A hybrid color mapping approach. Journal of Applied Remote Sensing. 2016;**10**(3):035024

[4] Kwan C, Choi JH, Chan S, Zhou J, Budavari B. Resolution enhancement for hyperspectral images: A super-resolution and fusion approach. In: IEEE International Conference on Acoustics, Speech and Signal Processing (ICASSP). New Orleans, LA; 2017. pp. 6180-6184

[5] Wang W, Li S, Qi H, Ayhan B, Kwan C, Vance S. Identify anomaly component by sparsity and low rank. In: IEEE Workshop on Hyperspectral Image and Signal Processing: Evolution in Remote Sensor (WHISPERS); 2-5 June 2015; Tokyo, Japan. 2015

[6] Zhou J, Kwan C, Ayhan B, Eismann MT. A novel cluster kernel RX algorithm for anomaly and change detection using hyperspectral images. IEEE Transactions on Geoscience and Remote Sensing. 2016;**54**(11):6497-6504

[7] Qu Y, Qi Y, Ayhan B, Kwan C, Kidd R. Does multispectral/hyperspectral pansharpening improve the performance of anomaly detection? In: IEEE International Geoscience and Remote Sensing Symposium (IGARSS). 2017. pp. 6130-6133

[8] Zhou J, Kwan C, Ayhan B. Improved target detection for hyperspectral images using hybrid in-scene calibration. Journal of Applied Remote Sensing. 2017;**11**(3):035010

[9] Kwan C, Ayhan B, Chen G, Wang J, Ji B, Chang C-I. A novel approach for spectral unmixing, classification, and concentration estimation of chemical and biological agents. IEEE Transactions on Geoscience and Remote Sensing. 2006;**44**(2):409-419

[10] Eismann MT, Stocker AD, Nasrabadi NM. Automated hyperspectral cueing for civilian search and rescue. Proceedings of the IEEE. 2009;**97**(6):1031-1055

[11] Khodadadzadeh M, Li J, Prasad S, Plaza A. Fusion of hyperspectral and LiDAR remote sensing data using multiple feature learning. IEEE Journal of Selected Topics in Applied Earth Observations and Remote Sensing. 2015;**8**(6):2971-2983

[12] Kwan C, Ayhan B, Larkin J, Kwan LM, Bernabé S, Plaza A. Performance of change detection algorithms using heterogeneous images and extended multi-attribute profiles (EMAPs). Remote Sensing. 2019;**11**(20):2377

[13] Kwan C, Larkin J, Ayhan B, Kwan LM, Skarlatos D, Vlachos M. Performance comparison of different inpainting algorithms for accurate DTM generation. In: Geospatial Informatics X (Conference SI113). 2020. DOI: 10.1117/12.2557824

[14] Ayhan B, Kwan C, Kwan LM, Skarlatos D, Vlachos M. Deep learning models for accurate vegetation classification using RGB image only. In: Geospatial Informatics X (Conference SI113). 2020. DOI: 10.1117/12.2557833

[15] Ayhan B, Kwan C. Tree, shrub, and grass classification using only RGB images. Remote Sensing. 2020;**12**. DOI: 10.3390/rs12081333

[16] Ayhan B, Kwan C. Application of deep belief network to land cover classification using hyperspectral images. In: International Symposium on Neural Networks. 2017. pp. 269-276

[17] Dao M, Kwan C, Bernabé S, Plaza A, Koperski K. A joint sparsity approach to soil detection using expanded bands of WV-2 images. IEEE Geoscience and Remote Sensing Letters. Dec 2019;**16**(12):1869-1873

[18] Nasrabadi NM. Kernel-based spectral matched signal detectors for hyperspectral target detection. In: International Conference on Pattern Recognition and Machine Intelligence. Berlin, Heidelberg: Springer; 2007

[19] Kwon H, Nasrabadi NM. Kernel RX-algorithm: A nonlinear anomaly detector for hyperspectral imagery. IEEE Transactions on Geoscience and Remote Sensing. 2005;**43**(2):388-397

[20] Bernabé S, Marpu PR, Plaza A, Mura MD, Benediktsson JA. Spectral-spatial classification of multispectral images using kernel feature space representation. IEEE Geoscience and Remote Sensing Letters. 2014;**11**:288-292

[21] Doshkov D, Ndjiki-Nya P, Lakshman H, Köppel M, Wiegand T. Towards efficient intra prediction based on image inpainting methods. In: 28th Picture Coding Symposium. IEEE; 2010

[22] Inpaint_nans. Available from: https://www.mathworks.com/matlabcentral/fileexchange/4551-inpaint_nans

[23] Zhou J, Kwan C. High performance image completion using sparsity based algorithms. In: SPIE Commercial + Scientific Sensing and Imaging Conference. Orlando, FL; 2018

[24] Roth S, Black MJ. Fields of experts. International Journal of Computer Vision. 2009;**82**:205

[25] Mansfield A, Prasad M, Rother C, Sharp T, Pushmeet K, Van Gool L. Transforming image completion. In: The 22nd British Machine Vision Conference; 29 August-2 September 2011. 2011

[26] Yu J, Lin Z, Yang J, Shen X, Lu X, Huang T. Generative Image Inpainting with Contextual Attention. arXiv:1801.07892 [cs.CV]. 2018

[27] Dao M, Kwan C, Koperski K, Marchisio GA. Joint sparsity approach to tunnel activity monitoring using high resolution satellite images. In: IEEE Ubiquitous Computing, Electronics & Mobile Communication Conference. 2017. pp. 322-328

[28] Burges CA. Tutorial on support vector machines for pattern recognition. In: Data Mining and Knowledge Discovery. Boston: Kluwer Academic Publishers; 1998. pp. 121-167

[29] Qian T, Li X, Ayhan B, Xu R, Kwan C, Griffin T. Application of support vector machines to vapor detection and classification for environmental monitoring of spacecraft. In: Lecture Notes in Computer Science, LNCS 3973. New York: Springer; 2006. pp. 1216-1222

[30] Bernabé S, Marpu PR, Plaza A, Benediktsson JA. Spectral unmixing of multispectral satellite images with dimensionality expansion using morphological profiles. In: Proceedings of the SPIE Satellite Data Compression, Communications, and Processing VIII; 19 October 2012; San Diego, CA, USA. Vol. 8514. 2012. p. 85140Z

[31] Mura MD, Benediktsson JA, Waske B, Bruzzone L. Morphological attribute profiles for the analysis of

very high resolution images. IEEE Transactions on Geoscience and Remote Sensing. 2010;**48**:3747-3762

[32] Mura MD, Benediktsson JA, Waske B, Bruzzone L. Extended profiles with morphological attribute filters for the analysis of hyperspectral data. International Journal of Remote Sensing. 2010;**31**:5975-5991

[33] Sun W, Du Q. Hyperspectral band selection: A review. IEEE Geoscience and Remote Sensing Magazine. 2019;7(2):118-139

[34] Kwan C, Gribben D, Ayhan B, Bernabe S, Plaza A, Selva M. Improving land cover classification using extended multi-attribute profiles (EMAP) enhanced color, near infrared, and LiDAR data. Remote Sensing. 2020;**12**(9). DOI: 10.3390/rs12091392

[35] Zhang W, Qi J, Wan P, Wang H, Xie D, Wang X, et al. An easy-to-use airborne LiDAR data filtering method based on cloth simulation. Remote Sensing. 2016;**8**(6):501

[36] Kwan C, Chou B, Kwan LM, Larkin J, Ayhan B, Bell JF, et al. Demosaicking enhancement using pixel-level fusion. Journal of Signal, Image, and Video Processing. 2018;**12**:749-756. DOI: 10.1007/s11760-017-1216-2